TECH-SAVVY PAREN

TECH-SAVVY PARENTING

A GUIDE TO RAISING SAFE CHILDREN
IN A DIGITAL WORLD

NIKKI BUSH
ARTHUR GOLDSTUCK

BOOK**STORM**

ISBN: 978-1-920434-90-8
e-ISBN: 978-1-920434-91-5

First edition, first impression 2014

Published by Bookstorm (Pty) Ltd
PO Box 4532
Northcliff 2115
Johannesburg
South Africa
www.bookstorm.co.za

Distributed by On the Dot
www.onthedot.co.za

Edited by Sean Fraser
Proofread by Wesley Thompson
Cover design by publicide
Book design and typesetting by René de Wet
Printed by Creda Communications, Cape Town

To all the parents who cross my path daily with their queries and concerns, and to the chief technology officers in our home, my precious sons Ryan and Matthew. We are all learning together.

– Nikki

For my teachers: Sheryl, Jayna and Zianda.

– Arthur

"As our children become increasingly technically proficient and preoccupied, it is vital for adults, parents and teachers to be aware of the world they frequent! Tech-Savvy Parenting *is a comprehensive, practical and insightful guide to understanding the possibilities and perils of this world, how to make it safe for our children, and how to embrace the opportunities it presents."*
– Keith Wilke, College Head, HeronBridge College, Johannesburg

"The authors celebrate and honour the essential nature of child development, how children learn and the digital media's place in it all. We know that screens should be used by children in moderation, but what does that mean? This book explains the concept of moderation so well. I cannot recommend it highly enough to every parent, educator and therapist."
– Cara Lee Weir-Smith, Occupational Therapist and founder of Impact Learning

"Invaluable information that all parents need to be aware of."
– Izabella Gates, author of the *Life Talk* series, MD of Life Talk Forum

"As parents we have a choice. We can either embark on this digital journey with our children or risk losing them to a world we do not understand. The earlier we begin, the better. Teach them the boundaries when they are toddlers, and hopefully by the time they are curious, rebellious teens, they will be able navigators, alert to the risks and alive to the opportunities that the online space offers. Tech-Savvy Parenting *is a compass every parent needs to navigate those digital waters safely."*
– Sally Burdett, eTV's parenting show, *Great Expectations*

"This book is a reminder of why it is so important not to allow the overuse of screens to hijack the first 1 000 days of a child's life, while at the same time setting the scene for healthy assimilation of screens as a child develops so that they are prepared for an increasingly digital future."
– Lynda Smith, CEO of BrainBoosters

"It is refreshing to read a book by a parenting author that supports parents by encouraging them to take advantage of the benefits of modern technology. Nikki gives sensible advice on avoiding the dangers that exist when used irresponsibly. She believes, like me, that trust is good but control is better!"
– Dr Dereck Jackson, Educational Psychologist and author of *Parenting with Panache*

"Tech-Savvy Parenting *empowers moms and dads in their role as gatekeeper and facilitator of all forms of media in their child's world. No parent should be without it!"*
– Sonya Naude, Editor, *Living and Loving*

"In our world of such re-aligned and re-negotiated relationships – often mediated by technology – there has never been more potential or more threat for children to learn and connect, or to find themselves hurt and excluded. Unless parents empower themselves, they could find themselves helpless bystanders. That's what this book provides: clear, sensible and informed empowerment."
– Marc Falconer, outgoing Headmaster of King David High School, Linksfield and author of *Notes From A Headmaster's Desk: The Challenges of Education, Parenting and Teenagers*

"Having just returned from presenting workshops to young adults in Manhattan, I feel that this book should be compulsory reading for every parent – even more so for parents of children from privileged backgrounds."
– Leonard Carr, Clinical Psychologist specialising in the psychology of appreciation

---

"Technology could be the miracle cure needed to transform education; conversely, it could lead to the disintegration of human relationships. In Tech-Savvy Parenting, *Nikki Bush and Arthur Goldstuck traverse the chasm of opinion that is so divided about the power of technology, and offer parents insights into how best to utilise technology for enhancing education and helping children to learn to get along."*
– Alistair Stewart, Boys Preparatory Head, St Stithians College, Johannesburg

CONTENTS

ABOUT THIS BOOK

If you've picked up this book, it's probably because you're a parent looking for help to make sense of a digital world that you're finding rather challenging. You've realised you are no longer the chief technology officer in your home and that you are not keeping up with the demands of technology. It's starting to feel like the kids are in charge and there seems to be a shift in the balance of power in your home. What happened to being mum or dad and feeling like you were the boss – of everything! When you don't know exactly what you need to know, why you need to know it or what you need to do about it, being a parent becomes even more daunting than it already was.

First up, may we congratulate you for wanting to know more and wanting to learn how to speak digital. Your children are lucky to have you.

Our aim with this book is to help you to get a handle on what's happening in consumer technology, what you need to do and to understand in order to navigate this new space together with your children with greater confidence. While they don't need to read manuals, you do. So we've distilled our experience, thoughts, research and observations into a beginner's guide that we have tried to keep practical and to the point.

It was even more important for us, however, to provide a human context: to place children's use of technology in the context of the relationship between parents and their children.

We know you want your children to be both safe and savvy in this fast-changing world, and that process starts with you. For families to remain connected, both online and offline, and for young people to develop into responsible digital citizens, parents need to bridge the digital divide to their children by understanding:

- how communication is changing
- how tech is changing the world
- what this means to their children
- why young people are so strongly attracted to social media and technology
- why digital skills are just as important as reading and writing
- the dangers posed by the digital world
- the new opportunities that the online world offers
- how to help young people to be responsible users of social media and technology
- how to help them navigate the information superhighway safely
- the importance of family relationships in keeping children safe online
- the importance of high touch (human-to-human contact) in a high-tech world.

As parents ourselves, we too are in the process of discovering and navigating this digitally connected world while raising our own wired children. Nothing is more important to us than the safety of our children and the emotional connectedness of our own families.

We hope this book will give insight and perspective to help you avoid the paralysis that fear of the unknown can bring. Be assured that real-world common sense still applies to the digital world. There are, however, several important questions you need to ask yourself:

- How teachable are you?
- How much do you want to stay connected to your children?
- How important are your family relationships to you?
- How important is your child's reputation to you?
- How committed are you to understanding their world and their new language?
- Are you avoiding parenting your children by hiding behind your own technophobia?
- Do you understand how important it is to give your children boundaries in both the online and offline world?
- Do you get that teaching your child how and why to protect themselves online is one of the best gifts you can give them?
- Do you want them to respect you and take you seriously?

Tech-Savvy Parenting is not a Social Media 101 lesson. Far from it. It is more about relationships than anything else. We'll hold your hand as we introduce you to this new language and connect you to the digital world. Let's bridge the digital divide together for the love of our children.

Nikki Bush & Arthur Goldstuck
Johannesburg, May 2014

ABOUT THE AUTHORS

NIKKI BUSH

Inspirational speaker and best-selling author, Nikki Bush, is highly regarded among parents, educators and business people alike. Her work is fuelled by her passion for play, connection and relationships. She presents a variety of talks and workshops and her digital safety presentations for parents and learners have become must-attend events. She has a way of helping parents to bridge the digital divide to their children, demystifying complex and scary concepts. Learners love her interactive style and ability to talk *to* them rather than *at* them.

Nikki is the co-author of two best-selling books: *Future-proof Your Child* (Penguin, 2008) and *Easy Answers to Awkward Questions* (Metz Press, 2009) and writes a weekly column called 'Parenting Matters 4 Schools', which runs in many school newsletters around the country.

She is a regular guest on radio and TV and is often quoted in the print media. She is the parenting expert on SABC3's *Expresso*, the family expert for *Longevity* magazine and on the advisory team for *Living and Loving* magazine. She is also a guest lecturer for the Wits Business School Executive Development Programme.

Nikki is married to Simon and has two sons, Ryan and Matthew, aged 18 and 14 at the time of writing, and they live in Johannesburg.

For more information visit: www.nikkibush.com

ARTHUR GOLDSTUCK

Arthur Goldstuck heads the World Wide Worx research organisation, leading groundbreaking research into how change is affecting business and society, and presents his insights to audiences across the globe. World Wide Worx produces the most widely accepted statistics for Internet use in South Africa, along with benchmark studies on social media, mobile technology and online trends.

Arthur is also an award-winning writer, analyst and commentator on Internet, mobile and business and consumer technologies. In 2013, the Institute of Information Technology Professionals South Africa named him recipient of the 2013 Distinguished Service in ICT Award, and made him an Honorary Fellow of the Institute. As a journalist, he was news editor of the *Weekly Mail* (now the *Mail & Guardian*), South African correspondent for *Billboard*, and a freelance feature writer for *The Times* of London, among dozens of local and international publications.

He publishes the online consumer technology magazine Gadget.co.za, and is author of 18 books, including South Africa's best-selling information technology book yet, *The Hitchhiker's Guide to the Internet* (Zebra, 1995). He has written six works on urban legends, published by Penguin between 1990 and 2010.

His weekly gadgets column is the most widely syndicated technology column in South Africa, and he writes a weekly technology trends column for *Business Times* in the *Sunday Times*. He provides commentary on technology and communications issues to both local and international media, and in March 2014 was appointed by the Minister of Communications to the National Broadband Advisory Council, which helps guide the South African government's broadband policy.

Arthur is married to Sheryl and has two daughters, Jayna and Zianda, aged 12 and 16 at the time of writing. They live in Johannesburg.

For more information visit: www.worldwideworx.com and www.gadget.co.za

HOW IT CAME TOGETHER

Collaborating on this book was a no-brainer after Arthur and I were interviewed together by well-known psychologist, Dr Dorianne Weil, on one of her radio talk shows about the challenges of parenting in the digital age. Arthur is a tech enthusiast and knows all the smart and technical stuff about technology trends, while I am popularly known as a creative parenting expert who finds creative solutions to 21st-century parenting issues. As we were responding to Dr D's questions, we found ourselves so on the same wavelength – but from two completely different perspectives – that when we left the interview we both looked at each other and said: "We have to write a book together!"

I had always had a dream of writing a book entitled, Mom and the Geek, *and had been casting around for my partner in crime for some time. Then in walks Arthur – and my technical expert had arrived! Interestingly, Arthur and I go back many years. I first met him when I did a freelance writing course he ran in his Rockey Street flat in Yeoville, Johannesburg, when I was in my early twenties. He was then famous for his urban legends book and has had a total of 18 books published while building a successful and well-respected research company called World Wide Worx.*

As a result of our collaboration, this book contains a mix of both mum and dad stuff as well as high-touch parenting insights, combined with high-tech digital speak. It is the result of many a long and meandering conversation and much research. We have so enjoyed sharing our experiences to put this together, and we hope that we have opened a door to understanding what can sometimes be a daunting and challenging world for us mere adults. But, more than that, we hope you take the necessary practical steps to help your children navigate this crazy new world with responsibility and insight.

We are both parents, just like you, navigating the digital divide. Our children are just like yours, curious and eager to learn and explore their world and that, today, also includes all that is on offer on a screen or online. Their playground just got bigger and we have to prepare them for a lot more. We – and our children – face many of the same challenges, debates and negotiations that are constantly being addressed by you and your own children.

As a dad of two daughters, and a mum of two sons, Arthur and I want our own children to learn to read, write and speak digital in a way that won't put them at a disadvantage in navigating the traditional world too. We want them to connect, to love and to be well-rounded human beings as they harness the power of technology. We want them to be safe and savvy while maintaining their curiosity about the world around them. We want them to be healthy 'switchers' between the on-screen and off-screen world. Our wish for them is to develop both high-touch and high-tech skills so that they can experience the best of what life has to offer them in the 21st century.

FOREWORD

BY AKI ANASTASIOU

As the Internet turns 25 this year, there is no doubt that this complex mesh of connectivity has changed humankind forever. The Internet has broken down barriers faster than any other communications medium in the history of civilisation, and it is symbolically significant that, in the same year the World Wide Web was born, the Berlin Wall came crashing down. In the ensuing decades, dictatorships tumbled and we saw despots being overthrown thanks to the power of connectivity in ordinary people's hands.

At the same time, the Internet, coupled with technological innovation, has seen massive advances in the power of computing. These giant strides have made telecommunications accessible to billions. The miniaturisation of computers has enabled mobility and there is some kind of connectivity on every corner of the planet.

Prices of computers and mobile phones have plummeted in the last decade and this has accelerated ownership of high-tech devices among those who previously could not afford them. That would be most of us. And, of course, these devices have also found their way into the hands of our children …

For the first time in history, children are using the same technology as their parents and they know how to use it better, although not necessarily responsibly. They have the same access to the world as we do. In fact, we are the first generation of parents that will never keep up with the prevailing technology and we find ourselves constantly on the back foot, playing catch up and desperately trying to understand the wired generation that is our children.

This is why this book is so important.

Tech-Savvy Parenting connects parenting and technology in an accessible way to assist understandably anxious parents, some of whom are suffering from a severe case of technophobia, as well as those who have decided to throw up their hands in surrender and allow their children to do what they like in the digital world.

Nikki Bush and Arthur Goldstuck take you on a journey from the biggest screens in your child's life to the smallest: from the passive entertainment of the television to the interactive nature of gaming and Internet-linked computers, to the realm of social networking – often accessed via a smartphone.

As parents themselves, Nikki and Arthur share their wisdom, insights, personal anecdotes and practical advice to help you make sense of this new high-tech normal that is making an impact on our children's development and the way we need to parent them. It is a much-needed guide from two people walking the same journey as you, that provides context and perspective.

It is reassuring to know that all is not lost – that parents really do still have a vital role to play in their children's lives, that we don't have to throw the baby out with the bathwater, and that common sense still applies.

Aki Anastasiou
Johannesburg, May 2014

Aki Anastasiou, aka The Greek Geek, hosts *Technobyte* on Talk Radio 702 and the television show *Tech Busters* on CNBC Africa. He also talks on disruptions and the impact that future technologies are going to have on the world. Follow him on Twitter on @AkiAnastasiou.

CHAPTER 1

A DIGITALLY NURTURED GENERATION

Our children, this generation, are commonly referred to as the digital natives – born with a computer mouse or gaming console in one hand and a cellphone in the other. We, their parents, call ourselves digital immigrants to this strange new world – a world that is entirely normal to our children.

We have given much thought to this classification of digital natives and immigrants and would like to put another, slightly contrary view on the table. Children are born human and therefore their first language is not digital, it is love. They are born into a human world surrounded by touch, multisensory stimulation and emotion. Our first and most important role in their lives is to marinade them in love.

But, by virtue of the fact that your child was most likely born in the 21st century or at the tail end of the 20th century, they have been surrounded by digital their entire lives. In other words, they have been digitally nurtured. As a result, they are wired for technology and there are no barriers to their entry into any new digital playground.

So, think of your child as a real human being floating around in a digital marinade. It consists of many new devices, constantly changing technologies, new ways to connect, live, work and play, and new rules of engagement – which themselves change all the time. This is a marinade you have not grown up with and you are only just acquiring a taste for it. Your children, on the other hand, have a voracious appetite for the stuff and can't get enough of it. Understanding the 'what' and the 'why' – and especially the 'how' – will help you to be a more tech-savvy parent.

If you buy into the notion of a digitally nurtured generation that is still human at its very core, with human needs, wants and desires with which you can identify, then all is not lost. There are plenty of ways of preserving and enhancing your connection with your children. While disconnection from your children can indeed be fuelled by technology, it is not primarily caused by it. It's our own behaviour, our desire to connect, and our ability to be fully human and present in the parent-child relationship that will determine the degree of connection or disconnection in our homes.

IT'S A PLUG-AND-PLAY WORLD

Today, if you can plug any device into the Internet, you can play in the digital world. Whether you live in the slums of India or Rio, or the posh suburbs of New York or Johannesburg, you have access to the same information and communication tools via the Internet.

If we or our children want to know anything, we just Google it. And, unless you live in a place like China or the Middle East, where the Internet is censored, no one stands between you and the information you seek.

This information freedom represents a massive shift in power from the days of the Crusades through to the era of colonisation, when information was held in the hands of very few. Access was controlled for good reason: information was power. Governments and religions controlled the creation and dissemination of information. That gave them the power to shape the world and manage – or hold back – change in the world.

As big businesses increasingly became custodians of knowledge and data, they started shaping our world and change happened more rapidly than ever before, for one simple reason: the speed of communication increased in direct proportion to the development of technology.

In the early 1990s, both the cellphone and the Internet – decades in the making – emerged as commercial realities. And now we have seen the next shift in power – and it is in the hands of the individual for the very first time.

This is an important part of our story because it is the reason why our role in our children's lives is utterly different to that of our own parents – and more critical than it has ever been. If our children can plug in and play, they have the power in their hands to change the world. The screen they hold in their hands today is shaping both their future and ours.

Devices are becoming more powerful all the time. Children are using devices that have more computer processing power than *Apollo 11* when it made its trip to the moon. And we often give them access to these devices without a moment's thought to the potential, in their hands, for both good and bad choices and outcomes.

The digitally nurtured generation may use or even own sophisticated pieces of technology but that doesn't mean it knows how to use them responsibly. When something goes wrong in the online world, the cry from parents and educators is often something like, "Block the Internet from our schools – it's evil!" We should, instead, be very conscious of the fact that the Internet is not a place: it is merely a channel, and a neutral one at that. It's what we humans do with it that makes it positive or negative.

In the same way as children need to learn etiquette, manners and how to keep themselves safe in the real world, they also need to acquire social skills for use on-screen so that they become responsible users of technology in a plug-and-play world. And that doesn't apply only to cellphones: it is a challenge from their first exposure to television and gaming to using computers, tablets, cellphones and more.

CHOICE COMES WITH RESPONSIBILITY

With such unprecedented access to information, we are surrounded by more choices than ever before – and our children even more so. When we look at some of the major stressors of living in the 21st century, the power to choose can be overwhelming. While we sometimes clamour for more freedom of choice, we don't realise how much it stresses us, not just once a day, but many times in a day.

Our children need to be made very aware of their power to choose and that choice comes with something called responsibility. It is one of our key roles as parents of digitally nurtured children to help them understand how to make responsible choices and to take responsibility for the consequences of their choices – and what those consequences might be.

Children live very much in the moment, in the now. And, for the most part, that is good. As adults, we would do well to emulate our children's ability to be present in the moment. However, they also need to learn from us that what they do today shapes the kind of future they will have. With access to digital technology, they can increasingly shape their own destinies.

With their future so far away, it's something of an abstract concept for them, which is why teaching how to be safe and savvy on-screen and online cannot be taught via a screen. It has to be conveyed face to face, human being to human being – and, where possible, parent to child.

Take your relationship with your child seriously. If you invest and parent wisely in the real world of human beings, you are building an emotional bridge to your child. You will need this bridge in the teen years. Your child will either use it to come back to you, or you will use it to connect to your child.

It is not your child's responsibility to build this bridge, it is yours. You need to make good use of the early years in order to build this emotional bridge before the pull of peer groups starts as they become tweens, with the addition of many and varied technological and emotional distractions in the teenage years.

Establish yourself early on as a hero in your child's life story, as a pillar of leadership and authority, as a source of unconditional love and a safe harbour to which they can come home when they are feeling tired, hurt, lonely or broken, as they can sometimes feel in the roller-coaster teenage years.

Know this about the new era in which we find ourselves raising our children and battling to keep up with a world changing at warp speed: it is a world full of paradoxes and contradictions. There are more ways to communicate but there is less connection. There is more healthcare but less health. There are more tools to save time, but less time to do more for ourselves and our families. The more we progress, the more we are stressed by the demands of progress. And the more technology progresses, the more people fall behind. This is commonly known as the Progress Paradox.

One of the key causes of this paradox is simple to understand: change that happens on one side of the world is felt on the other within minutes or hours. Snail mail gave us a chance to take a breath, to contemplate our answer. There was no demand for an instant response, and work and life were distinctly separate things.

Now the boundaries are blurred, because technology allows us to take our work wherever we go and we are contactable and accessible 24/7 by anyone, including our children and our boss, partner or spouse. There is both good and bad to this situation. Just as there are unbelievable opportunities down the line – think of new jobs and industries we have never seen before – so there are brand-new threats and moral dilemmas we will face for the first time. We and our children are living through a communication revolution that is making an impact on every industry and relationship in the world, including that between parent and child.

WHAT'S HAPPENED TO THE LIBRARY, THE POST OFFICE AND THE TELEPHONE?

We're sure you'd be ecstatic if your children asked you to take them to the library to borrow a book, or to visit the local post office to post a letter to a cousin or pen pal. You'd be over the moon, wouldn't you? Yes, of course – you still understand those things, so you're in your comfort zone.

The good news is that they are still doing just this, but in a very different way to what we regard as 'normal'. The new normal revolves around the Internet. Today the library is the Internet, the books are all the millions of websites out there (the good and the bad). Letters are the emails, SMSs, posts, Tweets and even likes and Retweets. The post office consists of a number of different digital platforms that are constantly growing and evolving, from Facebook to Twitter, LinkedIn, Instagram, Snapchat and the next catchy brand name – there will be many more before this book is even published!

Our children have hundreds of pen pals called 'friends' on social media, BBM, WhatsApp, Mxit and the like. And their curiosity is aroused by all that is on offer in the online world. For them, the Internet is like being on a permanent treasure hunt. Remember how they used to enjoy an Easter-egg hunt or a birthday treasure hunt in the garden when they were little? Well, that's the same excitement they feel when searching for something online, especially if it is a piece of free software that will help them access more of what they are hunting.

They have powerful new tools at their disposal and these tools exist in an exponentially changing world. Social media and technological advances are not fads that are going to disappear sometime soon, but rather part of a trend that is reshaping the world – permanently.

YOU CAN'T HEAR THEM!

Do you recall your mother berating you for hanging off the end of the phone chatting to your friends as soon as you got home from school? "But you've been with them all day, why do you need to talk to them now?" Our tweens and teens are not so different. They, too, have an insatiable need to connect with other human beings. It's what happens to them when they enter puberty – this urge to socialise and connect with others. The big difference, however, is that our kids text each other instead of speaking out loud. We can't hear the conversation, which quite literally freaks us out.

FOR THE RECORD

Here are a few social media statistics to blow your mind and convince you that this is not going away; it is the present and it is the future:

- In 2014, the number of active cellphone connections in the world was expected to pass the 7-billion mark – and there will be more cellphones in use than there are people.
- More than one in five of these cellphones will be smartphones, giving ready access to the Internet, apps, social media and mobile video.
- By 2008, there were 1 billion computers in use on the planet. That was expected to grow to 2 billion by the end of 2014.
- Facebook has 1.3 billion subscribers in March 2014.
- Twitter has 241 million monthly active users out of about 1 billion registered users. Of these, 184 million are active on Twitter via their cellphones, more than 70% are outside the United States. On average, 500 million Tweets are sent every day.
- YouTube has: more than 1 billion unique users each month; more than 6 billion hours of video watched each month; 100 hours of video uploaded every minute; and 80% of YouTube traffic comes from outside the USA.
- In South Africa, YouTube views grew by 90% in 2013. The good news is that 68% of South African users watch YouTube for education and learning – among many other purposes, obviously.
- WhatsApp has more than 450 million active users.
- Instagram has more than 150 million users and 5 million new sign-ups each week. About 60% of its users are outside the USA.

Bear in mind that these figures are already out of date because things are changing and growing so rapidly.

Many of these platforms are new tools we as parents don't understand, and yet our children are at the centre of this digitally driven world and for them this is all perfectly normal.

Our children have developed a brand-new language called digital. It consists of a lexicon of new words made up of short forms, such as 'gr8' for 'great' and 'cul8r' for 'see you later'. 'POS' or 'parent over shoulder' is a common one or – and far less common, we hope – 'GNOC' for 'get naked on camera'. Nikki used to think that 'LOL' meant 'lots of love', but then discovered that it means 'laugh out loud'. Ha-ha! (Go to Appendix 1 on page 212 for a list of common text acronyms.) In addition, they use emoticons – little smiley or frowny faces – to express their degree of emotion rather than using words. And adults are now learning this digital language from their kids.

Considering that we are undergoing a communication revolution, these developments are not surprising. What is new, however, is that kids can be sitting right next to each other, having a conversation on their phone via text – with each other. This is normal for their generation. They choose to 'speak digital', which means using text instead of having a verbal interaction. Let's dig a little deeper into the phenomenon that freaks out most parents.

MORE LAYERS OF COMMUNICATION

It's a complaint that has become a cliché: "What's wrong with these kids? They're sitting right next to each other in the same room and BBMing/WhatsApping/Snapchatting each other! What happened to good, old-fashioned talking to each other?" Very often parents don't even know what medium or app is being used for communication. Once it was only text, then smileys or emoticons were added, and now it is visual. Therein lies the real clue to what is happening here: a generation ago, before the cellphone and the Internet, verbal communication was all we had in a social setting. Today, many layers have been added to communication, and the digital teen has embraced those layers. This, in turn, means that a real conversation is playing itself out before adults' disbelieving eyes. More than that, it is a multi-layered conversation that includes voice, text, coded terminology, visual cues and content, and hints, insinuations and signals that make for a richer communications mix than we have ever seen before.

It disturbs us because we think that all of this is replacing communication, but instead, it is embracing the kind of communication that is reshaping the world.

BROADCAST TO INTERACTIVE

We are the TV generation. With our satellite TV or PVR, we feel all-powerful – because it appears to give us choice and control. But, think about TV for a moment: it is being done *to* us. We are passive viewers, and there is no interaction between us and with what is happening on the screen. In truth, we still only have limited choices – we get the bouquet for which we are prepared to pay.

On the other hand, our children are engaging in multiple forms of interactive media, not just static television, and this makes them actors in a digital world. They participate and interact with the online situation, site or social network with which they are engaged – often with other players or friends.

For many of us, television was the on-screen medium that dominated our childhood, but it is a one-way medium. For the most part, the message is predetermined, and is broadcast to us with no right of reply, no opportunity to interact. There was even less freedom of choice before paid-for channel TV arrived. Now at least you can choose to channel surf between programmes. Whoopee!

TV is characteristic of an era that was about command and control, top-down management. It has also been blamed for the rise of obesity in our generation – the generation that is supposed to be setting an example for the children we are now raising. So perhaps it's time to stop pointing fingers at the baffling preferences of the digital generation without first understanding what came before.

Most of us survived the threats posed by TV, from addiction to sloth to the dumbing down of culture. But then again, our own childhood was a simpler one, in a different time. Today, our children are at the centre of a new world of plug and play. It enables human beings to connect with each other – to network – something most of us really like to do, particularly from the teenage years onwards. TV was a medium that specialised in one-to-many transmission, while social media is about many-to-many. It enables us to collaborate, communicate, upload and download with many people – at will, whenever and via multiple media platforms. New media – whether they are apps, websites or our own video blogs – offer a vast range of interaction with content. Social networks, on the other hand, offer endless opportunities of interaction with people. That is both the wonder of it and its terrifying potential for harm. But where adults see only the threat, children see only the opportunity and the wonders of interaction.

It is for this reason, to a large extent, that children catch on to new technologies faster than adults. Because they are born into this environment, they assimilate it, while adults must accommodate – a different and much more difficult learning process.

Parents with young children have an advantage compared to other adults, however, because they can learn to navigate this new media landscape *with* their kids, who are natural authorities on the subject. That's not all good news, though. We are in a very different position as parents in that we are both the student and the authority in the same relationship. You need to get your head around the interactive space because it is revolutionising and changing everything, and especially our relationships with our children.

UPLOADING, DOWNLOADING, SHARING, COLLABORATING AND MORE

In the 2013 edition of the annual *Sunday Times* Generation Next survey, Linda Doke encapsulates one of the key trends reshaping communication:

"It's no longer cool enough to be telling the world where you are, what you're doing, and with whom you're doing it; now it's the norm to send them the photos to prove it. Using Facebook, Twitter, WhatsApp, BBM, Tumblr, Google+ and any other form of social networking media available, we send images of our daily doings and goings-on to friends and family across the world in seconds, imprinting a dialogue of our lives in cyberspace for our choice people to see … The fascination with photography seems insatiable, particularly among the youth. Sharing photos via social media is the hottest thing since Bieber was out of nappies, and there's not an urban teenager in South Africa who would not know how to upload, download, Tweet or tag to reach friends and followers."

But now listen carefully as Doke quotes one of the lead researchers on the survey, HDI Youth Marketeers communications and publicity manager Mokebe Thulo:

"This photomania is less to do with their interest in others' lives, and more to do with their desire to contribute to everything they can, and, wherever possible, control it. Just as teens and young adults like to download their own music, and choose their own mixes, which they upload and share with their friends, so they like to create and share their own images.

"Sharing photos online is just one of the ways in which they can express themselves, not only immediately but to a wide audience, and the youth find this particularly compelling. By posting pics to their Facebook wall or sharing them with friends, they're effectively putting their own stamp on the images they've personally created. It not only gives them recognition, but also instant gratification."

WE VIEW TECHNOLOGY DIFFERENTLY

Most of us, as adults, have cellphones, email, websites and social media accounts largely for work, productivity and improving both contact with our networks and access to information. Often, we have to be dragged kicking and screaming into this new form of networking. For our children, it's way more than this, and way easier. They readily communicate, share and collaborate with each other on a variety of platforms – things we are only just beginning to learn how to do. They live in a world that's always on and information as well as entertainment is available in an instant, anywhere, on any device, any time. This is the expectation that they have of their world and we are increasingly jumping on that bandwagon when and where it suits us.

FOR THE RECORD

From the 2013 *Sunday Times* Generation Next survey:
- 36% of 19–23-year-olds check their cellphones for messages every five minutes
- 32.7% of 8–23-year-olds send free messages every five minutes
- 43.5% of 8–23-year-olds still send SMSs at least once a day.

What they use their cellphones for every day:
- 8–12-year-olds: talk (46%), BBM/Mxit/WhatsApp (55.6%), MP3 (43.9%), games (41.7%), social media (25.9%)
- 13–19-year-olds: talk (49.5%), BBM/Mxit/WhatsApp (77.8%), MP3 (64.2%), games (23.5%), social media (50.5%).

Take cellphones, for example. They haven't been around for that long, but if you left your cellphone at home this morning, it's highly likely you would have turned around and driven back to get it. We are becoming more and more reliant on other devices too. While these gadgets may be brilliant and sometimes make us feel as if we have another brain outside our bodies, the ultimate test is whether we can remember where we have decided to store various bits of information!

But more and more of us are realising something that our children understand instinctively: our lives can be curated online. Teenagers don't worry about where they stored a photo or if they made a back-up of a hard drive: it's all online anyway. The open secrets are available to their friends and themselves in places such as Facebook. The closed secrets are locked down through services such as Dropbox.

Having said that, you may be surprised to learn that children don't know everything about the digital world – yet. Research conducted by World Wide Worx among schoolchildren over the past five years shows that, while children are far ahead of their parents and teachers in areas such as social networking and digital creativity, they are well behind them when it comes to using the tools for business productivity.

For that reason, it's not a great idea to ask a kid for advice on cloud computing: it is still largely a business environment and, until the 'consumer cloud' becomes one of the next big things, it is unlikely to interest our children. Although don't put it past them …

The decision-makers of tomorrow

Much of Chapter 1 has focused on explaining that your children have not become alien creatures who are lost to this world – your world. But if you want a truly positive perspective on the above, it is this: their digital lives and habits are preparing them for a future in a society that will demand these skills as a given, rather than as something you learn on a course or on the job.

Already, one of the most important skills demanded of a new generation characterised by mega-corporations – think Google, Apple and Facebook – is the ability to collaborate through digital means, and to work as part of a team, regardless of the medium the team uses for a specific project.

Your children's bad manners in having under-the-table text con-versations with their friends at dinner time is a consequence of your own child-rearing permissiveness. But their apparent poor etiquette in having a similar text conversation with friends with whom they are already chatting physically is a good example of an additional layer of communication. It is the style of communication and collaboration that will characterise the workplace of the future.

And that's only the beginning.

The ability to create, communicate and share through online networks will also be the basis for how businesses are put together, started and run. A great example that is already with us is the concept of crowdfunding: turning to a social network to provide financial backing for a new venture or product. Sites such as Kickstarter and Indiegogo have provided the springboard for projects ranging from smartwatches to movie productions, from gadgets to games. Investors benefit in numerous ways, from getting a credit on a movie or website to being the first to lay hands on a new product.

South African Mark Shuttleworth tried to have a new smartphone, the Ubuntu Edge, funded in this way. He challenged the community on Indiegogo to fund a production run of 40 000 phones, at a cost of $32 million – an unprecedented target in crowdfunding. He fell short, but reached an all-time record of $19 million in pledges.

It is that kind of example that will inspire our children to pursue their dreams online, rather than parents' whining about their children not having 'real' conversations. Already, a number of mobile games created by young South Africans have been fully crowdfunded on Kickstarter, showing the way to an entire crop of aspirant young developers still in school today (see page 104).

But seriously ...

There is no better example of how being digitally savvy has changed the world than in the election of Barack Obama as US president in 2009. The foundation of his campaign was built on digital tools for fundraising, voter activation and campaigning. It's a well-known fact that the campaign set records for fundraising, particularly in the amount of small donations from ordinary members of the public. Without digital savvy, and online and mobile tools, this would not have been possible. A less well-known fact is that these donations allowed Obama to become the first presidential candidate from a major party to turn down public financing since such funding became available more than three decades earlier.

Meanwhile, in just four years between his election and the following presidential campaign, a platform that had been in its infancy in 2009 had gone mainstream: social media. Twitter and Facebook had come into their own as campaign platforms, and Obama used them better than any other candidate, whether for the Democratic Party's nomination or for the presidency itself. And the results spoke for themselves: Obama won the majority of the popular vote for a second successive campaign – something no Democratic president had done since Franklin D Roosevelt in 1936.

In South Africa, politicians are only just beginning to discover the power of social media, so it did not play a significant role even in the 2014 elections. However, these elections can be regarded as a dress rehearsal for 2019, when most South African voters will be using social media in one form or another.

ALONE ON THE INFORMATION SUPERHIGHWAY

With more and more information at our disposal and more devices with which to access the information, at speed, we are travelling on the information superhighway even when we don't realise it. Our children are not just passengers or learner drivers in our cars on that highway. From the first time they master the use of the family PVR, your cellphone, the home computer, your new tablet or a gaming device, they are also driving without your supervision.

We wouldn't allow our toddlers to cross a busy road without adult supervision and instruction. We don't let them cross the road alone until we have instilled the rules of the road in them and feel they are competent enough to do so without us. We teach our children not to hitchhike or accept lifts from strangers, because that's dangerous. And yet we allow them to use very powerful and sophisticated devices long before they are reliable, responsible users of them.

Usually, we do so out of ignorance, because our children are ahead of us, or we haven't had time to give it much thought. Some parents are technophobic and give their children carte blanche with technology because they are never going to catch up. The attitude is: "Do what you like, I have no idea how to protect you."

Other parents are so paralysed and fearful of new technology that they try to prevent their children from using it or accessing information via technology. They simply deny access and then their children find conniving ways to access what they want anyway, once again without appropriate guidance and lessons in responsible use.

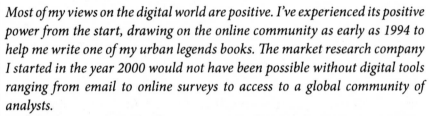

In my regular presentations of 'The One Thing You Need to Remember', I tell tweens and teens that, for me, there are only two kinds of people who hitchhike on the highway in the real world: those who are desperate and those who are ignorant. Desperate because they are out of options, or ignorant because they don't know any better.

Without guidance, our children may well land up being desperate or ignorant, both of which are dangerous to their physical, mental and emotional well-being, as well as to their reputation on the information superhighway.

Most of my views on the digital world are positive. I've experienced its positive power from the start, drawing on the online community as early as 1994 to help me write one of my urban legends books. The market research company I started in the year 2000 would not have been possible without digital tools ranging from email to online surveys to access to a global community of analysts.

But at every step of the way, I encountered cases where people's lives were all but ruined by cyber-bullying, by addiction to online pornography or gambling, and by betting everything on a speculative Internet venture. The Internet is no different to the real world: as much as it has unlimited potential for great things, it also holds unlimited potential for harm.

The real peril here is that the dangers remain invisible. The countless bad-news stories disappear into the background as headlines are grabbed by massive purchase prices paid for the likes of Instagram and WhatsApp. But make no mistake: the dangers may become invisible, but they are not disappearing.

SO, WHAT'S THE ATTRACTION?

On-screen technologies are attractive to children across the board for a variety of common reasons. They:

- are easy to use (for them, anyway)
- offer children a sense of control, so that they may become masters of their universe
- offer a lot of programming choice
- are entertaining and hold their attention
- are alive with colour, music, sound, lights and fast-paced action
- feed curiosity and the need to discover
- stop boredom
- provide relaxation

- are a source of education
- feed special interests
- encourage creativity (children can create their own films, publish their stories, work with Photoshop, compose music and more)
- allow children to connect with their world
- provide social opportunities by keeping them in constant contact with their peer group
- are always available even when their parents are not
- fill the emotional void when parents are absent or friendships sour
- either stimulate or pacify the child
- can produce endorphins or feelings of achievement, even if these are false
- offer a sense of independence
- connect them with others or provide an opportunity to play alone
- can be competitive, offering reward systems (in order to get to the next level of a game, for example)
- provide children a platform on which they can express themselves and share ideas
- provide an opportunity for children to hide from society but still take part
- require less conscious thought and energy than real-life play because there are constant visual and audio prompts telling children what to do next.

Children are wired young

We talk about kids of all ages being screen-hungry. They can't seem to get enough of on-screen technology and they sure don't have to be taught how to use it. They are intuitive about any form of technology, from television and using a PVR to the latest cellphone. They are definitely wired young.

At a recent party, Nikki asked a seven-year-old what he wanted for Christmas. He very clearly told her he wanted a Wii and started reeling off all the specs, from the price to the games that were to come with it, as well as details of Nunchuks and so on. The words and perfect descriptions just poured out of him like water over a waterfall. He didn't skip a beat, and he comes from a home where the use of technology is well monitored and kept to an age-appropriate minimum. His mother's eyes grew wide as she eavesdropped on the conversation. She had never imparted any of these details to him and neither had she taken him window-shopping for a Wii. Nikki asked the young man how he knew so much about the Wii, where had he got all his information from? "Oh, from my friends and I have also played Wii at my cousin's house." Well, with the depth of his knowledge, combined with his enthusiasm for the topic, this seven-year-old would do a much better job than most of the sales assistants we have encountered when shopping for a Wii!

And then Nikki's sister phoned her in disbelief, because her seven-year-old daughter had announced that she had just Googled 'Disney' on the family computer. "I didn't know she knew how to Google! How does she know how to do it?" Now this is a child who has had more access to technology than most other seven-year-olds, and whose parents are very tech-literate, Googling on their iPhones all the time, and Facebooking from wherever they are. Nikki's niece had learned how to navigate an iPhone within just a couple of days at age six, with no adult instruction at all. Smart, intuitive and technologically wired would be the description.

Technology kicks in young and, whether or not you promote the use of it with your children, they are into it anyway. This is not to say that you should give in and hand over control of the remote or any on-screen device. Indeed, you need to remain the gatekeeper and determine how much exposure your children have to technology and the online environment. In the preschool and primary school phase, children need to move as much as possible because the body is the architect of the brain and overuse of technology and on-screen media doesn't encourage physical movement. When your children become tweens and teens, they need to understand how to be discerning users of media to enjoy all the benefits of technology while protecting themselves from the potential dangers.

It's not surprising, really, that many people attending our digital safety presentations, which are actually targeted at parents with tweens and teens, have much younger children. Our children are wired young. You need to understand and manage their attraction to technology and social media from as early as you can.

THE DIGITAL PLAYGROUND

Children of the 21st century are increasingly viewing their world via one screen or another. Screens have become ubiquitous; they are everywhere – in our living rooms, bedrooms, studies, our handbags, briefcases or computer bags and in our back pockets. They are in shopping centres, restaurants, shops, at stadiums, in cars, trains, buses and planes. They are increasingly being incorporated into children's toys and games. Wherever you look, there is a screen offering myriad activities, from passive viewing such as television to interactive gaming, learning, entertainment, socialising and networking.

Televisions are getting bigger and bigger and the functionality of TV, your computer and social media will increasingly be accessible on a single screen, allowing you to send Tweets and respond to emails while watching TV on the same screen. And then there is also the miniaturisation of digital technology, bringing us ever-smaller screens on mobile devices, even incorporating television or cellphone technology into wristwatches. Many parents own a DStv Drifta, enabling them to watch up-to-the-minute international rugby or cricket matches while sitting on the side of a field watching their children play sport.

All this is possible on the digital playground. In Chapter 2 we take a look at the attraction between children and some of the more common on-screen devices in our lives.

- Our children's first language is love, but digital is close behind.
- The digital world is changing part of our children's internal operating system.
- Children are naturally wired for technology because they are marinaded in it right from the beginning.
- It's a plug-and-play world.
- We are going through a communications revolution.
- The library, post office and telephone have changed.
- The era in which we live is characterised by the fact that power has transferred to the individual due to unprecedented access to information.
- The Internet is not a place; it is a neutral channel.
- How we use the Internet determines whether it is good or bad.
- Owning a sophisticated device does not make children responsible users.
- With choice comes responsibility.
- Communication has shifted from broadcast to social and interactive media.
- Our world is one of paradoxes and contradictions.
- Children are wired young.
- Children need us to be their guide alongside them.

CHAPTER 2

THE BIG PULL OF THE SMALL SCREEN

While the younger generation has access to a greater variety of on-screen technology than ever before, TV viewing is still a pastime that takes their fancy in a big way and how you control its use in your home will have a significant bearing on how you teach your children to manage other devices in their lives as they get older.

The 2013 *Sunday Times* Generation Next survey tells us that the most popular pastime for youth in the peri-urban and urban categories in South Africa is still watching TV. Second to that is surfing the Internet on their cellphones, then listening to the radio, followed by accessing the Internet on a home computer. Right at the end of the list is the reading of magazines and newspapers.

FOR THE RECORD

Television abounds in South African homes. According to the 2013 *Sunday Times* Generation Next survey (urban and peri-urban youth aged 8–23):
- 48.1% have at least three TVs at home
- 78.7% have at least two TVs at home
- 55.5% have a TV in their bedroom
- 31.5% say the TV is always on.

Satellite or cable TV and the PVR have revolutionised the medium of television. Often, the only people in your home who know how the PVR actually works are your children! Because there is more choice of programming available than before, the variety keeps them glued.

Today we have children who channel surf whenever they lose interest in the programme at hand. They have become used to shows in technicolour with fast-moving scenes. Now think of that versus an old Western movie in which guns are pulled so slowly you may often wonder if the actors are ever going to shoot the damned things! There are no such slow scenes in modern television.

This generation is used to quick cuts, zooms and edits and, if something doesn't grab them they don't watch until the end. They simply switch the channel or multi-task with a cellphone or tablet in hand at the same time.

FOR THE RECORD

The South African Audience Research Foundation conducts the largest survey of South African media consumption habits, and reports its data every six months in the All Media and Products Survey (AMPS).

AMPS data show a dramatic rise in TV viewership, even as the Internet reaches into every income and age group. Over a five-year period, the following proportion of South Africans aged 15 and older confirmed they had watched TV the day before – indicating that they watched daily:

- 2008: 83.7%
- 2009: 85.5%
- 2010: 88.5%
- 2011: 90.8%
- 2012: 91.5%

During the same period, DStv daily viewership went up from 16.8% to 28.3%.

There is one simple conclusion from these numbers: TV is not going away anytime soon.

Television has long been blamed for our children's dwindling attention spans, falling literacy rates and a reduction in face-to-face time in families.

Once again, the problem lies less with the technology than with our indiscriminate use of it and lack of boundaries for our children's use of devices.

Parents have fallen into the trap of using television as a babysitter. There isn't a busy parent who hasn't worked out that, when children are in front of a TV, they generally sit still and behave. If you need to take a few moments for yourself or get dressed and be ready on time, plonk your child in front of a TV and you buy yourself time. However, because it is so convenient, the problem is that parents are defaulting to a screen more and more.

Kristen Jordan Shamus echoes this in her article in the *Detroit Free Press* entitled, 'Maybe it's Time we Turned off Technology and Tuned in to our Kids': "How many of us have parked our kids in front of *Dora the Explorer* or *Good Luck Charlie* for 20 minutes of uninterrupted time to make a work call, prepare dinner in peace, get something done? How many of us have flipped on the Wii or the Xbox and said, 'I just need a few minutes, kids,' but by the time we return our attention to them, inadvertently a full hour has passed?"

WHAT THE EXPERTS SAY

So what happens to the brain in front of TV?

Children go into stare mode in front of TV. They are mesmerised and engaged. Even hyperactive children generally pay attention in front of the TV. This is not to say that TV stimulates brain growth, however ... In fact, according to the research of Juliet Schor, published in her book, *Born to Buy* (Scribner, 2004), from the first time a child watches TV, an automatic feedback loop is created. The stimulus and response come from the same source, so there is no need to turn the information over in your brain or to really think, unless someone on the screen instructs you to. This means that TV doesn't grow new neurological pathways in the brain unless a parent or caregiver is sitting with the child and asks questions about the content, for example: "How big was that animal? What does it eat? What sound does it make?" or "What do you think about the man? What do you think is going to happen next?"

The controversy around brain development is illustrated well in the example of the *Baby Einstein* baby video/DVD series that claimed to make your baby smarter if you let them watch.

"No Einstein in your Crib? Get a Refund!" was the headline in *The New York Times* following a court ruling in 2009 and the announcement that the developers – Disney, no less – were offering a refund to anyone who had purchased a *Baby Einstein* video/DVD after being convinced that it would make their baby clever. This was a coup for the Campaign for a Commercial-Free Childhood (CCFC), which had been lobbying for this for some time, and it put the spotlight on the issue of when to introduce on-screen activities to children.

Moderation and common sense are imperative when raising children, but they seem to be in short supply unless there is a conscious understanding of and perspective on how children learn. What most parents do not know is that:

- Children need to move in order to learn (from birth right through to Grade 7), because the body is the architect of the brain. This is why a sedentary baby or child has a limited learning experience when placed in front of television for lengthy periods.
- Children need concrete learning experiences by interacting with real games and toys, with real people who respond to them, touch them, connect and communicate with them. In other words, children need all their senses stimulated.

If we look at real life versus on-screen images, a mouse and an elephant can be exactly the same size on TV. A child can only appreciate how large an elephant is if she sees one in real life. Then she realises that the elephant is a lot bigger than her parents' car, and that a mouse is smaller than her own foot.

Watching something on a screen is no substitute for the real thing, but it can be a wonderful reinforcement of what a child has already seen and experienced in real life.

A child's brain goes through three phases of learning successively and simultaneously:

- The concrete phase: This is anything real that can be experienced via the senses of taste, touch, smell, vision and hearing (as well as the two hidden senses, called vestibular and proprioception). The vestibular sense (located in the inner ear), tells us about balance, direction, gravity and where our body is in space, such as whether we are stationary or moving, upright or upside down, coordinates our eye movements with our head and determines normal muscle tone. The proprioceptive sense sends information through the muscles and joints to the brain, telling us where our body parts are in relation to each other, helping us to plan our movements and judge speed, force and distance, such as how hard to hit or kick a ball, and allowing us to climb a jungle gym without having to look at our feet.

  The concrete phase lasts right up to the age of 12. It doesn't end the day your child learns to read and write at around the age of seven. This is an important element of learning, because children only create meaning of their world if they personally engage with it, as opposed to seeing pictures or being told about something second-hand.

- The semi-concrete phase: This is a picture of the object in question, say in a book or on a screen.

- The abstract phase: This phase of learning would be symbols such as numbers, words, letters and dots.

Overuse of technology in the childhood years, up to the age of about 12, could create learning gaps due to lack of personal experience with the real world, insufficient repetition (which can lead to a child's inability to master a skill, such as cutting with scissors or manipulating puzzle pieces), and lower levels of social maturity (because of the solitary nature of television). Of course, because our children are naturally wired for technology, you don't have to teach them much about how to navigate a remote control or a computer. It stands to reason, then, that you don't have to start too young either. So when is the right time to 'expose' them to television?

The American Academy of Pediatrics recommends no television for children under the age of two as exposure to television interferes with brain development (because they are not moving or interacting with people).

In these times, however, that is easier said than done.

Many parents allow children to flop down in front of television to relax after a 'tough' day at school. Just think of yourself. Why do *you* watch television if not to let go at the end of a busy day and allow yourself to go brain dead? You don't have to think in front of TV unless you're watching a game show and pitting yourself against the host or a contestant. Watching television generally increases the size of the theta brainwaves, the relaxation ones, which is why we let go and often even nap in front of TV.

While there are families who are extremely vigilant and keep their young children as screen-free as possible, which is admirable, it can also become a practical nightmare – think of a household with multiple children. As soon as the eldest is allowed to watch television, the youngest will soon follow. In the same way, it is easy to keep an only child away from sweets and junk food, but not so easy with the second child because the eldest is now allowed to taste the forbidden fruit.

Keep the exposure of really young children to TV short and sweet and be very aware of the type of content they are watching. Pre-schoolers can watch a show or two a day, but preferably not back-to-back. That's what video recorders and PVRs are for. An hour of TV a day for primary school children is certainly not going to harm them if it is part of a balanced day filled with plenty of physical activity, and provided the content is appropriate and they are not up late at night watching beyond bedtime. With academic and co-curricular demands, high-schoolers don't have much more time available to them than primary schoolers, although they might make up for it on weekends.

WATCH WHAT THEY'RE WATCHING

Parents are not only using television as a babysitter; it has now evolved into a bodyguard too. Parents think that if their kids are watching TV then, because they know where they are, they must be safe. What a misconception this is! While there is so much good content on this medium, which is often really entertaining or educational, what children shouldn't see in real life they should never see on TV.

Because TVs are on 24/7, like moving wallpaper in many homes today – even replacing artwork on the walls – children are regularly exposed to 24-hour news reporting, which is often full of scary imagery. And then there are all the trailers for adult programming to be aired later in the evening. These often contain high-energy moments that are sometimes violent, as are news reports. But, because our kids might not be sitting and watching – perhaps they are just passing through the living room to the kitchen – they get to see shootings, stabbings, muggings and more. Young children can be scared beyond belief by what they see on a screen because they cannot always separate real life from what is happening on a screen, and as children get older and are exposed to more and more violence, for example, they can become hard-wired to be inured to it – it no longer shocks them and this impacts on their view of the world and their value system.

The human brain is a very impressionable organ. Everything we see, hear, smell, taste, touch and experience is filed in some nook or cranny and shapes us in some way. Children's brains are particularly elastic and have few filters, soaking everything up like a sponge.

The point about how television can help shape us was proven at a Grade 12 Life Orientation cook-off in which my eldest son, Ryan, was involved. The 'MasterChef effect' was clearly evident, even at a school where Consumer Studies (Home Economics) is not taught, as each group of six young people cooked and served up their dishes to the judges. These 17- and 18-year-olds could easily have been mistaken for people who had had years of lessons in food preparation, cooking and presentation. I'll not detract from the fact that many of them, like my son, may have been cooking with their own parents for years, but it was the very professional little touches, such as the way they wiped their plates and garnished their dishes before serving, that was the cherry on the top.

I was sitting with a group of teachers and parents towards the end of the competition and my comment to them was, "So, from this display we can conclude that television does indeed teach, influence and mould our children!" to which they completely agreed.

Nikki's example above is a very positive one and there are plenty of other good ones. Think *Minute to Win It* and the fun and games that particular game show has spawned. A more recent favourite, *Downton Abbey*, stimulated enthralling conversations in families about social classes, social norms, social prejudice and much more. Think *Barney* and his successors if you have little ones and all the good values that are being taught to young children through music, song and dance.

FOR THE RECORD

But not everything on TV is good for children. An increasing amount of very graphic violence and sexual content is contributing to shaping their minds, values, beliefs and culture over and above what we as parents are doing. Just consider the following statistics from the Campaign for a Commercial-Free Childhood:

- Nearly two out of every three TV shows contain some violence, averaging about six acts of violence per hour.
- Violence is more prevalent in children's TV shows, which average 14 acts of violence per hour.
- More than half of the music videos aired contain acts of violence, usually against women, and on average contain 93 sexual situations per hour, including 11 'hardcore' scenes depicting behaviours such as intercourse and oral sex.
- By the time a child is 18, he or she could have witnessed, on average, 200 000 acts of violence, including 40 000 murders, on TV.

The 2013 *Sunday Times* Generation Next survey found that 31.5% of urban and peri-urban youth between the ages of 8 and 23 in South Africa say that the TV is permanently on in their homes, which means that it has become like moving wallpaper. We, as parents, are setting fewer and fewer boundaries concerning TV, and we haven't even touched on gaming and cellphones yet.

Remember that a child's brain is very impressionable and not everything has a positive *MasterChef* effect. We really do need to watch what they are watching – both good and bad – so that we can help them make healthy media choices that will shape them in the best way possible.

THE BRAND-CONSCIOUS CHILD CONSUMER

The plethora of media today has enabled marketers to draw our children into the centre of the marketing equation. They use every touch point imaginable to connect to our children and build relationships with them. They invest billions globally in understanding how children think and learn, what their needs, wants and desires are, and where the chinks in their armour lie – whether it be the need to be cool, or growing up in a time-starved home. In the USA in 1983, companies were spending $100 million targeting children. Now they are spending $17 billion per annum.

We are raising the most brand-conscious generation in history. Babies can recognise brands, toddlers ask for products by brand name and, according to the BratTrax Research Survey 2007/8 (the last known local research on this topic),[1] by the age of 10, children could recognise 400–500 brands. Television and movies have been very effective in creating brand disciples of our children from a very young age, and brand disciples recommend products to each other. Brands and products are not just items to be purchased, used or consumed; the intention is that they actually become part of one's lifestyle. They are a form of self-expression, part of who we are. Think Nike, Levi's, Adidas, Apple, and Samsung, among many others.

According to the BratTrax Research Survey 2007/8, children were already then bombarded by no fewer than 5 000 value-laden marketing messages each week on TV alone. With more media now in the mix, this figure today would be far higher. Brands and products make promises that buy into children's needs: "If you have this then you will feel more loved, you will be cool, you will be the envy of all your friends." Strategic product placement in movies, sponsorships, overt advertising and branded merchandise, and covert campaigns are included in online activities, of which parents are rarely aware.

Star Wars was the movie that changed childhood. Few parents realise that the first *Star Wars* movie, launched in 1977, was one of the key events to change childhood, ushering in an explosive advance in kids' consumerism. It was the first movie to launch a range of merchandise, including toys and games: The Star Wars Collection. So what? Well, the movie grossed $307 million and the merchandise made twice that – a signal to the marketing world that there was a fortune to be made out of theme merchandise linked to a movie.

Star Wars started a new movement – movies and TV shows that sell toys. Movies are now created specifically to sell character or branded merchandise. The movie has become just another advertising vehicle. The same goes for children's programming on TV. Just think about it – most of the popular shows have merchandise attached to them, from *Care Bears*, *Ninja Turtles*, *Power Rangers* and *Masters of the Universe* to *Bob the Builder*, *WWE*, *Hannah Montana*, *High School Musical* and *Ben 10*. Today, parents need to ask themselves this question: Is TV programming entertaining and educating my children, or selling merchandise?

Children today are big business, influencing 60–70% of household spend, from the food that lands up in the shopping trolley to the make and colour of the family car. This extraordinary situation is known as 'kidfluence', and parents need to understand how it works in order to be able to help their children grow into discerning consumers and savvy users of media. Your children are born with a computer mouse or cellphone in one hand and your wallet in the other. Without parental guidance, The Force is definitely with the marketers: you are putty in the hands of your children and you just listen to your wallet go '*ka-ching!*'

There is a war out there for a share of your child's heart and mind, as well as your wallet. But you are still the gatekeeper; hold on to that role and all the responsibilities that come with it. It will save both you and your child in the long run.

With so many more media touch points available to marketers today via all the gadgets at our disposal, children are caught in the crosshairs of marketers who, if they are worth their salt in financial turnover, all have a youth marketing strategy. The adage is, "Catch them young and hold them for life." Our children are becoming part of cradle-to-grave marketing and the earlier marketers can hook them the better.

There is a lot of white noise out there that runs interference between us and our kids – the noise of technology and the clutter of consumerism and all the stuff it brings into our lives, both necessary and unnecessary. Childhood is being reshaped into a process of learning how to consume and children are taught that pester-power works – especially when parents are feeling tired and guilty ...

We have to rise above all of this noise and clutter in order to stand out, to be noticed and heard by our children and to connect with them emotionally. On-screen media provide opportunities for our children to achieve instant gratification in so many ways. This feeds into their materialistic nature, resulting in an "I like this, I want it, and I want it now" generation.

It is vital that parents understand the connection between marketing to children and the plethora of media our children have at their disposal. We are not the only ones raising our children today. Big brands and technology are also big contributors to shaping who our children will become. Be awake and be aware and remember that a good CEO understands his or her competition. As CEO of your family, you need to do so too.

SEXUALITY AND STEREOTYPING ON A SCREEN

The media per se are drowning in sexual images and sexual innuendo. Just flick through magazines, watch TV adverts and listen to the suggestive nature of radio advertising. Add to that the easy availability of sexual content on TV and the Internet, and there is a distinct possibility that your children are seeing sexually explicit material – intentionally or unintentionally – before it is age-appropriate. Watch young children at parties or in the playground and, as they play out roles with each other, there is glaring evidence of having seen things that they shouldn't have.

A child's first exposure to information about sexuality or their own physical and emotional development should come from conversations with their parents or caregivers and not from viewing sexual acts on a screen that have no context. Marketing campaigns are, in fact, well known for encouraging younger kids to aspire to being older than they are.

Beware of racial, ethnic and gender stereotyping in TV programmes. For example, men are often portrayed as the village idiot, the dunce in the family or the bad guy, while women are often portrayed as mean-spirited and domineering alpha females or sex objects. All of this is great cannon fodder for some healthy family conversation. How do these issues fit in with your own family value system and worldview?

ASKING PERMISSION

From the time your child is tall enough to press the *On* button on the TV set or has worked out how to use the remote control, you need to teach them to ask for permission before watching TV – and this should continue right into the teenage years. If you don't, you risk raising children who believe they can watch anything, anytime, whenever they want to. If you give away your control of their TV consumption from an early age, you won't be able to regain it at a later stage, which, in turn, will have a serious impact on your ability to influence their use of cellphones and social media in the future.

FOR THE RECORD

The Youth Dynamix BratTrax Research Survey 2007/8 revealed that 7–15-year-olds in South Africa's upper income brackets were watching 3.4 hours of TV per weekday, rising to 5.8 hours on a Saturday and Sunday and rocketing to 7.8 hours per day in the school holidays. In 2006 the Kaiser Family Foundation pegged toddler TV viewing at 1.5 hours per day. According to specialist youth researcher and child development psychologist Carol Affleck, local, unofficial research indicates that this figure is now closer to three hours per day.

Even more alarming is the fact that these statistics are from before cellphones became commonplace and tablet technology even existed. What these figures reveal is that children are definitely not moving or playing enough. Whether they are in the care of their parents or a caregiver, these figures need to be reduced for healthy child development to take place. Moderation is the key. Children need to play more in the concrete sense rather than the virtual sense – it's how they learn best. Bingeing on TV (and other on-screen media) can affect your child's beliefs, values and culture; it also makes discipline harder, and affects their attitude towards you.

You need to be in control of how much TV they are watching as well as the content they are exposed to. Just a few words of advice:

- Do not set up a TV set in your child's bedroom – that's the quickest way to lose them. In my experience with busy families today, the average parent has little time and energy to monitor their family's viewing on one screen let alone screens in each child's bedroom, although some active, very vigilant parents can make it work (see Arthur's comment below).
- Record desirable TV programmes for viewing at times suitable for you as a family (as your children get older you can choose content together). Pre-recording also helps you to get around the invasive advertising between programmes that is aimed at getting your child to want more stuff, ultimately influencing what you buy.
- As often as possible, watch programmes together, so that you get a feel for the content and underlying messaging. You might be surprised to know that kids' TV programmes contain twice the number of violent acts as adult programmes and there is a lot of contradictory messaging. The Nickelodeon channel puts out a brilliant message that says, "Every day in every way we are part of everyone," while the underlying messaging in many of its shows is that adults suck and kids rule.
- If your relationships are important to you, then turn the TV off if you are not actively watching it. Studies have confirmed that a television left on in the background is detrimental to one-to-one interaction between parent and child. The Seattle Children's Research Institute in America offers a shocking statistic: parents say an average of 941 words per hour to their children when the TV is off, and only 171 words when the TV is on (and that's only when it's on in the background). And we are supposed to be talking our children clever!

I had often heard the advice that children should never have TVs in their bedrooms, but that always struck me as a blunt argument that did not take into account specific circumstances or ability to control viewing.

At one point, we were wrestling with vastly different viewing habits in our home – especially on a weekend when my big soccer match was on, but Jayna and Zianda had their favourite series on at the same time, or Sheryl wanted to watch the Crime & Investigation channel, and the 'family' TV was anything but ... So we decided to get a couple of small sets for the girls' bedrooms, with a strict proviso: they had to have permission to switch on the TVs, and we had to approve what they watched.

The key to the success of this approach was that the parameters were put in place before the TV sets were. The ground rules were accepted from the ground up, not suddenly superimposed over a set of habits that could no longer be broken. As a result, we've never had excessive TV viewing in the bedrooms.

This experience holds an important lesson for the time when smartphones start to become a part of children's everyday lives: the ground rules must be put in place first, the smartphones second. Insist on the boundaries (more about those later) from the start, and you avoid half the battles that most parents fight every day.

Your children need you to teach them how to become discerning TV viewers from a young age so that they, in turn, become responsible consumers of media both in duration and type of content. Teach them to ask permission before they press that button! You do not have to give up control of the remote control.

FROM THIS CHAPTER ...

- Watching television is still one of the most popular pastimes for South African children.
- The media habits you create around TV viewing will set the basis for gaming, social media and cellphone habits moving forward.
- Children do not know how much is too much and need guidance in order to learn how to become savvy users of media.
- Do not give up control of the remote control.
- Watch what your children are watching – content matters.
- Television can impact on a child's values, worldview, attitudes towards gender issues and more.
- Make constructive use of television.
- Don't replace physical activity and real play and learning opportunities with time spent in front of television.
- Don't overuse television as a babysitter.

CHAPTER 3

ON-SCREEN FUN GOES INTERACTIVE

From having just one small screen to manage in your child's life, there is now a different screen everywhere you turn. There are approximately two billion computers on the planet and children increasingly access the world via the Internet. Computers are useful tools for entertainment and learning. The need for printed encyclopaedias has fallen away as the Internet has given us access to more than a trillion websites, both good and bad. Everyone knows that if you want to know something, whether it is a fact or how to do something, just Google it and the answer will appear, like magic. This is the power of the world of computers, search engines, cellphones and the Internet.

Home has morphed into a multimedia entertainment centre and children can take their pick from the family computer to gaming devices and gaming consoles (which now also include cellphones). The gaming industry is burgeoning, with profits way exceeding that of big-screen movies in Hollywood today.

If parents thought they found buying real games and toys confusing, now they have to consider on-screen devices and all the games and apps that go with them too.

Let's take a look at the digital playground that our children find so exciting and engaging and why.

COMPUTERS, GAMING DEVICES AND CONSOLES

As with television, computers and gaming have provided children with more entertainment choices than any previous generation of children has ever had. While much of it takes place in the home, with mobile devices children can continue to play in any environment.

All forms of on-screen interaction are open to constructive use or abuse. It is vital that parents understand the addictive nature of on-screen activities in which their children are engaged (see page 38), but the focus of this chapter is on what makes this kind of technology attractive to children.

WHAT'S THE ATTRACTION?

Home computer games have had a compelling attraction for children since they first emerged commercially in the 1980s. They have evolved dramatically since then, to the extent that 'computer game' and 'video game' have become meaningless labels. In reality, they are digital games, and the platforms range from PCs to notebooks to tablets to consoles to smartphones to TV screens.

The advent of gaming apps on tablets and smartphones has resulted in an explosion in the number of people playing digital games. But rather than kill off other formats, it has also spurred even greater interest in 'serious' gaming. Quite unexpectedly, then, sales of gaming consoles are reaching an all-time high. Have a look at the numbers and forecasts from technology consultancy Gartner in the following table.

Video game market revenue worldwide, 2012–2015 (millions of dollars)

Segment	2012	2013	2014	2015
Video game console	37.400	44.288	49.375	55.049
Handheld video games	17.756	18.064	15.079	12.399
Mobile games	9.280	13.208	17.146	22.009
PC games	14.437	17.722	20.015	21.601
Total video game market	**78.873**	**93.282**	**101.615**	**111.058**

(Source: Gartner – October 2013)

The figures in this table confirm, therefore, that gaming is hardly a dying market. Rather, it means that even as mobile-games spending more than doubles in three years, cutting-edge gaming devices will become even more ubiquitous than they are today, and revenue from consoles still dwarfs that of mobile or PC games. This, in turn, means that names like Sony PlayStation, Microsoft Xbox, and Nintendo Wii will become household names as they invade your home – or at least your child's wish list.

Console games in themselves provide wonderful entertainment, but they are also immensely addictive. While it is easy to limit screen time on most devices for most purposes, a different dynamic kicks in with console games: it's called time. While someone can spend 10 minutes playing a mobile game or half an hour watching an episode of a TV sitcom, that doesn't seem possible with console games. Especially when first played, these games tend to have lengthy introductions, a period of learning the rules and tricks of the game, and then exploration of the game's environment – all before actively embarking on the quest, adventure or battle that is the core of the game. That is not going to happen in half an hour, or even an hour.

Once you open the doorway to games that play themselves out on a TV screen, via handheld controls, you also open the door to lengthy absorption in the game. Again, this is not necessarily a bad thing, if you have set boundaries of time and activity, and such lengthy engagement is not a daily occurrence or a school-day norm.

The related dynamic that tends to be different on mobile games is the level of escape from reality and 'immersiveness' of console games. It is hard to wrest a child's attention back to reality when they are in the midst of an interactive big-screen adventure. How you manage both the child's immersion and the child's retrieval from that immersion will dictate what effect console games have on children's behaviour. Not managing it at all is the only certain source of harm.

ACTIVE GAMING

There is an exception to the 'escape-from-reality', insular aspect of console games: games that require energetic activity and allow full family participation. Nintendo started the trend with the Nintendo Wii, which offered various fitness-oriented accessories like the Wii Balance Board. Microsoft followed up with the Xbox Kinect, a motion-sensing system that allows what is described as 'full-body gaming'. Sony then responded with the PlayStation Eye camera and the Wand controller, which allow extensive interaction that is not possible only with a handheld controller. Between these three platforms, there is no end to options that enhance rather than reduce physical activity. Gaming is no longer only for couch potatoes – although, of course, it can never truly replace physical exercise and all the sensations that would usually flood the very important proprioceptive and vestibular systems mentioned in Chapter 2.

IT'S LIKE A TREASURE HUNT AND MUCH IS FREE

Allowing access to the Internet is like sending children on a treasure hunt. Their sense of curiosity is piqued and they are off, searching for something (preferably for free) – a game, a piece of software, a list of cheats, information. With an Internet link, anything is possible. The world is their oyster.

It starts rather benignly. Children see the latest animated movie, and quickly discover that the movie has an extended life online. They find the official website, download the official screensavers, wallpapers or games, and even sign up to a limited 'club' that allows them to interact with other fans of the movie.

From there, they gravitate – and graduate – to more established online locations, with broader social environments too. Now they begin to interact with a broader public, typically under nicknames, but with the possibility of sharing personal information with strangers.

Then children progress to sites such as Moshi Monsters and Club Penguin, which are free at first … They set up a personal profile, and it's like a Facebook platform. Even your credit card is now at risk, as they discover that in-game purchases are the quickest way to progress.

Finally, they begin to see the Internet as their playground – with the same sense of safety and even authority that comes with mastering playground equipment.

Along the way, they gain control of the family or personal tablet, or are allowed to play with a smartphone. And they discover the world of apps. While many apps will be downloaded, tried out and discarded, some will become deeply addictive. Temple Run was downloaded 100 million times in 2013, and has been known to occupy children for many hours without a break – ignored by parents who are relieved to have found a new babysitter.

Offline activities and games are now available online and you can interact with and play against others in real time. This opens an exciting new gaming dimension for children, tweens and teens – with the realism, levels of violence and potential credit-card traps rising exponentially through the age groups. But it's not only bad news.

Blokus is a strategic-planning board game that incorporates chess-type thinking but in a fast-paced game. My boys loved playing the game and then discovered that it was also available online. They had their first online gaming experience with Blokus, playing against another player from Washington when they were about eight and 12 respectively. As part of the game, you fill out your player details, including your name, age and where you live. There is also a chat-box feature. I took this opportunity to teach my children that, for their own safety, they did not need to reveal too much personal information about themselves. As they were playing with a stranger, who could be anyone, with good or bad intentions, I told them not to use their own name or only to use their first name, not to put in their age and, at most, to say that they lived in South Africa with no further details. The boys were enthralled with the fact that they were playing with someone who lived so far away. Technology does make the world a very small and exciting place.

Skylanders, the most popular children's video game of all time, has quite literally brought real toys to life by doing something that has never been done before. Real figurines are provided for fantasy play and, when placed on the 'portal of power', they magically appear on your gaming screen. They provide a child with strategy, problem-solving and creative opportunities as they face challenges in the game. This digital breakthrough has been such a success that other industry players are rushing to apply similar technology. Disney, for example, launched Disney Infinity in 2013. Children are now able to take Buzz Lightyear to play in the Monsters University world, and connect Jack Sparrow with The Incredibles, and much more! Gaming platforms such as these are like an extension of the movies, but now your child gets to script the scenes and play roles in them.

"Just five more minutes, please!"

Reward systems make gaming a very attractive pastime for youngsters. They have a driving need to get to the next level. "Just five more minutes, please!" is a regular refrain from youngsters when Mum calls them to dinner or to finish up with what they're doing. And any parent who has had experience with gamer children knows that five minutes is actually 20 minutes, or much more than that, because the next level is usually some way away. Children lose all sense of time when playing computer games. They get caught up in the rush and excitement of it all. They become so engaged and immersed in the world in which they are playing that they don't really hear their parents at all.

Reward systems fuel the fervour and stimulate the pleasure centre of the brain, which is why these games are so addictive. We already know how effective star charts can be in the real world, so it should come as no surprise that their power online or on-screen is even greater, because the rewards chop and change all the time and help gamers move ahead to the next level.

In their guide, *Facing the Screen Dilemma: young children, technology and early education*, the Campaign for a Commercial-Free Childhood and Teachers Resisting Unhealthy Children's Entertainment explain how new neuro-imaging techniques provide biological evidence of the addictive properties of some screen media over and above television. "Dopamine, a neurotransmitter associated with pleasure, reward and alertness is released in the brain during fast-moving video games in a manner similar to its release after the consumption of some addictive drugs. In a survey of children 8–18 years old, one in four said that they 'felt addicted' to video games."[1]

Young parents entering the market were themselves the first gamers, so gaming is a natural part of their make-up. If you yourself are a gamer, you will understand that urge to continue playing and playing. If you are not a gamer, you will simply find this behaviour extremely irritating and not conducive to family relationships. Either way, children need to learn that there is a time and place for gaming and that they need to be able to control their gaming habits. And parents need to play a role in managing this learning process.

Children can acquire amazing skills through gaming, which we would do well to harness, and formal education is even looking at the 'gamification' of learning where it makes sense. Minecraft is a good example of a game that is being encouraged for its strategic thinking value in various schools around the world. Some of the skills enhanced by gaming include:
- eye-hand coordination and manual dexterity

- following complex instructions
- balancing short-, medium- and long-term planning
- strategic thinking and problem-solving
- patience (because you set goals and play to earn your reward)
- visual literacy (some of the newer, more complex games require a lot of reading)
- collaboration (including setting common goals and working together to achieve them)
- responsibility for looking after homes, families, buildings, crops, pets, armies and more in various games.

Familiarity with apps and their possibilities is also spawning a generation of young developers who think nothing of creating an app before they reach high school (see Chapter 7). Of course, not everyone can be a developer or come up with a winning concept at the age of 12, but there is a broader issue at stake here: familiarity with the ways of the world of communication and interaction means that children today are becoming far better equipped to enter the world of work, study, creativity and even relationships than those of a generation ago.

The answers to the kind of embarrassing social questions we could never ask our friends, parents or teachers are now a Google-click away. Sometimes there are far too many answers, and sometimes online advice is downright dodgy, but that is where parents – and teachers – once again have a role in guiding children to discern between credible sites and those that are, frankly, incredible.

YOU TAKE THE LEAD

Children need to understand that they shouldn't believe everything they see or read on the Internet. They need to know that not everything you see on the Internet comes from a credible source or is true. There is a lot of misleading content out there and kids need to be made aware of this and be encouraged to question and interrogate information, developing their critical-thinking skills. The Internet, with over a trillion website addresses, is the new library. The web is used to promote factually accurate information as well as opinions ranging from mild to extreme that can whip up hysteria and encourage antisocial or even dangerous behaviour. Children should not take everything they read at face value. They need to learn how to assess the quality and accuracy of information.

Of course, there are some wonderful child-friendly laptops and many great programmes and sites. Some are entertaining, others highly educational. Be selective about content and ensure that your child is not glued to the screen and attached to the mouse for hours on end. From the ages of about four to six, 20–30 minutes is ample – and this need not be a daily occurrence. Primary school children may want more time, but beware of them becoming hooked and being unable to disengage. *You* need to determine when your children are allowed to play on the computer and what programmes they are using and sites they are accessing. Make sure you enable security features on your computer and install additional cyber-protection if necessary. Children who play online games can quite innocently land on unsavoury websites by misspelling a word in their Google search. Of course, there are those children who will do it on purpose, however …

INAPPROPRIATE CONTENT AND PEOPLE

Access to inappropriate content and unsavoury people is always a danger on open systems. People can profess to be one thing on a screen but in real life turn out to be someone entirely different. Children need to learn to be discerning. Not trusting digital personas is a fundamental rule they need to take to heart to protect themselves, no matter what those people promise them.

There is an internationally accepted argument that when children spend more than two hours a day online, their exposure to predators and paedophiles rises exponentially. As they are surfing the net without their parents looking over their shoulders most of the time, they need to be made aware of this, so that they make responsible and sensible decisions about who they will allow to connect with them.

According to the 2013 *Sunday Times* Generation Next survey, South African youth in urban and peri-urban areas spend two hours on the Internet daily, with 62.73% accessing the Internet using their cellphones and not home computers. Imagine that: nearly two out of three young people in South Africa have a device they can use at any time of day, largely unsupervised, to explore the world of information and entertainment. It is natural that a fair proportion will also be tempted to explore forbidden fruit. From pornography to pirated music, the temptation is there, in the palms of their hands, for several hours a day.

Whether children actively seek out inappropriate content or whether they come across unsuitable or upsetting content inadvertently, such as via a search engine or by innocently clicking on a link or pop-up, or by reading distasteful comments on social media, they can be exposed to things you would probably rather they weren't. Think violent or pornographic images, gambling websites, unmoderated chat rooms (with no adult supervision), or even video-sharing websites and forums that encourage antisocial and reckless behaviour, such as substance abuse or vandalism.

Just as you might not want your children watching an age-restricted movie, or reading an adults-only magazine, so you should be concerned about what they view on the Internet, their cellphones or gaming console. Just because it is on a screen doesn't mean you have no jurisdiction or say in the matter.

Inappropriate games are often readily for sale to children way below the recommended age guidelines. In large toy stores with gaming departments, children of all ages can easily purchase games with 16 and 18 age restrictions without the salesperson batting an eyelid. The premise is that if you have the cash, you can get the game. Many parents do not supervise their children's tech-shopping experiences and are unaware of what their children are purchasing.

Because the brain remembers everything it sees, children cannot easily erase a disturbing or uncomfortable gaming experience from their minds. They have to be helped to assimilate and understand it for it not to have a negative impact. Let's face it, in how many households are parents there to witness what their children are actually playing? And, of course, many children are exposed to such games in other people's homes too, in the same way they may view movies they would not generally see at home. Value systems differ from home to home and children need to know what is and is not okay for them to play or view. Not that it will always stop them, but at least you have brought the issue to their attention, enabling them to make conscious choices. More about this in Chapter 11.

The gaming landscape explained

When you visit a bookshop or video store you usually know exactly where to look for different genres. Then your children take you into a gaming shop

– their eyes light up as if they're in a candy store and you feel completely lost and out of your depth. Sections called 'New releases', 'Best-sellers' and 'Pre-owned' tell you nothing. How do you help children make a suitable purchase beyond just adhering to the age ratings on the back of the game? And you thought buying games and toys was confusing!

Like puzzles, games and toys, there should be a variety of different types of video games available to children to ensure that they don't get stuck on one genre – 'smash-and-bash' games, for example. You need to ask yourself two questions before making a purchase:

- What will this game get my child to do, e.g. match shapes, race cars, build or kill?
- What kind of world will this game encourage my child to step into, e.g. criminal underworld, fantasy, Disney movie? You need to be happy with the type of imagery your child will be playing with.

Generally, there are five main categories of games. The following list was adapted from Teresa Orange and Louise O'Flynn's *The Media Diet for Kids* (Hay House, 2005). We hope it gives you more insight and confidence to help you make wiser choices for, and with, your children.

Fast action games
- These include maze, 'zapping', sports and racing games.
- They are simple games that are often good for eye-hand coordination.
- These are not necessarily intellectually stimulating and can be very repetitive.
- Examples include MotoGP, FIFA and Gran Turismo.

Strategy and creative games
- These include family/quiz games, creating virtual worlds, sports management, flight simulation, strategic war games and educational games.
- They are designed to get kids thinking and planning strategically.
- Examples include The Sims, RollerCoaster/Zoo Tycoon and Minecraft.

Adventure games
- These include adventure games, such as film fantasy and original fantasy.
- They usually involve a voyage or mission with tasks and obstacles to be overcome.
- Many are linked to a film or TV programme.

- They are good for learning decision-making skills.
- Examples include James Bond, Lord of the Rings, Tomb Raider, Doom, Sonic the Hedgehog and The Simpsons.

Fighting and war games
- These include beat-'em-up games, combative war games, destruction games, wrestling and even murder games.
- Players are challenged to complete a number of missions.
- The heart of the experience is about fighting and destruction.
- Some are good, clean fun, others are okay played in moderation, but many are not suitable for young children and carry age ratings of between 15 and 18.
- Look out for exceptionally realistic and graphic imagery.
- Examples include Grand Theft Auto, Mortal Kombat and Street Fighter.

Educational games
- These include fun ways to learn perceptual skills such as matching, categorising, working with colour and shape, literacy and numeracy skills and music.
- Most are subject-specific and designed to support schoolwork and revision, but you will need to check that they are compatible with the school curriculum.
- They enable learning through fun and play.
- They reinforce educational skills learned in the real world.
- There are creative and multi-activity programmes with a wide appeal, but should not replace real games and toys.
- They facilitate IT literacy, typing skills and language learning.
- Check whether there is a feedback or assessment mechanism to report on your child's progress.
- Examples include Mathletics and Big Brain Academy.

Keep in mind, however, that marketing buzzwords can be misleading. While games and activities that can be played on various devices might be billed as 'interactive' versus the more 'passive' nature of old technologies such as television, for example, many such games and digital activities still only allow a choice between a predetermined set of options, choices or responses, which has been shown to diminish creativity.

Remember, too, that children still need multisensory, whole-body experiences with their world to enable them to work with their very own original thoughts rather than following someone else's programme, train of thought or idea on-screen. Child-initiated play is an essential component of healthy childhood development versus being constantly directed by an adult in real life or prompted on-screen.

Visit www.commonsensemedia.org for trusted gaming reviews and lists of recommendations.

The effects of video-game violence

Modern warfare is increasingly being fought remotely. Soldiers may be sitting in the USA but are able to control a drone flying over a warzone in Afghanistan and make aim-and-kill decisions on screens that look extremely similar to those our children interact with when they play computer games.

The training of soldiers includes on-screen training that is used to condition them and desensitise them to killing. These training methods also have built-in reward systems and involve repetition to myelinate the neurological pathways in the brain. The more a pathway is myelinated the faster the neurological impulses can flow, improving reaction times and decision-making. A soldier's inhibitions to kill are thus lowered. The same techniques are at play in our children's computer games too.

A review of 50 years of research on the impact of violence in TV, movies, video games and on the Internet concludes that watching media violence significantly increases the risk that a viewer or video-game player will behave aggressively in both the short and the long term. About 60% of TV programmes contain violence and 40% contain heavy violence. Most video games contain violence. Video-game ratings are a poor indicator of content and constitute a conflict of interest, because the rating is allocated by the video-game industry itself. The authors of the review state that the impact of violent electronic media on public health is second only to the impact of cigarette smoking on lung cancer.[2]

Of course, young children are most vulnerable to media violence because they are more impressionable, can't distinguish between fantasy and reality, cannot discern motives for violence, and learn by observing and imitating.[3] They can also be at risk of suffering Post-Traumatic Stress Disorder (PTSD) just from watching or engaging with inappropriate violent – or sexual – content, even if they have been exposed unwittingly at a friend's house, for example. In many such instances, a child is unlikely to tell their parents what they have seen for fear of getting into trouble or having their devices confiscated so they simply live with the pain and fear that PTSD creates. There is a whole genre of violent computer games that require murder, killing, torture and more. You need to have a handle on the content your children are playing with, and watch out for symptoms such as aggressive outbursts, impulsive behaviour, apathy, lethargy, withdrawal, depression and antisocial behaviour that may need to be dealt with by a professional – or may disappear completely if you help your child to make better choices. Stay tuned in to your child, it could save you a lot of family heartache.

WHAT THE EXPERTS SAY

We know many parents may feel out of their depth when assessing appropriate technology and content, but a helpful trick is to put a human face on whatever it is that you are assessing. This will bring common sense back into play, as it would if you were assessing a new friend your child has made. In the friendship scenario, you very quickly start evaluating whether you are happy for this person to be your child's playmate, the influence of this new person on your child and his or her mood and behaviour, and whether this friend energises or drains your child. If you get a negative response to any of these questions, you usually find a way to discourage and even end the friendship.

So, what about the television programmes your child watches or the computer games he or she plays with? They are your child's companions too and, in many instances, replace play dates or social interaction with other children. You need to consider whether they are good or bad company and how they might be influencing your child. Children cannot make these assessments themselves.

When putting a human face on content, insert the word 'person' instead of 'game' or 'programme' and ask yourself these questions:[4]
- What learning does my child take from this 'person'?
- What does this 'person' motivate my child to do?
- How does this 'person' influence my child's energy levels?
- What language does my child adopt as a result of this 'person'?
- What role model does this 'person' offer my child?
- How does this 'person' influence the mood of my child?

> • Does this 'person' encourage my child to be social, and if so, in
>   what way?
>
> This trick of personalisation was inspired by Teresa Orange and
> Louise O'Flynn in their book *The Media Diet for Kids*. It should help
> you feel like you are on more familiar turf and decision-making will
> become that much easier. We must help our children on the journey
> to become discerning users of media content.

DOES THE ATTRACTION FOR BOYS AND GIRLS DIFFER?

In media usage, girls take the prize when it comes to socialising. They tend
to use chat facilities more than boys, and want and 'need' a cellphone earlier than boys do. Boys, on the other hand, are generally more competitive
and are drawn to the more compulsive nature of computer games. They
love macho imagery and fast, aggressive action scenes. They are always
looking for cheats and ways to get to the next level of the game. Speed,
smash-and-bash, and violence seem to be attractive to boys. Think Gran
Turismo, FIFA, Need for Speed and Minecraft. Walk into any gaming shop
and notice the masculine appeal. Many computer games have a single goal
and this works well for boys.

Girls, however, are more attracted to games that entail creating characters and situations in a fantasy world, or games with a social dimension.
Think The Sims and all its spin-offs. In Arthur's home, both his daughters, Jayna and Zianda, came to serious computer games via this franchise.
Girls are also more comfortable than boys with games that have multiple
goals or outcomes.

According to EU Kids Online, "There are … gender differences in
risk: boys appear more likely to seek out offensive or violent content, to
access pornographic content or be sent links to pornographic websites;
girls appear more likely to be upset by offensive, violent and pornographic
material."[5]

Balance your child's real and virtual experiences – they need both. Just as an example, some years ago I picked up my six-year-old son from a play date and he was having the time of his life. His friend's parents were doing an alteration to their home and the boys had found a plank of wood and a few bricks with which they made a seesaw ramp for their bikes. What incredible fun they had for over two hours. The exercise was creative, challenging and very physical. It entailed thinking, planning and problem-solving to set it up, and then the gross motor skills of balance, coordination and spatial planning (how fast or slow to go and when to accelerate so that you don't fall off the ramp). This was the perfect balancing act to the hour spent playing a computer game earlier in the day.

That hour of on-screen activity itself was also well spent playing a simple game called Hugo. This entailed fine motor coordination to move the cursor over the screen, helping the worker ants collect food for the queen. On depositing food in the anthill, my son then had to decide on his reward – select either a worker ant or a soldier ant. This introduced thinking skills and strategy to the game. From time to time, the anthill came under attack from enemy ants, so there needed to be a good spread of worker ants and army ants to deal with whatever situation arose. This game involved basic thinking, planning and problem-solving skills in a virtual environment.

It's amazing how quickly children work out how the game is played and what the rules and consequences are – and all of this without actually reading a rules booklet! Come to think of it, there was no rules book or adult supervision with the bike ramp game either! Aren't children so naturally resourceful?

It is so important for parents to help their children develop a balanced approach to on- and off-screen activities. We must ensure that they are able to switch easily between the real and virtual worlds with which they engage, because they do need to master both to survive in today's hi-tech world. While it is possible to do things and visit places via technology that would never be possible in real life, there is no substitute for real-life experiences with real-time consequences.

A world in one room

With so many screens vying for our children's attention, one of the dangers to avoid is that they substitute human companionship for a screen. It is easy to do and a child's world can become very small even though they may be connected to many people online. We call this living in a world in one room. It's probably close to the worst image you have of an anaemic-looking solitary teenager in a dark room alone, with remote control in hand and growing roots into the couch.

With your guidance and help, your child needs to become a healthy switcher between the on-screen and off-screen world. We need to ensure that they keep it balanced and real.

WHAT THE EXPERTS SAY

In 2008, leading US psychiatrist Dr Jerald Block suggested that there are four common characteristics of obsessive Internet use:[6]
- excessive use – losing track of time or neglecting to eat or sleep
- withdrawal – e.g. feelings of anger, tension or depression
- tolerance – wanting a better computer or more hours online
- negative repercussions – e.g. arguments, lies, isolation and tiredness.

During their research for *The Media Diet for Kids*, authors Teresa Orange and Louise O'Flynn ran focus groups of parents, children, caregivers and grandparents. Interestingly, most kids interviewed sensed that too much screen time was a bad thing. They were looking to their parents to take the lead. As one 11-year-old boy said, "If you don't get told to come off, it's hard to know when to come off."

Most kids in the survey – apart from serious media bingers – thought their parents were far too weak. "They say 'no' and don't mean it," was a frequent comment. They were also determined that, if they had children one day, they would be stricter and do more to control the screen at home.

VIRUSES, FILTERS AND RISK

One of the security risks in the online world is that we and our children may inadvertently download viruses onto our devices. Criminals are also constantly finding innovative ways to install malicious software (known as malware) onto our computers that can damage them, cause them to run slowly, gather your personal information, harm your reputation or access your bank accounts.

When it comes to managing your family's online/digital risk, there are extremes. You can be a parent who takes no precautions at all or one who believes that the best protection is to switch of the device or unplug it and lock it away in a cupboard. In between these two there is a vast range of precautions that you can take based on the extent to which you want to manage your risk and exposure. Like real-life risk management, the more you implement the more complex it all becomes.

Very simply, the average family needs standard risk management, which consists of the following:

- Antivirus to protect you from viruses and malware (malware masquerades as something safe but it can take over functions of your computer). If you have the right software, you will receive warnings such as, "Are you sure you want this programme to make changes to your computer?", before you download a piece of software or an update, for example.
- Security software that protects your computer from others having access to it from outside, and protects you from clicking on bad links.
- Firewall software offers complete security from outside intrusion much like burglar bars in your home. You can also set firewalls to block certain activity.

These three products can be purchased separately but are often combined in the same product for standard levels of safety. If you are looking for free online safety programmes to download, AVG and Avast! are recommended. In addition, safe online behaviour is just as important. Discuss the following with your family:

- Practise safe surfing online, which includes not clicking on links that tell you to log into your bank account (commonly known as phishing), or entering lotteries, for example. Phishers want access to your passwords so that they can control your computer.

- Don't click on strange links sent to you by people on social networks, for example, and especially if they haven't told you what's behind the link. Common ones that both youngsters and adults fall for include, "Have you seen this funny video?" Just by clicking on something as innocuous sounding as this can result in a third-party gaining access to all your passwords. In most cases your 'friend' did not post this. They fell into the trap before you and now their account is being used to forward the same message to all the friends in their network.
- If a company calling themselves Microsoft, for example, phones you out of the blue and tells you that they have been monitoring your computer and have picked up that there is a virus in your system that they would like to help you with, ignore them – it's not Microsoft. Once again, they will ask you for passwords and will guide you through downloading software that will 'fix' your system, but in reality will enable them to control your computer and shut it down at will. This results in extortion when they tell you that you will need to pay them if you want to use your computer again.

With all forms of Internet-linked on-screen media gaining such momentum we will never run out of topics to discuss around the dinner table with our children, and teaching them to make choices that are good for them has become an important parenting objective.

ⓘ

Which websites should a parent block – based on a child's age?[9] Net Nanny, the world's number-one-rated parental-controls software, recommends the following based on years of experience and feedback from customers.

Notes
- 'Block' – the person browsing the web will be blocked from viewing (not allowed to view) the web page requested
- 'Warn' – the person browsing the web will be warned that the website requested is not recommended, but the person can proceed to viewing the web page, if desired
- 'Allow' – the person browsing the web will be allowed to view the web page requested

Child: Ages 4–7
- Categories to block: abortion, alcohol, anime, dating, death/gore, drugs, gambling, lingerie/swimsuits, mature, nudity, pornography, profanity, provocative, proxy, sexual health, suicide, tobacco, weapons
- Profanity: Block

Pre-teen: Ages 8–12
- Categories to block: abortion, alcohol, death/gore, drugs, gambling, mature, nudity, pornography, provocative, proxy, suicide, tobacco, weapons
- Categories warned: anime, dating, lingerie/swimsuits, sexual health
- Profanity: Mask

Teen: Ages 13–17
- Categories to block: alcohol, drugs, gambling, mature, nudity, pornography, proxy and tobacco
- Categories to warn: abortion, death/gore, sexual health, suicide, weapons
- Categories to allow: anime, dating, lingerie/swimsuits, provocative
- Profanity: Mask

Adult: Ages 18+
- Categories to block: pornography, proxy
- Categories to warn: none
- Categories to allow: abortion, alcohol, anime, dating, death/gore, drugs, gambling, lingerie/swimsuits, mature, nudity, profanity, provocative, sexual health, suicide, tobacco, weapons
- Profanity: Allow

- Children are screen-hungry and have more entertainment choices than ever.
- Gaming is big business today.
- Gaming is fun and can be educational, but is also addictive.
- Gaming is highly absorbing and takes time.
- Children can acquire beneficial skills from gaming.
- Built-in reward systems are an intrinsic part of what motivates children on-screen.
- Supervise your child's gaming purchases and downloads.
- Balance your child's real and virtual experiences.
- Implement necessary risk-management measures to protect your child.
- Help your children to make good choices.

CHAPTER 4

DEVICES GO SMART & MOBILE

While the trend is towards miniaturisation of computers, mobile devices are now in fact reversing this trend, becoming ever larger as their displays increase in size. The rise of 'superphones' or 'phablets' – smartphones with large screens – has gone hand in hand with the rise in popularity of video content viewed on smartphones. The medium evolves with the message, and content drives innovation. The future of technology can be described as any content, on any device, anywhere, any time.

The App Store for Apple's iOS operating system opened on 10 July 2008, and the world was forever changed. Today that store houses more than a million apps, as does Google's Play Store, while Microsoft's Windows Store and BlackBerry World add a few hundred thousand more.

In the meantime, more than half of all cellphones sold globally and in South Africa in 2013 were smartphones, and eventually there will be no such thing as a basic phone. With entry-level smartphones falling below R500 in price, it will make little sense for manufacturers to keep making basic phones that sell for only a little less than that.

Think of that for a moment: in a few years' time, the only phones you will be able to give your children will be smartphones. The world will be accessible in the palms of their hands.

Mobile devices really do bring greater meaning to being connected to the digital skin of the world through the use of convenient and very powerful devices. As parents, we need to understand the capabilities of these devices and their possible uses to ensure our children's safety and responsible use of them.

Toddlers easily navigate their parents' mobile devices. They already know how to access movies on their parents' phones and tablets, which buttons to press, and how to slide their fingers across a touchscreen. It is second nature to them and they don't seem to forget. In fact, give a magazine to a toddler to flip through and she will look for the buttons and try to use it as a touchscreen. Toddlers simply come to the conclusion that a magazine is a tablet that doesn't work! This illustrates the degree of digital immersion in certain homes.

Children are not just playing on their parents' phones and tablets, but are increasingly being given their own devices of a similar nature at younger and younger ages. Kiddies' laptops and tablets fill toy store shelves and schools are rolling out tablets into the classroom at a rapid rate. Regular questions from parents include, "At what age should we be giving our children cellphones?" and "Is the use of tablets in schools really necessary and good for our children?"

WHAT CHILDREN WANT FROM YOUR PHONE OR TABLET

We need to understand that children want to play with whatever it is that they see us engaging with regularly, and today that means on-screen devices and gadgets. Haven't children always wanted to play with their parents' toys? Think back to our own childhoods when we had pull-along phones that were the kiddie version of the telephone in our homes. Same, same. When our firstborns were toddlers, they would climb onto our office chairs and bang on our keyboards, calling out "'puter, 'puter", with great glee. Many had toy versions of a cellphone. By the time our other children came along, their toy cellphones looked so realistic that they could have been mistaken for the real thing!

The fact that today's toddlers want to play with their parents' gadgets is perfectly normal because children like to copy what their parents do. If you consider how much they see you interacting with such devices, it's little wonder. The problem is that your 'toys' are actually quite expensive and are not child-proof. They have also become vital to the effective running of both your personal and professional life. They have become your external brain or mobile filing system. In a very real sense, they are another hard drive carrying all your vital personal and business information, so you don't actually want your kids playing with them.

However, when you are busy or out and about with your children, or just need to get them to sit still and stop moving for a minute, there is nothing like technology or a screen-based game to engage them in an instant. The result is that technology has become part of our parenting default setting, with parents' devices morphing into convenient playthings.

Reading the trend, toy manufacturers are now churning out laptops, tablets and many other gadgets for babies, toddlers and children. There are protective cases to child-proof your tablet and smartphone (to a degree, anyway). Increasingly, toys are also looking more and more like the real thing, with similar capabilities: with built-in cameras and MP3 players, a variety of apps already installed and more that can be downloaded off the web. Toys can even access the web directly through 3G capabilities, opening up extensions to the offline play experiences online. Parents have had a tough enough time making choices around the plethora of real toys and games, and now along come tech-toys.

Toys, like everything else, are changing to incorporate the real and virtual world, evolving and merging with technology, such as incorporating the capabilities of parents' smartphones and tablets into a game. This new generation of toys and games is referred to as Toys 3.0, whether it's a helicopter or car that can now be controlled by a smartphone, figurines that can be brought to life on a gaming console (think Skylanders), or even board games that can now be played on a tablet computer (there is a new version of Monopoly that utilises an iPad in the middle of the board).

Then there's the Barbie Digital Makeover Mirror that pairs an iPad with a mirror for augmented reality play, enabling a little girl to apply make-up in the mirror without actually putting it on in real life (or making a mess), but it's her face in the mirror with the green eyeshadow! Mums, this is the same technology you will find in clothing shops in the future, where you will no longer try on clothes under ghastly lighting in fitting rooms. Rather, you will simply look in a virtual mirror and, at the swipe of a touchscreen, the clothes will appear on your body! Your children are already preparing for this world.

Portability is a big trend in Toys 3.0: play any game, anywhere, on any device, any time. Take, for example, the AppVentures iPad Play Case, which turns your iPad into an interactive firehouse or dollhouse. You are able to decorate your house, rearrange furniture, water plants, slide down a fireman's pole, put out fires, and a whole lot more. The best part is that you can take your entire playhouse with you wherever you go. If a toy manufacturer can create both an online and offline experience of their game and toy, they'll be playing right into the hands of their target market – because that's what children today want so that they have maximum play flexibility.

In the workplace of tomorrow, our children will expect to find the same kinds of options, and will be able to log onto any device, using their credentials to pick up on a project where they left off on a different device in a different location.

Already, any device can now become a toy, and this is even extending to areas like our cars. Car manufacturers SAAB and Ford are installing technology to make car windows touchscreens on which children can play during a car journey. Opportunities and applications are endless. And the future use of such technology is already becoming clear.

The key to healthy assimilation of tech-toys into a child's life is that parents need to choose the platform, the medium and the toy, ensuring that it is age-appropriate. For example, does a two-year-old need a real tablet or a tech-toy specially designed for her age and stage that is also unbreakable? (A two-year-old doesn't understand the value of a tablet, and dropping toys is part of exploring how gravity works.) Should a six-year-old begin gaming online on a computer or cellphone, or would he be better off with an educational gaming console where you get to control the content?

While on the topic of children from birth to six years of age and technology, mention must be made of the potential overuse of technology, which can impact negatively on their acquisition of essential life skills.

BEWARE! DEVICES CAN HAMPER LIFE-SKILL DEVELOPMENT

If children are to become independent, they need to learn to self-regulate and manage their own daily routines. This includes basics such as sleeping in their own beds and being able to fall asleep without much outside assistance. One of the traps parents fall into today is that they often put their children to bed watching something on a smartphone or tablet in lieu of a bedtime story, a lullaby or two, a quick tickle and then lights out.

Children are becoming addicted to screens for regular activities such as falling asleep, eating meals, and self-soothing after they have been angry or upset. Many a parent claims they cannot get food into their toddler unless they are sitting in front of the television or playing on an iPad. This may seem innocuous at first, but the ramifications are deeply disturbing and will almost certainly have long-term consequences. Screen addiction for sleep may ultimately be replaced by sleeping-pill addiction, for example. And if a child doesn't learn how to deal with the full emotional catastrophe of life, how do they develop emotional intelligence (EQ)? On-screen activities from movies to gaming can overstimulate children or replace their ability to find inner happiness and satisfaction because they become dependent on an outside source for that. On-screen activities can also hamper the development of resourcefulness in children. Be aware that children need to learn how to:

- be happy in their own company
- put themselves to sleep
- create their own fun without a screen
- combat boredom without the use of a screen
- be their own internal source of happiness rather than relying on a screen
- be able to soothe themselves when they are upset.

Get the above right in the early years by creating healthy media habits and not replacing human contact with you with a screen, and your children will have a solid foundation on which to become healthy digital citizens. Teaching them how to make good media choices will be so much easier.

As children progress to becoming tweens and teens, their appetite for on-screen connection with their peers, via messaging services, social media or gaming, increases exponentially with the biological need to connect more with others. They are not just engaging for fun any more, but with more purpose. They are on a journey to independence and on-screen media provide a very strong feeling of operating independently from their parents.

The technology also fits in well with the increased desire to take risks, do new things and try on different personas that come with puberty and adolescence. Computer games stir up emotions, create excitement and tension, or provide an opportunity for a good laugh.

At all stages of development, parents should be concerned about the amount of time their children spend interacting with on-screen media, the content and activities they are engaging with, as well as the digital personas with whom they connect. Parents are still the gatekeepers, despite the fact that they are digital immigrants. Teaching kids to make safe and savvy choices around their media usage is an important role for parents today.

A sound understanding of children's technology journey, combined with some insight into their development and the changing world, is imperative to help you to keep perspective and make good decisions in this regard. A greater conscious awareness of your own technology usage and possible adult addictive tendencies in the online realm is also recommended.

WHAT PHONE AT WHAT AGE?
The single most common 'official' reason for parents giving a child a cellphone is safety and security. The unofficial reason, of course, is that the parents have finally given in to their children's nagging.

Not surprisingly, one of the most common questions asked by parents whose children do *not* have phones, is what the most appropriate age would be to put one in their hands. And along with this question goes the one about what type of phone a child should have.

First things first: safety is indeed the best reason to give children a phone. Especially if they use public transport or school buses, or are involved in extensive extramural activity, a phone becomes an essential tool for coordinating meeting and pick-up times, or providing updates about delays from either side.

There are two general age levels at which this need seems to kick in: at age 10, when children typically move out of the junior grades at school, and involvement in sport and cultural activities begins to take off; and at age 12, when their social lives become a complex maze of events, activities and negotiations.

Increasingly, children are getting their own phones at a much younger age. A recent study by Elizabeth Englander among 20 000 children in

Massachusetts showed that one-fifth of eight-year-olds already had phones.

Most parents have their own reasons, with nuances drawn from their own lifestyles and environment, for giving a child a phone. But they still find themselves at a loss when it comes to choosing the right phone. Here, at least, the guidelines are more clear-cut …

If you must give a child of eight a phone, make it a basic phone that offers only voice and SMS. If you give a child of that age an Internet-connected device with chat and app functionality, you're almost guaranteeing tears. The Massachusetts study found that 20% of eight-year-olds with phones had experienced cyber-bullying. At best, you're still expecting little children to take responsibility for an expensive device that many parents have often not mastered.

For this very reason, the phone should be pre-programmed with key numbers of family, caregivers or school authorities. Clear rules must dictate when and how the phone may be used, and usage must be monitored.

At age 10, basic phones are still recommended, but smartphones become more of a norm, especially when they are hand-me-downs. Here parents have a responsibility to understand the parental controls on the device, and to ensure that children only access age-appropriate content. A strict budget on voice and data must be imposed.

From 12 onward, the pressure is on to get a decent smartphone, particularly to use chat apps that allow youngsters to coordinate their social lives. No matter the sophistication of the phone, also provide a cheap basic phone as a standby to take along to parties, field trips and other outings where there is a high chance of a phone being lost.

Above all, remember that the phone is your property, and only on loan to your child.

Using a smartphone presents both risks and opportunities. Setting a few ground rules before you hand over the phone will provide much-needed peace of mind for you *and* your child.

- Set a password for the phone and stress that they are not to share it with anyone but you.
- Add important contacts that are necessary for daily and emergency use.
- Set up the email account correctly for older children.
- Establish rules of use – when and where they are allowed to use it and what they can do with it (see Appendix 2 on page 214 for a copy of a cellphone contract you can use in this regard).

- Check the school's cellphone policy and make sure your child understands it.
- Establish rules for Internet access, app downloads and in-app purchases.
- Discuss the costs of using the phone and how you will limit these.

AVOID BEING AMBUSHED BY APPS

There is another very different reason adults need to understand their children's digital activity – one that will affect them more directly than any other. And that is the temptation to buy products within a game or app, which in turn leads to the temptation to 'borrow' parents' credit cards. The rise of virtual products – intangible goods that cannot be re-sold – has been highlighted in a study conducted by MasterCard across 20 countries, including South Africa. The card company's 2014 *Online Shopping Behaviour Study* included the top six sites most often used by South Africans for shopping online in the past three months.

The first three were no surprise: the Naspers-owned Kalahari.com, the social shopping site Groupon, and the online auction site Bidorbuy. co.za. Of South Africans shopping online, 35%, 13% and 12%, respectively, bought on these sites. In fourth place, relative newcomer Takealot.com saw the biggest rise in share of shoppers of any site in the country, increasing from 4% a year to 11%. It was followed by Amazon.com, the biggest foreign site in the local mix, and classifieds site Gumtree, with 10% and 8% respectively of online shoppers saying they shopped there.

And then the virtual elephant in the room: from almost nowhere, suddenly claiming 7% of local online shoppers, came Apple's iTunes and App Store. But that was just the tip of the elephant's trunk. All respondents, representing 4.6 million highly active Internet users in South Africa (according to research by World Wide Worx), were asked whether they were aware of virtual items, credits, or upgrades within games or apps. A full 91% were aware of these. And a quarter of respondents – more than 1.2 million South Africans – had made a purchase in this way.

Such items are also known as 'in-app' purchases, and are usually invisible in the virtual storefront of app stores, games sites and download platforms. Even when a game is free to download and play, users often find themselves faced with the option of making a purchase during the game to advance more quickly, or to unlock more levels, characters or scenes. That was the key to the massive valuation that the 'free' Facebook game, FarmVille, afforded its creator, Zynga. It is the key to the huge valuation of the maker of the Candy Crush Saga mobile game, King, as it rakes in close to a million dollars a day from inside the app.

'Shopping' is almost too dignified a term to describe this form of impulse buying. We call it 'ambush retail': it is the one form of purchase that the user does not expect to make or even want to make, but is faced with the choice, suddenly, at the moment when the need for instant gratification is highest.

How much more so will that need be felt by teenagers? If they can, they will use airtime to trade for in-app attractions. Many youths also have a debit card, typically given to young people as the 21st-century equivalent of a savings account. Soon the banks will give such cards the functionality to make online purchases, and suddenly pocket money will have a very different meaning. So, don't forget to check the apps on your child's phone – and yours – and keep an eye on your monthly cellphone and iTunes accounts.

- Almost anything you can do on a computer you can now do on a smartphone or tablet device.
- You have spent time and money securing your computer; you need to take the same care with your mobile devices too.
- Understand how to child-proof your devices.
- Implement safety measures to enable your child to safely use your devices, limiting their access to inappropriate or harmful content and activating parental controls and installing filters.
- Beware of in-app purchases.
- Establish rules of use for your own devices.
- Make a thoughtful and educated decision about when to give your child a cellphone.
- Provide your child with age-appropriate functionality on whatever device you decide to buy them.
- Engage your children regularly in conversations around cellphone safety issues.

CHAPTER 5

CHILDREN IN SOCIAL MEDIA:
NO, YOU HAVEN'T LOST THEM

"A real conversation is playing itself out before adults' disbelieving eyes … It disturbs us because we think that it is replacing communication, but instead it is embracing the kind of communication that is reshaping the world." This is the argument Arthur puts forward in Chapter 1. These lines represent the best of social media and messaging. But they also indicate the worst of what social media can mean. We can find case studies aplenty about children who find the virtual world of online communications so compelling that they abandon the real world and withdraw from social interaction with family and friends.

In most of these cases, however, the withdrawal already began before technology intervened. Lack of communication within the family and absence of parental interest in the child provide fertile ground for cyber-withdrawal.

That, however, is the exception rather than the rule. Almost every new fad in social networks among children is driven by peer-group pressure. While that does, of course, imply the impulse of children to follow the crowd, it also denotes social engagement with friends and peers. And that is exactly what social networking represents.

It offers a benefit to parents as well: if you understand social media, you have an additional window into your child's world. You may not be able to control this world or even your child's behaviour in it, but with knowledge, you can guide and manage your child's place in this world.

TWO KINDS OF SOCIAL ANIMAL

Two broad types of social platform form part of children's social activity today: instant messaging (IM) and social networks.

IM started out as a simple messaging application that used a computer or phone's data connection, rather than a phone's SMS service. That means, in most cases, a message costs a fraction of a cent, while an SMS to personal contacts has typically cost between 50c and 80c in South Africa. It is astonishing that children tend to embrace the concept before adults, who should be setting the example in cost consciousness.

IM can evolve into social networks, as with Mxit in South Africa. In general, social networks are content-oriented. They are typically a more rich and complex environment for sharing experiences, photos, videos and links to even more content. When children are engaging in social networking, they are not only chatting; they are also sharing. This is the fundamental basis for Arthur's argument that layers of communication are being added. Think of it as a multimedia form of communication, compared to one consisting only of verbal and visual cues contained in face-to-face contact. Even the emotional component of conversation, which adults assume is far richer in real life, is enhanced with emoticons (smiley faces), images and symbols that allow children to express feelings they have a hard time articulating verbally.

This does *not* mean all forms of virtual communication are richer or more positive; only that this is more often the case. It doesn't give parents an excuse to be less aware or vigilant of where their children go when they disappear down the virtual rabbit hole.

Let's examine each of the major social networks, why they are so compelling, and why they can be so dangerous.

FACEBOOK

Facebook was the first of the major global social networks. It started in 2004 as a social website for a single university, and quickly expanded to universities and colleges across the United States, and then to schools and workplaces. In 2006, it became available in South Africa, and take-up was instant and exponential. By April 2014, more than 11 million South Africans were using it, mostly on their mobile phones. Far more adults than children use it now, and it is common for grandparents to use it to keep in touch with their children and get the latest photos of their grandchildren within minutes of pics being taken.

Facebook, fraud and fear

For the first five years or so in this country, Facebook was regarded as the domain of teenagers. Facebook's rules require that one be 13 or over to use it, but numerous under-13s lied about their ages to show how cool they were. That was to be expected. What was not expected was how many parents aided and abetted them in this flouting of a rule that was intended to protect children.

A far deeper form of dishonesty underpinned this form of digital permissiveness. For children to go onto Facebook, they must identify themselves with a school. In most cases, they would wish to name their own school, while lying about their age. This means they – and their parents – drag the school into their dishonesty. If they were 'merely' providing fraudulent information to allow their poor darlings to nibble on forbidden fruit, one could argue that as a parenting choice. But once other institutions are associated with this fraud, a line has been crossed. No parents should expect to be able to pull their children back across that line once they have allowed them to wander free in a world designed for older individuals.

That's the first of the downsides. The second is that children do not know how to cope when faced with entirely new situations in which new dynamics apply and for which they have never been prepared. We're talking, of course, about cyber-bullying. Much is written about it elsewhere in this book.

In the context of this chapter, bear in mind that cyber-bullying is most vicious on Facebook, where it can draw in not only a peer group, but a global gang of vicious young thugs who take enormous pleasure in the anguish of others. Suicides as a result of Facebook harassment are reported throughout the world. Absent from the headlines, however, is a high level of nervous breakdowns and social dysfunction as a result of Facebook experiences. Allow your children into this environment when they are still finding their social and technological feet, and you multiply their chances of falling victim. Allow them onto Facebook without yourself being in there as both a friend and social explorer in your own right, and you are abandoning your responsibility.

Facebook calls contacts on their social network 'friends', which in some instances can be a complete misnomer. When 13-year-olds first sign up on Facebook they spend the first year or two trying to connect with as many people as possible so that they can boast about the number of friends they have on the social network. It is a 'badge of honour', so to speak. But how many of their 'friends' do they really know in the real world? When asking young people this question in our talks and workshops, it is clear that many, if not most, are strangers. This is tantamount to hitchhiking and catching a lift with a stranger.

This is risky behaviour typical of teenagers. It is often difficult for them to get their heads around the fact that many of the people they are connected to could be posing as someone they are not – that digital persona can lie and use pictures of someone else. A 'friend' could be a 50-year-old man posing as a 16-year-old girl, for example, and your child would not have an inkling of who they have invited into their world and what potential danger they could be opening themselves up to: stalking, predators, paedophiles and cyber-bullies, for example. This is a real danger not to be taken lightly. Make sure your children know they are making conscious choices with consequences when they either invite someone to be their friend or accept an invitation to be a friend on Facebook. And just because one of their friends is friends with someone doesn't mean they have to be, as this mother who uses Net Nanny Social to keep tabs on her daughter's online activities discovered:

"A few days ago I got an alert regarding my daughter's friends on Facebook. After checking it out, I discovered someone who had requested her as a friend was someone she did not know, but she had accepted the request because some of her other friends had. The 'friend' was just over the age limit I felt was inappropriate to be hanging around my teenager, even virtually, so I checked around with other parents. It turned out none of these kids knew the man. They all assumed the others did!

"I did a little more digging and discovered the 'friend' in question lives in our neighbourhood and is on the sex-offender registry. Obviously, I shared this information with the other parents, reported my concerns to Facebook and watched my teen 'unfriend' this character."[1]

Do make sure that your child knows how to unfriend people on Facebook and other social networks.

The positive power of Facebook

Nothing has sent the world a stronger message about Facebook's power for good than the Arab Spring that shook Tunisia and Egypt in 2010. While Facebook was not the catalyst for the revolutions in these countries, it was used to spread the message, coordinate protest activity, and give the world a window into repression as it was happening. Former Egyptian president Hosni Mubarak tried to shut down the Internet in his country for three days to prevent word from spreading – to no avail.

Of course, children are not typically trying to foment revolution on Facebook. But they do know – even if only subconsciously – that it allows them to become participants in the world rather than merely actors or consumers of other people's communication and content.

More and more, adults turn to Facebook to campaign against wrongs in the corporate world. A few years ago the Woolworths chain made the ill-advised announcement that it was removing Christian magazines from the shelves because they were not selling. The obvious strategy would have been to announce removal of all low-selling magazines. Instead, they were seen as attacking a special-interest group, and one that is highly vocal. On Facebook, 'highly vocal' translates into 'socially powerful' and from there into 'public relations disaster'. The subsequent Facebook campaign forced Woolworths to reverse its decision.

Buoyed by such examples, more and more children are turning to Facebook to campaign for causes, to raise funds for charities, and to create support groups for anything from an ill classmate to a persecuted activist. The experience children have on Facebook today means that tomorrow they will be far less likely to be the passive consumers that their parents tended to become.

The message in the duckface

It is sad, then, to see how many children still use Facebook purely as a platform for narcissism and a home for their selfies. The 'duckface' pose – children puckering up their lips in an exaggerated kiss for a camera –

is the symbol of social stupidity, sending a signal of herd mentality, lack of self-respect and unwitting desire for sensual experience with anyone viewing the image. There is only one word of advice for the duckface pose: *Don't!*

However, lurking within the duckface is what makes Facebook compelling for kids:

- It is a place for expressing their personalities in a way that is usually not possible in the home environment.
- It is an environment they feel they can make their own.
- It is a world that their parents tend not to inhabit as intensively as they do, so chances are that their random comments, posts and photos will go unnoticed, unlike their untidy bedroom or sloppy clothes.

In other words, on Facebook, children believe they can make a mess without being told off. That's all very well, except that the mess is visible to the world, and sometimes the messiness spills over into inappropriate behaviour that can destroy a child's image or self-confidence, or that of others. And it can take years to repair such damage.

The call to action for parents is simple: Facebook (as with its successors) is a very active space that you have to inhabit. It's not a place where you can fall asleep.

MXIT

Mxit was South Africa's answer to Facebook, even before Facebook arrived in this country. Very quickly, it had more than 10 million users, mostly school children and students. One of the most compelling aspects of Mxit was that it was a J2ME (Java 2 Micro Edition) application, meaning it could be installed on any phone that was capable of an Internet connection. Even the cheapest of phones could run Mxit, as long as it had GPRS (general packet radio service) – the slowest form of mobile Internet connectivity, available on most feature phones.

As compelling as its compatibility across so many devices was how little a message cost. While Mxit did not give direct access to the Internet, it used the phone's data layer, and the mobile network's WAP (wireless application protocol, or gateway – a network function that allows for data use) capability to allow for cheap instant messaging. Because Mxit was originally almost entirely text-based, it used even less data than subsequent instant messaging apps such as WhatsApp.

For children with a limited airtime allowance, Mxit was a miracle: it allowed endless text conversation for the cost of a single SMS. Again, it is astonishing that adults, who should be far more budget-conscious, remained almost oblivious to this massive benefit while their children embraced it.

Mxing with the dark side

However, there was a very dark side to Mxit. Adult predators, knowing that Mxit was largely populated by children, saw it as a happy hunting ground. Newspapers reported case after case of a schoolgirl being befriended on Mxit by someone who masquerades as a boy, then admits is an adult, and persuades the child to hook up with him or even run away with him.

The newspapers fail to mention, of course, the culpability of parents, who did not even know their children were on Mxit, let alone befriending strangers. Even when they do, rarely are the social dynamics of the home mentioned. In most cases in which a child runs off with a stranger, there would have been warning signals in the home environment, or a crumbling relationship between parent and child.

Naturally, there are exceptions, and one cannot simply write off the family of a runaway child as careless or reckless in their parenting. Many a parent of teenagers can tell horror stories of destructive incidents despite every precaution and despite every attempt at instilling values.

However, those values are the best defence against predators who stalk social networks. The problem for Mxit was that it came at a time when most parents hadn't a clue about social networks, and had no idea about the rights and wrongs of how to handle their children's entrance into this environment.

Mxing with the right crowd

The power of Mxit lies in its very broad appeal in lower-income areas and schools. It gives children in these environments access to a communications tool and to new layers of communication that would otherwise have been available only to the privileged.

More than that, though, it also gives them access to communities of interest and resources that would otherwise not have been available. By adding an organisation as a 'contact', any Mxit member can interact with it or receive information from it.

An excellent example is an initiative started by Marlon Parker, a young social activist from the Western Cape. His Angel drug-counselling service on Mxit is now referenced worldwide as a case study in interventions among disadvantaged communities.

In a less well-known case study, the HIV-intervention organisation Cell-Life, along with the LifeLine suicide helpline, teamed up with Parker to make HIV counselling more accessible to young South Africans "in a medium that is comfortable and familiar to them".

Research had shown that users sometimes struggled to call the National HIV/Aids Helpline from a landline because it was difficult to talk about certain things for fear of someone overhearing. They felt more comfortable if it seemed like they were just chatting with a friend on Mxit. The service worked like this:

- The team created a contact on Mxit called RedChatZone.
- A web-based system was created to enable counsellors to provide text-based counselling from their PC to Mxit users.
- A small amount of 'splash-screen' advertising was done on Mxit to inform users about RedChatZone.
- Users then added RedChatZone, allowing them to chat with a trained counsellor.

Counsellors were also trained to understand 'chat' language, so that they could communicate on the same level as the users, and were able to handle up to 10 conversations at the same time. Due to the less personal nature of this kind of chat, counsellors found that users would get to the point far quicker.

The typical hoax calls that are a big problem for South African helplines – up to 80% of calls to the National HIV/Aids Helpline were hoax – decreased dramatically on Mxit, and counsellors could easily ignore them and carry on with genuine conversations.

The only shortcoming of the project was that there were not enough counsellors to meet the staggering demand for the service.

Mxit's future
Mxit has been through a radical shake-up since Facebook became the dominant social media platform and WhatsApp the main instant-messaging service in South Africa. It has evolved into a full-fledged social network in its own right, and introduced a number of innovations in micropayments – very small payments for content and services accessed through Mxit.

With a maturing audience – more than half are adults – Mxit has also become a powerful marketing tool, both for brands and for organisations. The ANC, for example, used it as a tool to mobilise young voters in the Western Cape during the 2014 general elections. While it may not have swung the vote their way, it was an excellent example of using a specialised social network for a specific campaign.

Will Mxit survive the onslaught of international competitors? During 2012 and 2013, it maintained an active user base of about 6.5 million users, signing up new users as quickly as it lost old ones (although appearing to fall back significantly in 2014). Innovation continues at its headquarters in Stellenbosch, and we can expect more surprises from Mxit – as well as challenges for parents – in the future.

BBM

BlackBerry Messenger (BBM) was, for a few brief years from 2010 to 2013, the instant-messaging tool of choice among the 'cool' crowd, the influencers who dictated the social trends among their peers.

Initially, it took off at private schools across South Africa, to the extent that social arrangements were made almost exclusively on BBM. This also meant that it was tailor-made for subtle forms of cyber-bullying, such as social exclusion, ganging up on an unpopular kid, and even 'publicly' gossiping about someone. The consequences for children's self-esteem has been as disastrous as it is in Facebook-based cyber-bullying.

On the plus side – and in its dominant mode of use – BBM represented a remarkable enhancement of family communications. In numerous cases, at the time, the breadwinner of the family had acquired a BlackBerry phone for business communications. From around 2007, many companies insisted on issuing the BlackBerry to staff, as it was specifically designed to be integrated with corporate networks, offered higher levels of security than any other phone, and prioritised email and other forms of communication, such as BBM.

Suddenly, as if on a signal, from late-2009 teenagers began demanding a BlackBerry from parents. The catalyst was the BlackBerry Curve 8520, still as of mid-2014 the single most widely used smartphone across Africa. It cost a quarter of the price of a high-end BlackBerry, came with unlimited Internet usage for R59 a month, and BBM offered a rich range of emoticons to spice up text chats.

Overnight, Mxit disappeared from higher-income segments of the market, and BBM took its place. By 2012, BlackBerry was voted the coolest brand in South Africa in the 2013 *Sunday Times* Generation Next survey among youth. It had even overtaken Coca-Cola.

The result was that many families had both a child and a breadwinner on BBM, while the other spouse and other children were typically still using SMS to communicate. The absurdity of paying 80c for a message between some family members while others were incurring no additional expense was obvious. By late 2010, South Africa began seeing the emergence of BlackBerry families – with every member of the family using the same brand, and all communicating via BBM.

For the following three years, at least on this platform, families were on the same page – but only in communications within the family. Outside of that nucleus, children were finding ways to communicate in styles and codes that were a mystery to their parents.

Cyber-bullying was rife on BBM. Aside from the examples already mentioned here, it became common for one child to pick up another child's unguarded phone and send abusive messages to the other child's friends. It was called 'hacking', despite being generations removed from true hacking, but the term made it seem cool. Moreover, it denoted an exercise of power, and was the ultimate form of cyber-bullying.

At the same time, though, the platform was no longer a mystery to parents or teachers. This time, they had no excuse for technophobia, as they were using the same tool as their children. Schools quickly embraced cyber-bullying rules, seemingly able to cope with the arcane nature of BBM bullying far more easily than the more obvious nature of Facebook bullying.

BBM's fall from grace has been equally fast. With the appeal of Apple's iPhone on one side, and the rapid rise of Android smartphones on the other, BlackBerry's cool factor vanished overnight. By the end of 2014, according to World Wide Worx research, 6.5 million of the country's 18 million smartphones in use will be Android devices, mostly from Samsung. BlackBerry will have dropped from a high of 5.7 million in 2013 to below 5 million, and falling.

BBM lessons learned
It may no longer be the 'cool tool', but the feverish growth of BBM and its vital social significance hold many lessons:
- Make sure you know what social networks or instant-messaging apps your children are using, and use them yourself – if only to understand

how they work, and to be able to respond to abusive situations. This can apply to your child being both the victim and the perpetrator.

- Even if you are on the same network as your children, be vigilant about their activities, experiences and moods that may be a result of messaging activity.
- Ensure that your children have been briefed on the potential consequences of abusive behaviour in social networks or instant messaging, and how to respond if they are victims.

In my family, the first advice we gave our children in this regard was not to delete abusive messages, but to bring them to our attention. That way, we could firstly counsel them. Secondly, we would have a record of abusive activity, and would be able to take it up with other parents or with the school. Don't imagine that if it happens outside school hours the school can wash its hands off one child being abused by another in the same school. Thanks to BBM, many schools now have an understanding of these ground rules.

WHATSAPP

WhatsApp is the big new giant in communications. When Facebook paid $19 billion to acquire it in 2014, the deal was derided by many as an absurd overpayment. However, the value was not related to the commercial status of WhatsApp as at January 2014, but rather to its likely status by 2020. At the time of the announcement, WhatsApp had grown from 200 million users to 450 million in just nine months. In another year or two, it was expected to overtake Facebook's 1.3 billion users.

WhatsApp is a simple instant-messaging app that allows anyone to connect with anyone else who also uses WhatsApp simply by having the person's mobile number. Your number is associated with your WhatsApp account, so there is an immediate element of identification built in. Most phones with an Internet connection can run WhatsApp, and it works on all smartphones.

WhatsApp, like BBM, allows for rich layers of communication, with a wide range of emoticons depicting emotion, attitude or objects. A WhatsApp birthday message can look like a joyous celebration in a way that an SMS or even a voice message can rarely do. Talking of which, voice messages, sound files and even video clips can also be attached to a WhatsApp message, meaning that a rich form of communication is now available to most mobile users.

Like BBM, WhatsApp also allows for groups, and a wide variety of content within these groups. WhatsApp groups have become a basic building block of coordinating sports teams and study groups in schools and universities.

The positive lessons learned from BBM have given WhatsApp an instant boost because even its newest users have a support structure for getting the most out of it. At the same time, of course, that means that the negative elements of such platforms also come into play. The same threats and dangers that beset BBM now apply to WhatsApp, with a bit of Facebook-style visuals thrown into the mix. The upside is that WhatsApp is quickly becoming a universal tool, and even old-school parents – and principals – have a sense of what it is and does.

SNAPCHAT

There is always a new dark horse galloping in over the threat horizon. The 2013 edition, and still going strong in 2014, is Snapchat. It looks and behaves a lot like WhatsApp, except that it is designed to delete any message received within five to 10 seconds of it being viewed. The concept behind the app is that kids sometimes just want to have fun in chat, and send a one-off message or image without the encumbrances of lengthy dialogues or trying to figure out how the sequence of conversation went in a group chat. In particular, it is intended to get round the embarrassment of a personal photograph that is sent to one person on a whim, being sent on to a broader circle and from there to random and remote contacts.

The basic Snapchat action is to take a pic on the spur of the moment and send it to a friend. You set how long the pic can be viewed once opened, but the default is eight seconds. Then it is automatically deleted. The same applies to text messages. It's a brief, once-off message that is intended to be read quickly before it vanishes.

When it first took off like wildfire among teenagers, adults typically threw their hands up in horror. With little evidence to support the idea, Snapchat was almost instantly cast as the new bad guy of social media. It was obvious, went the argument, that children would use it to photograph themselves naked and send the pics to their friends. Or it would be used for sexting – sexually explicit text messages. Clearly, this was just what kids had been waiting for to conduct their illicit activities in secret! Apparently.

Well, the fact that it *can* be used for such a purpose is hardly evidence that it *does* get used primarily for it. No doubt some kids have pursued this avenue. But then some boys have also invited girls home – or vice versa – when their parents are out, and we don't throw our hands up in horror over the existence of homes containing adolescents, do we?

Once again, the core principle of this book applies: if your children have the values in place for how they should behave, or appreciate the reputational risk of overstepping these kinds of boundaries, then Snapchat is exactly what it is intended to be: a fun approach to instant messaging that redefines 'instant'.

THE NEXT SOCIAL THING

For the foreseeable future, there will always be a 'next big thing' in social media. At the time of writing, Instagram has been subverted from its original role as a platform for amateur and professional photographers to show off their work and share compelling images to become a narcissistic gallery of selfies and meaningless 'look-at-me' snaps. Many image-obsessed teenagers prefer Instagram to Facebook, because it allows them to cut through all the timeline and newsfeed intrusions in their lives and place the focus squarely on the most important thing in their lives: themselves.

In most cases, teenagers are not even aware of the nature of their own behaviour. They simply think they're being cool. Because their parents do not share these aspects of their lives with them, and are usually oblivious of what this kind of behaviour represents, there is no one to serve as a guide – moral or technical – in this world of emotional and reputational risk.

It is your role as a parent to be that guide. However, to guide them effectively you must also understand them. You need to understand that social media is a new layer of their social lives. However, when it becomes obvious that it is beginning to replace a social life – no direct interaction with friends, no social activity in the physical world – it is your role to retrieve them from down that rabbit hole where they imagine they are experiencing an equally real world.

- Social media and instant messaging represent the latest in 'cool tools' enabling teens to connect with each other.
- 'Virtual' and 'instant' are the buzzwords in this form of communication and socialising.
- These tools enable networking with vast numbers of people either generally or in very specific groups.
- Social media has created the biggest public stage on earth, with the biggest potential audience.
- Social networks can be used positively to campaign for causes.
- They are the quickest and most cost-effective way to communicate.
- Social media open up a world of potential moral and reputational risk.
- There are degrees of personal privacy on social media – the choice is up to the user.
- Being your child's 'friend' on social media is essential.
- Be alert and awake but not hysterical about your child's involvement in social media.
- Invest in your offline relationship with your child – it's their best protection in that it helps them to make better choices online.
- All text on instant-messaging networks or social media provide a body of evidence if need be – warn your children not to delete it.

CHAPTER 6

THE
EVOLUTION
OF LEARNING

As we have been at great pains to illustrate, the way the world *was* and the way the world *is* has changed dramatically over the past 100 years or so. Our kids are particularly attuned to this and they experience the 'disconnect' between a changed world and the one being presented to them in the classroom. To prepare learners for the new world of work, the dynamic in the classroom needs to be more reflective of the real world out there. Interestingly, it is not only about bringing technological change into the classroom but also about embracing social shift – the way we think about and relate to the world and each other. Just as good parenting cannot be effectively accomplished via a screen, neither can the goals of providing a relevant and holistic education be achieved without teachers, although that role is needing a considerable amount of reinvention.

Schools, parents and teachers remain at risk of implementing quick-fix approaches to bridging the gap in the education space, often without the necessary understanding of the bigger picture. In many schools today, technology is being used as a Band-aid rather than a real solution. While the presence of technology allows schools to claim that they are on the right track and that they are able to prepare children for the 21st century, in truth, many of these interventions are simply IT supporting traditional learning, reinforcing what was needed 50 years ago.

INDUSTRY DETERMINES WHAT WE DO
IN EDUCATION

Industry creates an environment that needs to be addressed by education. This has always been the case. A hundred years ago, children were being educated in a specific way to prepare them for the production lines of the industrial era. And so Classroom 1.0 was born.

Classroom 1.0: Children needed basic literacy and numeracy skills, so education focused on teaching the three Rs – reading, writing and arithmetic – often by rote and through much repetition. Mastering these three areas of learning constituted learning almost entirely. The teacher was the only authority and was a powerful gatekeeper to all knowledge and resources; this was characteristic of information being in the hands of the very few. Unfortunately, most schools in South Africa are still stuck in Classroom 1.0.

Classroom 2.0: The focus remained on teaching the three Rs, but with the addition of critical thinking and problem-solving to match the needs of industry in this era. A good example of why this was necessary can be seen in the shift at IBM. It was once one of the world's largest computer companies, but it no longer sells computers. IBM has evolved to solve companies' information challenges, helping them to become more competitive through the use of information systems. This requires critical thinking and problem-solving, working out how to sell products and predicting what people will need next. Technology is supporting this work. It is being used to construct systems and processes that get the user to the answer quicker and more efficiently.

Airlines, a more consumer-oriented industry, have experienced the same evolution, although still dependent on physical hardware in the form or aircraft. But the vehicles are no longer the core focus, since every airline tends to source its planes from a few major manufacturers, such as Boeing and Airbus. If it were only about the hardware, all airlines would operate in the same way, and be indistinguishable from each other. The real differentiation is in their operations, from the logistics of routes and hubs to the human resources issues revolving around pilots, cabin crew and ground staff.

A badly run airline does not stay in business – unless it is a subsidised state-run operation – and it is these soft issues that determine which airlines are more profitable and therefore more competitive.

Similar challenges face the automobile industry, food and agriculture, health and medicine. Constant access to new skills and information is at the heart of 21st-century competitiveness.

The advent of Google in 1998 was the culmination of Classroom 2.0. Information was now available at the click of a button, heralding a new era in freedom of access to information. For the first time learners were able to know as much as or even more than the teacher. Children now question the teacher's ultimate authority on knowing everything.

If all the world's information is available at your fingertips, then knowing stuff is less important than knowing how to access it and manipulate it for some greater purpose. This is a trend that is redefining what it means to teach and learn if knowledge acquisition is no longer the core goal.

Teachers have largely become delivery systems – deliverers of information to children. If the goal has changed, then teaching now becomes a more creative, interactive profession. The teacher needs to remain central to a more dynamic learning process that is facilitated by technology and is student-centric. Leading us to Classroom 3.0.

Classroom 3.0: Because our youth are increasingly using technology in their personal capacity to connect with the world, play online and on-screen games, and find information they need, there is less need to teach them technology skills in the classroom. Remember, this is the digitally nurtured generation. Rather, education needs to use technology to develop meaningful experiences for young people. This has a strong connection to one of the key drivers of youth, as the following mantra illustrates: "Give me an experience and only then will I promise you a relationship." This is what the smart classroom can achieve with a smart teacher.

For teachers to earn the respect of learners and to truly connect with them, they need to become specialists at creating learning experiences, using not just the technology of the day, but also positioning these experiences or lessons against a relevant social backdrop. This is about creating a context for learning. If something means nothing to young people, if they can find no personal connection, then they will remain unmoved and un-changed. We have to try to find ways to connect them to the information at hand. We need to create reasons for them to engage.

"If you can light the spark of curiosity in a child, they will learn without any further resistance, very often. Children are natural learners," says educationalist Sir Ken Robinson. Great teachers, throughout every era, have always been those who have piqued the curiosity of their learners. Learning to read, write and solve mathematical problems is still an essential part of education. They remain important foundations, but that is all they are: foundations. Critical thinking and problem-solving skills are the goal for Classroom 2.0. Now, in Classroom 3.0, collaborative learning and creativity must be the aim.

Once again, we see industry driving demand for these skills. If you want to work for Google today, you are expected to be able to collaborate at an intense level and have high levels of creativity. In its recruiting efforts, academic qualifications are less important than collaborative and creative skills, which are identified through a rigorous interview and assessment process.

THE SOUTH AFRICAN SCENARIO

The vast majority of schools in South Africa are still struggling just to be Classroom 1.0 compliant. Most progressive schools – comprising some of the top government schools and many of the private schools – are Classroom 2.0 compliant. Smartboards are being rolled out as the most common first step to introducing technology in the classroom. Unfortunately, many teachers do not know how to use them effectively and they become glorified white boards, often resulting in little more than death by PowerPoint, and continuing the age-old chalk-and-talk model of learning from the industrial era, but in a new form.

Schools and teachers need to embrace and understand the shift from broadcast to interactive discussed in Chapter 2. Children don't want edu-cation to be 'done' to them. They want to be actors or active participants in their own educational journey. They are able to do this on their personal digital devices, so why can't they do this in the classroom too?

If your children are still being taught in a school that focuses on the mechanics of learning, a Classroom 1.0 school, then they are being prepared for a world that doesn't exist. If they are being educated in a Classroom 2.0 school, then you are creating a great corporate citizen. Unfortunately jobs in corporations will be less and less the norm as the trend to downsize and outsource needs to individuals steadily increases. The era of the entrepreneur is dawning and it requires a whole new mindset. So even the most well-intentioned schools that have incorporated technology as part of their curriculum, often at great expense, are still mainly using it to enhance traditional learning. They still haven't made a full shift to match education to the needs of the world that is emerging.

Admittedly, because change in the world and technology are moving at such a pace, it is difficult for schools to keep up, even for those that are committed to their own evolution. And, while we should be applauding schools that have stepped up to the plate and are opening up conversations around all things new, we also need to be pushing for a new paradigm. It goes without saying that the paradigm shift needs to be taking place concurrently at home and at school, while also keeping the human in the middle. This is no small task and it needs to be done consciously, because Classroom 3.0 is, in truth, a live experiment. There is no historical research; there are only recent case studies. We need to engage with watching and reading the trends that will shape the classroom of the future.

When it comes to the national vision, change in education remains slow and schools always seem to be playing catch up. The classroom of the future was a vision for our national education system as early as 2007. Believe it or not, the South African Department of Education (DoE) put forward a vision in that year of the "transformational use of ICT [information communication technology] to redefine the role of the teacher and classroom environments".

It wouldn't happen overnight, of course. It would evolve through five levels, starting with Entry level, followed by an Adoption level for newly qualified teachers, then Adaptation, and culminating in Appropriation and Innovation.

All students leaving higher education for teaching, said the DoE, should be at the Adoption level: "They should have the knowledge and skills to use a computer and application software, the ability to use various ICT, including a computer, to support traditional management, administration, teaching and learning, and be able to teach learners how to use ICT."

Further, all practising teachers who have access to ICT should, at minimum, be trained to the Adoption level.

"The Adaptation and Appropriation levels focus on the knowledge, skills and values to integrate ICT into teaching and learning. At least 60% of teachers with access to ICT should reach the Adaptation level and 20% should reach the Appropriation level."

With these levels still a pipe dream, the Innovation level remains a distant ideal: "At this level, entirely new learning environments that use ICT as a flexible tool for whole-school development and for collaborative and interactive learning are developed."

Sadly, we are only in the preliminary Adoption phase of implementing basic computer skills to support traditional administrative and management roles. It is tragic and even criminal that a government department that was able to develop a vision of this scope almost a decade ago remains bogged down in the most basic of Classroom 1.0 needs, such as delivery of textbooks.

It is for this reason that we cannot wait for the authorities to do it for us: we have to grasp the future of education in our own hands.

THE CLASSROOM OF THE FUTURE

Canada, Australia, Sweden and Singapore have been pioneers in the classroom of the future. They generally allow children to bring their own devices to school, which means that there is a real mix of technology in the learning environment. This is something that wouldn't yet work in South Africa due to slow adoption rates and lack of teacher experience when it comes to using or managing multiple devices in the classroom.

Efforts at creating Classroom 3.0 are experimental and evolving. We can't fully trust it, and must be wary of technology taking over from quality teaching. While there are no clear solutions, what we want to sketch here are some basic principles that need to be applied to Classroom 3.0 and the education that takes place within it.

Parents and teachers are allowed to be confused here, but you do not have the choice to be phobic about change and technology if you want children to be prepared for the future.

A SMART CLASSROOM NEEDS A SMART TEACHER

The idea is not that the classroom becomes fully automated and replaces the teacher. Far from it. The teacher is an essential part of facilitated learning – the chief excitement officer, if you will. Teachers need to facilitate and encourage curiosity with whatever tools they have at their disposal *right now*, whether that be a smartboard, tablets, cellphones or just a traditional blackboard. But … teachers are in trouble – and that's because they are:

- not teaching themselves
- not collaborating
- resistant to change.

Change is a fundamental state of society. The only way to cope with it is to be open to learning and collaboration.

In his book, *Future Shock* (Random House, 1970), Alvin Toffler states: "The illiterate of the 21st century will not be those who cannot read and write, but those who cannot learn, unlearn and relearn." There has never been a more appropriate quote when it comes to education. It applies to all adults in society, but particularly to parents and teachers. The way we have always done things is not the way we are going to get to the future. What got us here is not going to get us there.

When faced with change, one of the greatest dangers is to act with yesterday's logic. The rules around success and failure are changing across every industry in the world. Disruptive change is being brought about by technology everywhere, and education is no different. Our open-mindedness about writing the new scripts necessary to operate and thrive in this new world of work will determine our children's preparedness for their future.

It is estimated that approximately 60–70% of the jobs our children will do have not yet been invented, and at least 70% of our kids will be entrepreneurs in a fast-changing world where information, skills and jobs – as we know them – are going to become obsolete at a rapid rate.

It is for these reasons, among many others we have already mentioned, that our children need to be prepared with skills and character traits over and above good grades. It starts with how we parent and educate our children. Everything we do and don't do counts.

In their book, *Future-proof Your Child* (Penguin, 2008), Nikki Bush and Dr Graeme Codrington assert that the new mantra in the future world of work will be: "Who you are is far more important than what you do or what you sell."

If you think of a constantly changing world, what we need is children of substance who are highly adaptable, flexible and resilient in order to cope with regular and disruptive shifts that will characterise their working lives.

Bush and Codrington identify five key X-factors for success above and beyond good grades that employers of the future will want:

- creativity or thinking outside the box (the world is looking for ideas and new ways of thinking to tackle and solve both existing and emerging problems facing humankind and the planet)
- a love for learning (learning is a lifelong process in a fast-changing world)
- resilience (being able to adapt to new situations and cope with change)
- knowing themselves (self-knowledge is the pathway to effective emotional intelligence)
- relating to others (both offline and online).

The reality of the new world of work, according to Richard Soderberg of the National Technological University,[1] is this: "People mistakenly think that, once they've graduated from university, they are good for the next decade – when they're really good for the next 10 seconds." An education and a qualification might get you an interview but it no longer guarantees a job – this is the new reality, and so employers will want all of the X-factors mentioned above showcased in future CVs or what the authors call Talent Profiles. Acquiring technology and information-processing skills goes without saying as fundamental prerequisites for operating in the 21st century. Children need to know how to navigate numerous devices and operating systems as a matter of course. These are the communication devices of the day, as quills and inkwells, slide rules, pens and paper were in previous eras. But they also need to be open to learning the next operating system. And the next.

The thing about these X-factors for success is that most of them are caught and not taught – caught through personal experience and by watching role models like parents and teachers. X-factors are difficult to teach to the test, so to speak, which is why children today need parents, teachers and schools to partner effectively.

THE LEARNER AND THE LEARNING ENVIRONMENT REINVENTED

"The destination is different and so is the route the kids must take," says Don Tapscott in *Growing Up Digital* (McGraw-Hill, 1998). Kids can now connect with anyone on the planet and can access any information. This demands a different way of teaching. If we want to keep children contained in a box and sitting on their hands, they are bound to get frustrated and fidget, when they know that as soon as they get home and onto their devices, the world is their oyster.

More and more knowledge is being made public. Just look at the development of MOOCs (massive open online courses) which are being offered by top universities and learning institutions such as Harvard, Yale and MIT. They are aimed at unlimited participation and access, enabling learning to be a lifelong experience and levelling the playing fields so that those who could not previously access such content are now able to do so, often for free.

The best lessons from the best teachers and lecturers in the world are being curated online for all the world to share. Just Google 'Coursera' or 'The Khan Academy' and you will be amazed at the extent of what they have to offer the general public today. Even iTunes University, as close as your computer or phone's music library, offers a new world of education in any discipline you could consider.

MOOCs are not just for use by school leavers or those in tertiary education; we as adults can continue our education for as long as we wish. There is no excuse to get mentally old when we can continue learning new and fascinating things for the rest of our lives, and much of it is free. You just need a decent Internet connection. And, for many of these, you're only expected to pay when you want to write exams or earn a formally certified qualification.

To keep up with the revolution underway in education, we need to accept that children are demanding a different way of learning in the classroom, and the world of work is demanding a different kind of learner too.

A note to teachers:
You need to keep up if you want to remain relevant, if you want to grab the attention of your learners and if you want to achieve a memorable or 'sticky' factor. You must leap across the digital divide, reinvent yourself and embrace the exciting new tools that you now have in order to bring learning alive – far beyond being able to type on a keyboard and use a mouse. Think tablets, cellphones, the Internet, YouTube, MOOCs and more.

NEW KEY PERFORMANCE INDICATORS FOR TEACHERS

Teachers have traditionally been:

- transmitters of information – "I decide what you will learn and how you will learn it; this is a one-way communication transaction."
- measurers of knowledge retention – "I test how much you can remember of the information I have imparted to you."
- judges of performance – "I assess how well you can put the knowledge I have taught you into practice" (proof is often sought through projects or setting of tasks that are then marked with little scope for individual interpretation).

In a changing world, where brains and knowledge will be the source of wealth in the global economy rather than muscle and physical human stamina, and where media are the tools of the day, learning needs to shift toward helping children discover information and participate in their own learning. This makes them more invested in both the process and the outcome and creates a partnership between teacher and child in the learning process.

Says Mark Treadwell, "To successfully change the attitude to learning we must ensure that learning opportunities are challenging, engaging and are focused on the excitement of understanding and experiencing the 'aha' moment, where learners respond with 'I get it!' rather than 'Whatever!'"[2]

Just as Google is looking for more than academic qualifications in their employees, so teachers need new Key Performance Indicators (KPIs):

- Willingness to learn – be teachable yourself and grasp new learning opportunities with both hands. You might just reinvent yourself.
- Willingness to collaborate – a new space for teachers who are accustomed to building little empires and not sharing their techniques or knowledge. Collaborative and cooperative teaching helps fill the gaps you may have in areas where others can do better than you and vice versa. You cannot know everything about everything these days, so split the stress and share.
- Willingness to change – unlearning the way you have done things for a long time is tough, much tougher than learning something new from scratch. You have to erase a well-worn neurological pathway and it takes time, practice and dedication not to fall back into the same patterns or ways of doing things.

LEARNING IS SOCIAL

"Education is not a mechanical system. It's a human system. It's about people," says Sir Ken Robinson. One of the big shifts in society today is that kids are able to connect directly with anyone on the planet. This has made learning social. The fact that children can share information with each other and collaborate means that they can help each other to learn. Where one child in a group has knowledge about how to build a website, say, another child will have greater knowledge about how and where to access information about something specific, while still another will be better at building an online community or know how to conduct a digital survey. When kids collaborate and pull all their skills and knowledge together, social learning shows its power.

The old saying that the whole is greater than the sum of its parts has new meaning in learning today. One of the things that this generation does better than adults is that they share with each other; something adults, particularly teachers, are not so familiar doing.

In his presentations on 'The Classroom of Tomorrow', Arthur terms this process 'Digital Peer Group Learning'. There is nothing new to peer-group learning – it is standard in universities – but throw 'digital' into the mix, and put the tools in the hands of youth, and you can watch it in action. This is precisely why children often appear to learn an entirely new operating system, game or device in no time at all: they are asking and telling each other, getting and sharing tips, and are – possibly most important – open in their enthusiasm.

Teachers tend to keep their best practices to themselves, a little like parents who keep the household chores to themselves and don't invite kids to participate at an early age. If you don't share with other teachers or your students, you will be left carrying the whole load yourself. If you share, you can both learn more and split responsibility, each doing what he or she is best at and learning from those better at other aspects.

Collaborative and cooperative learning is not a new concept, it just hasn't caught on in a big way yet. It can be used in both high- and low-tech teaching environments to great effect. It can bridge learning gaps in children through peer-to-peer learning, bring learning alive through active dialogue and group participation, and is entertaining, social and time efficient. It takes a load off the teacher and is a smart way of learning for both the educators and learners.

The example below, which illustrates this point, involves no technology whatsoever:

When English teacher Jill Worth was head of the English department at St Stithians College in Johannesburg, she taught a Shakespeare class and used to divide up the class into groups consisting of about five boys each. She would teach the lesson and then the groups themselves would workshop different aspects of the lesson, or be given a different section or chapter to analyse. She says that the discussion was always lively and entertaining and, by splitting the work up between groups, each group's work was shared with the whole class, making studying the entire setwork far less tedious for all.

Jill moved on to the Lebone II College of the Royal Bafokeng Nation in North West province, where she still teaches today. There she is teaching Shakespeare to learners whose mother tongue is Setswana. All their lessons are in English. She gets around the language barrier by teaching in English, allowing the groups to work in Setswana in order to create meaning for themselves, and then invites group feedback in English, so that she immediately knows whether they have grasped the concepts.

In both instances, students learned to cooperate, work in teams, solve problems, and take responsibility for their own learning – by doing it themselves. In cooperative team work, if there's something they don't understand, they must ask everyone else in the team before asking the teacher. This is called peer-to-peer learning and would also happen very effectively in a more high-tech situation.

TEACHER AS FACILITATOR NOT TRANSMITTER

In an era of information overload, finding information will not be the problem, deciding what to do with it all will be the real challenge. This is where the changing role of the teacher comes in.

In her 2013 research paper, *The Rewired Generation: Stepping Into the Gap that is the Digital Divide*,[3] specialist youth researcher and child-development psychologist Carol Affleck writes: "The youth have the information at hand, but it will become the task of their teachers to direct the youngsters' skills in organisational abilities, such as scanning multiple sources of information, discerning the relevance and veracity of the sources, and then compiling the various sources of information into a cohesive flow that does not smack of Cut and Paste tactics. In addition, these educators will have to teach critical thinking as young minds are put to work challenging the authors from an academic, personal or even ethical perspective."

In essence, teachers need to be teaching children how to use technology to help them to learn, but they need to keep up with developments, as learners are already starting to regard smartboards and PowerPoint as old technology. The bar has been lifted and teachers have to stretch themselves in an attempt to engage their classes in learning traditional material that is fast losing its appeal.

Teachers are trained to understand child development and the stages of cognitive functioning and this is still an important role they need to play. This child-development information needs to be married to what technology has to offer in the learning space. Because of the enormous amount of time children spend on digital devices, they have developed far more efficient neurological pathways than adults have in this regard.

"However, we must not expect such efficiency across all levels of cognitive functioning. Proficiency in technology should not be confused with developmental maturity," says Affleck. She is very clear that, while their skills may be different to those of previous generations, our children still have to progress sequentially through the developmental phases to attain full maturity.

Developmental theorist Jean Piaget[4] is famous for his theory of cognitive development, which suggests that there are four distinct stages through which all children must pass sequentially in order to reach a more mature stage of reasoning. It is important to note that, although the order of the stages is fixed, the age at which each stage occurs can vary. In addition, one stage builds on the stage before, so there is a natural timetable. The four stages are:

- the Sensorimotor stage (approximately 0–2 years)
- the Pre-operational stage (approximately 2–7 years)
- the Concrete operational stage (approximately 7–11 years)
- the Formal operational stage (from approximately 11–12 years onwards).

Each child must master the cognitive milestones attached to each stage before moving into a higher-order level of cognitive functioning.[5]

While our youth may well be able to multi-task across various digital devices at the same time, way more proficiently than we can, proving that they can focus when they *choose* to, it is also vital that they develop the self-control necessary to *choose consciously* to shut out activities that may be more pleasurable, such as Facebooking or gaming, in favour of focusing on another more laborious task, such as homework.[6]

This level of self-control comes with maturity, training and discipline and, to get it right, it must start from as young an age as possible. Good habits are created over time, and when it comes to children, sometimes that can take many years. Parents have a significant role to play in their children developing the ability to self-regulate and manage the plethora of media in their lives, which highlights how important it is for parents to partner with schools and teachers on this matter.

Where there has been no discipline or few boundaries around when it is appropriate to use technology at home, it will be increasingly difficult for teachers to change attitudes and behaviour in this regard.

Self-regulation takes place in the frontal lobe of the brain – the higher-order reasoning centre responsible for self-control, reasoning, decision-making and organisational ability. It is one of the last parts of the brain to mature fully, at around the age of 25. Until then, it is extremely plastic and elastic, making it very sensitive to the impacts of digital technology, both good and bad.

BLENDED LEARNING

Formal learning programmes that combine face-to-face learning with computer-based learning or online content and instruction are termed blended-learning programmes. It is one of the easier ways for teachers to introduce technology into lesson planning. One of the upsides is that learners can learn at their own pace, and remediation exercises or extra practice are easy to include. Face-to-face time with teachers is still required, but technology is incorporated into the learning process, which enables data on a learner's performance to be captured and assessed. Beware, however, that technology is not being used just to teach old stuff in a new way.

In some schools in the Classroom 3.0 mode, physical walls between classrooms are being broken down, creating large open-plan learning spaces where learners bring their own devices and follow online or computer-based curricula at their own pace. When there is teacher instruction, it often takes place outside this space, in smaller meeting rooms or classrooms. They take small groups of learners out to workshop concepts face to face. Learners then go back to the communal learning space, which has very flexible seating arrangements and workstations: anything from a formal table-and-chair set-up to couches and beanbags, or the floor, if you wish. There learners get to collaborate with each other and share their learning and ideas in the style that suits them best.

THE FLIPPED CLASSROOM

The flipped classroom takes the traditional learning process and turns it on its head. Usually, the teacher would instruct first, followed by discussion, worksheets, projects or homework. In this model, learners are expected to do their own homework first, in preparation for what the teacher will be discussing. They are usually exposed to the content via pre-prepared video or audio material. In a nutshell, pre-recorded lectures are followed by in-class lectures and activities.

Due to the self-discipline required, this kind of instruction is more suitable for older children and in tertiary education institutions. It offers learners the time and opportunity for reflection on the information being presented, because the pause and rewind button can be pressed when necessary, which is not always possible with a real teacher.

It does require effective preparation by the teacher and all links to content must work. Mobile devices and ongoing development of technology will increasingly allow learners to access this content wherever and whenever it is most convenient to them. The flipped classroom thus encourages interactive learning and engagement by learners.

GAMIFICATION OF LEARNING

Games make learning fun. As our technological capabilities improve, so virtual gaming is finding a place in the learning space. Apps make this a reality on a daily basis.

Minecraft is a good example of how gamification is crossing over from pure entertainment to education. Creating virtual cities in the game is not massively different from learning how societies work, in the context of history, social studies and even business economics. In fact, at one middle school in Sweden, students are required to take a Minecraft class, in which they create virtual cities to learn about electricity grids, water supplies, urban planning and, of course, design.

At the Viktor Rydberg School in Stockholm, says one of the teachers involved in this programme, the emphasis is on how this new world can be used to teach about the existing world. The game is customised to existing lesson plans, and provides new insights into environmental issues as well as problem-solving for the future.

However, gamification of learning is not only about applying computer games to learning. It is about turning learning into a game. The most fundamental form of gamification in parenting is the star-chart concept, where children are rewarded with a star or smiley face for a particular activity or behaviour. Adjust the behaviours, ages and rewards, perhaps by offering badges of the kind available in current app-based games, add an element of competition, and ... you're practically reinventing the concept of tests and performance prizes. The difference is that you're not doing it as a daunting once-a-year exam or quarterly cycle tests, but building it into daily activities, so that the incentive is ongoing. Exactly as in computer or app games.

APP-BASED EDUCATION

Increasingly, we will find printed textbooks being replaced by digital ones on tablets. In many cases, apps will replace textbooks. Rather than increase access to educational content, however, this evolution has highlighted the gaps.

The ironies in inequality have seldom been so stark. As the education crisis deepens for the South African government, for the Department of Basic Education and for teachers and learners in isolated parts of the country where they may not even have classrooms, more privileged schools have never been more spoiled for choice.

The most pressing issue facing the privileged is in which direction to take the evolution of the classroom. Do we embrace iPads immediately across all subjects, or phase them in? Which form of flipped learning should we embrace – combining teaching with general Internet tools, or with a mix of apps and textbooks?

An alarming reality lurks behind such privilege, however: the majority of schools considering technology-based enhancement of classrooms are clueless about where to start. Whether they are considering embracing smartboards, iPads or smartphones in teaching and learning tools, they tend to be doing so because it is expected, rather than because the educational process itself requires it. And, because flipped learning – the blend of traditional teaching with technology aids – is still a matter of debate around the world, there are no clear and agreed guidelines, rules and processes that will ensure success in achieving teaching goals.

The quest for appropriate apps is haphazard, and sometimes teachers even create their own apps to ensure that they meet curriculum demands. The greatest need, it turns out, is not the technology itself, but resources to guide teachers through best use of the technology.

The educational arm of the South African Apple distributors Core Group, Think Ahead Education Solutions, has produced two guides to teaching and learning apps that cut down dramatically on the complexity of app selection.

First off the presses – and, yes, these are printed books – was *The Primary School Education App Guide*, providing a comprehensive and categorised guide to apps for the iPad, iPhone and even iPod Touch. It splits apps between those for Grades 1, 2 and 3, and for Grades 4, 5 and 6. Each listed app, in turn, indicates the device at which it is aimed, the price and a brief summary.

It's not focused only on the duller aspects of education either. For the youngest children, it includes the likes of bedtime stories and games on one hand, and literacy and ebook-reading apps on the other. For older kids, Eco Footprint, Mr Thorne Does Phonics and Fraction Math underline the serious intentions of the guide.

The guide was a revelation for many teachers who had been wrestling with homemade versions of app guides produced randomly by colleagues. The moment high-school teachers laid eyes on it, Core was met with a chorus of demand for an equivalent guide.

They duly obliged, and *The Secondary School Education App Guide* was produced – double the size of the primary version. Again, the apps are split into two groups, for Grades 7, 8 and 9, and Grades 10, 11 and 12. They are further divided into subject categories, specifically for Maths, English, Physical Science and Life Science, and categorised according to their fit with the national curriculum.

These are textbooks that represent the beginning of a true educational revolution in South Africa – one that is happening despite the incompetence of officialdom to resolve the educational crisis, rather than being thanks to their efforts. More important, they provide educators at more fortunate schools with the tools they need to escape their dependence on the whims of party-political appointees. They represent what is possible in education, rather than what we are forced to accept because it was foisted upon us by unthinking bureaucrats.

While they represent the tools that will for the foreseeable future be out of reach of those still waiting for textbooks, they also send a signal to government that the world is moving on while it dithers with our future.

Some final words of advice for teachers and schools aiming for Classroom 3.0:

- You don't need to be technology-centric, but you must understand how to use technology to facilitate learning.
- You are not aiming for a fully automated education system that gets rid of the teacher: humanity, flexibility, child development and creativity are still your domain.
- You need to support the educational goal of good basic academic foundations with critical thinking and problem-solving skills added to the mix, together with relationship and creative skills. The latter can all be used to enhance the former.
- Teach or workshop small groups at a time and then allow group learning to take place in between. Make peer-to-peer learning work to everyone's advantage.
- The old must meet the new.
- Create a rich, blended-learning environment that has both high-tech and high-touch, time to learn alone and time to collaborate in groups, time to use technology and time to use high-touch face-to-face skills.
- Be an engaging and involved teacher.
- If you are using technology, know your technology and never let it replace you.
- Never underestimate the power of face-to-face communication. It is your high-touch advantage.

The solution to upgrading education does not lie solely with the implementation of more and more technology. These are just the necessary tools of the day. Computer literacy is not a substitute for basic literacy. But the focus needs to shift from top-down command-and-control teaching where the teacher is still the sage on the stage, to co-creating learning spaces with the children themselves, integrated with technology. This repositions the teacher as the guide alongside and will go a long way to helping reinvent school itself as a learning organisation, and capturing the imagination and attention of learners.

We are fast shifting from the information society to the connection economy. We are moving beyond the basics of what, why, where, when and how, and beginning to ask, "What's next?" We need kids who are invested in, and fascinated by, this question. As Don Tapscott reminds us in *Growing Up Digital* (McGraw-Hill, 1998),[7] "Never before has it been more necessary that children learn how to read, write and think critically. It's not just point and click. It's point, read, think, click."

FROM THIS CHAPTER ...

- Industry leads education and learning.
- Computer literacy is not a substitute for basic literacy.
- The student is reinvented.
- Classroom 3.0 is the goal, embracing both technology and social shift.
- Critical thinking, problem-solving, collaboration and creativity are necessary outcomes for Classroom 3.0 to ensure children will be ready for the changing world of work.
- Don't fall into the trap of using technology just to teach old skills better.
- Teachers and schools must buy into change.
- Children need to be taught what to do with information.
- The teacher must remain central to the learning process.
- Parents must partner with teachers by taking responsibility for teaching their children healthy media habits from a young age.

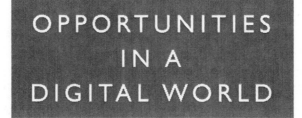

CHAPTER 7

OPPORTUNITIES IN A DIGITAL WORLD

Opportunities exist in this new era that have never been possible before because of the convergence of new technologies, the Internet, instant communication through social networks and a new paradigm in the learning space. With unprecedented opportunities to create and invent using these new tools, pioneers, inventors, thought leaders and change agents will take their ideas public, seeking buy-in from supporters for a cause or financial support for a concept.

Participation in these ideas is not limited to the elite in society, however. Because the playing fields have been flattened, anyone can get involved as long as they have access to the Internet. It's as simple as that.

This chapter definitely does not deal with jobs of the future but rather principles and trends that are behind the potential jobs and roles of tomorrow. Both you and your children are very likely to participate in or make use of some of these opportunities.

CROWDSOURCING

While information is available everywhere, at our fingertips in a plug-and-play world, we are not only downloading but also uploading information and contributing to the creation of the total body of knowledge on the planet. Every human being connected to the digital skin of the world is able to do this.

FOR THE RECORD

'Audience participation' is the name of the game for many Internet-based information and data sources, but two such institutions have taken that to a whole new level: Wikipedia and InnoCentive.

- One of the most powerful examples yet of inviting people to contribute content, ideas and their time is Wikipedia, the free online encyclopaedia that in effect killed off the venerable old *Encyclopaedia Britannica*. It is a collaboratively edited, multilingual, free Internet encyclopaedia supported by the non-profit Wikimedia Foundation. Volunteers from around the world collaboratively write Wikipedia's 30 million articles in 287 languages, including over 4.4 million in the English version.

  Anyone who can access the site can edit almost any of its articles. It is not expert- or academic-driven – in fact, Wikipedia is the largest and most popular general-reference work on the Internet. In February 2014, *The New York Times* reported that Wikipedia is ranked fifth globally among all websites, stating, "With 18 billion page views and nearly 500 million unique visitors a month … Wikipedia trails just Yahoo, Facebook, Microsoft and Google."

- Want to know how NASA finds solutions to its problems and challenges? Just visit www.innocentive.com. InnoCentive is the global leader in crowdsourcing innovation problems to the world's smartest people who compete to provide ideas and solutions to important business, social, policy, scientific and technical challenges.

  Their global network of millions of problem-solvers, proven challenge methodology, and cloud-based innovation management platforms combine to help their clients transform their economics of innovation through rapid solution delivery.

  For more than a decade, organisations such as AARP Foundation, Air Force Research Labs, Booz Allen Hamilton, Cleveland Clinic, Eli Lilly and Company, EMC Corporation, NASA, Nature Publishing Group, Procter & Gamble, *Scientific American,* Syngenta, *The Economist,* Thomson Reuters, and several government agencies in the USA and Europe have partnered with InnoCentive to generate innovative new ideas and solve problems faster, more cost-effectively, and with less risk than ever before.

CROWDFUNDING

Crowdfunding is exactly what it says it is – allowing the 'crowd' out there to fund projects instead of developers having to raise funding for projects and ideas through formal channels and stringent processes. Essentially, you trade on an idea, put it out on the Internet and ask people to invest in your project. There are usually incentives for early investors.

FOR THE RECORD

The Micro is a 3D printer for the average consumer, like you and I. It can print small household objects, from buttons to pieces of Lego and toys. It went on to Kickstarter to raise funds recently with a target of reaching $50 000 in 30 days. It reached its target within 11 minutes, raised $1 million within three days and exceeded its target beyond the wildest expectations. At the time of writing, it had pushed past the $3 million mark, with over 10 600 backers pledging their money to the project.

The way a crowdfunding project works is that members of the public 'purchase' the still-to-be-made product at a price that makes sense and with incentives that make them want to be one of the first to get it. This funding gets the prototype to market. M3D priced the first 250 pledges for the Micro 3D printer at $199, helping to drive early momentum to the campaign. The price rose to $249 and then $299, but the pledges still rolled in to the last day. It is the fifth-fastest Kickstarter project to date to hit the million-dollar mark. The product was due to reach the market in August 2014 and, regardless of its success on the open market, will remain a landmark in what a creative idea can achieve in the crowd.

Fundraising

Social media and instant messaging can be a very expedient and visible way of launching a fundraising campaign for a cause. It is a traditional idea that uses technology and innovative means to get the word out. Twitter and Facebook are used actively in this space. You are asked to repost or Retweet a message, which then links back to a website where contributors can make a donation. It could also be as simple as putting out a message about a winter blanket drive on social media and where they need to be dropped off. In fact, one of South Africa's first crowdsourced fundraising projects was exactly that.

#TBDZA, a Twitter-driven blanket drive, was South Africa's largest social media-fuelled fundraising initiative of the early years of Twitter. It began in 2009 when Melanie Minnaar Tweeted about her wish to collect blankets for the homeless living on the cold streets.

In 2010, the South African Twitter community held eight nationwide events and collected more than 500 blankets. In 2011, the figure rose to 11 national events, and the collection of over 4 000 blankets and more than R30 000 in donations. It has even expanded to neighbouring countries, and keeps growing, with many corporations also supporting the drive.

The Live Below the Line challenge is a campaign that's changing the way people think about poverty by challenging ordinary people to live on the equivalent of the extreme poverty line for five days. That would be approximately R12 a day if you were participating in South Africa, or $1.25.

The Global Poverty Project coordinates the Live Below the Line challenge internationally, running the website, supporter journey and media campaigns in support of more than 70 participating charities in the USA, UK, New Zealand and Canada.

People hear about the challenge from charities, participating friends and in the media. They sign up to participate at www.livebelowtheline. com, and choose a charity to support. The Global Poverty Project provides them with a personal fundraising page, tips and tools about how to succeed in the challenge – from recipes to advice on how to ask for donations. Participants are sent regular emails with updates, and are part of an online community that shares their experiences.

They share what it feels like to be hungry for the five days to which they have committed, and make requests for donations or sponsorship via their social networks. Donors simply click on a link, make their pledge, enter their credit card details and it's done.

A recent Facebook campaign, a breast-cancer fundraiser, dared women to take a selfie with no make-up on and post it on Facebook for all their friends to see. They also had to make a donation to CANSA and nominate specific 'friends' to do the same.

LANGUAGE IS NO OBSTACLE

Technology allows real-time translations when you need them in an instant. Giving instructions to a taxi driver in Japan, as an English speaker, is really easy today. You speak to an app on your smartphone, and it will do an instant translation for your taxi driver. Users of the Samsung Galaxy S4 and S5 open an app called S Translate, and talk or type into it, get an instant translation, and can then choose to show the translated text or play it back as a voice clip.

Much is made of Apple's Siri voice-activated 'assistant', but the truth is that this functionality had already been widely available via Google services and on Android phones: it had simply not been integrated as tightly with phones. That is all changing now, as a wide range of voice assistants and translation apps are emerging.

On a recent trip to Israel, Arthur was able to use an Android app simply called Translate to take photos of Hebrew signs, have the image converted to text, and have the app translate the text. The same app will translate text from English into Hebrew, and allow the phone to 'speak' it.

In the near future, you will be able to speak into services such as Skype to someone who does not understand your language, but who will hear it translated into their own. Today it sounds like little more than a useful gimmick for travel, but in future it will be a key to unlocking close collaboration with anyone in the world, regardless of their chosen language.

COMMUNITY BUILDING

It has never been easier to build communities with a special interest in something. We both send out monthly newsletters to our databases and followers. This is a way of building a community or following. If you haven't already done so, please sign up with us!

FOR THE RECORD

Commercial brands are using social media to create communities of followers who become brand disciples and talk about the brand to their friends and contacts. But non-profit organisations and social groups are also using social media successfully to get the word out about causes and events.

- The Share a Virtual Coke functionality on the Coca-Cola site allowed members of the public to create a Coke can with a personalised name on it. This virtual Coke could then be shared via Facebook, Twitter or Mxit. It created a real buzz both online and offline, because you could also purchase a real Coke in store with a random name on it. Nikki has kept a can with her name on it that she received at a restaurant as a memento!

  By the end of January 2014, over a million virtual Coke cans had been created on the www.shareacoke.co.za website, while 485 000 cans were shared on Facebook, according to Coca-Cola's head of marketing Marius Vorster. In December 2013, Coke grew volume by more than 9%, and single-serve transactions grew by 5% – and that from a brand that had been well-established for more than a century.[1]

- According to Anthony Sharpe, in his article #occupythestreets published in the April issue of *Khuluma*, #moonlightmass takes place in the city of Cape Town, starting and ending at Cape Town Stadium at 9pm every full moon. What started out as a social experiment on Twitter has mushroomed into something much bigger than co-founders Daniel Graham and Elad Kirshenbaum could ever have anticipated. Over a cup of coffee, they casually discussed how much fun it would be to cycle along the promenade at full moon. They then took it to Twitter to gauge support for the idea. The first night 35 people pitched up, then 80, then 160. Today more than 1 000 people do the Moonlightmass cycle. These are not Lycra-clad professionals; it is simply a social night out on the streets of Cape Town that has fast become an institution. There is no cause and it doesn't raise funds. It's just for fun. That, too, is about the opportunity of a connected world.

NOT LIMITED BY GEOGRAPHY

Because the Internet crosses global boundaries, it has enabled many a virtual miracle to happen. People can work for companies without living in the same town, city or even country. Virtual meetings can take place between people from a number of different countries at once using web-based technology such as Skype, Google+ Hangouts and even Facebook. We often speak at conferences where there is live streaming of our presentations to different parts of South Africa or the world simultaneously. It is now possible to be operated on by the best surgeon in the world without being in physical contact. All that is needed is a reliable Internet connection so that the surgeon can connect with the computer that is doing the operation.

The most immediate example for Nikki and I was the way we completed the writing of this book. I was out of the country on a long-planned family holiday overseas as the final deadline approached. Due to the short time frame we'd given ourselves, sections of the book still needed completion after I'd left. I agreed to talk through what was in my head, while Nikki agreed to do the 'heavy lifting' of writing down those thoughts and making them look coherent. It was all done through Skype, with one of the co-authors making a contribution while talking into a tablet and gazing out over a bay in Eilat, and the other focused on a computer screen with the view of a wine farm while on a business trip to Cape Town. In future, far more work will happen this way, even when it doesn't seem like work!

NOT LIMITED BY AGE

Young people are becoming inventors and starting up business during their childhood and teenage years. This has rarely been possible before, but the Internet has changed all that.

South African Nadav Ossendryver was just 15 years old when he developed the Latest Sightings website, which later became an app. He never imagined that it would be a full-time business before he had even finished school. He also couldn't have imagined that it would lead to him meeting Barack Obama and Kingsley Holgate, or that it would take him into the boardrooms of Microsoft and Nokia.

What started as a blog to satisfy his curiosity about the best animal sightings in the Kruger National Park in South Africa developed into the Latest Sightings wildlife-tracking website and app for iOS, Android and Windows Mobile devices. It provides real-time animal sightings by using crowdsourcing to collect information from current park visitors on what animals have been spotted where.

Now that more than half the world's population is armed with a cellphone, this type of data collection is becoming increasingly easy and effective. Visitors can immediately send updates via the app alerting other visitors to the park.

The idea itself has been copied many times since, but the integrity that was an essential part of the original idea – a passion for sharing – was a lot harder to copy. The result is that, at the time of writing, the YouTube channel for Latest Sightings was the sixth-most visited in South Africa. That is not just a number designed for boasting; it also translated into serious advertising revenue from YouTube – enough to turn Latest Sightings into a serious business.

ANYONE CAN BECOME AN AUTHOR

The realm of book publishing is being completely reinvented with the advent of the ebook. In 2012, the sales of ebooks overtook the sales of printed books in the USA for the first time. Traditional bookstores are closing down all over the world. Anyone who wants to publish ideas in a book can do so today. There are numerous programmes available online to take one through the motions of what to do. Amazon's CreateSpace is one of the most popular, since it gets the author into the world of the Kindle e-reader. Once complete, you simply create an account with Kindle, upload it and you are done. If you plan to sell the book in the USA, however, you would still need to make arrangements with the Internal Revenue Service

(IRS) in that country, which gets a little more complicated. But for South African sales, it is as easy as …

We recently came across this story of a local teenager who had published a very useful ebook:

Early in 2014, teachers and principals at various South African schools received the following email letter:

Good morning Mr …

My name is Tanya Meyer. I am in Grade 11 at Northcliff High School. I have written an ebook on how to use an iPad at school. In 2012, I started using my iPad in the classroom. I now do all my homework, projects and studying on the iPad. This approach allowed me enough time to play two first-team sports for my school and become the top academic student in my grade.

I noticed that learners are keen to use technology but don't know where to start. That's when I decided to write a *Teen Guide to School iPad Use* based on my experience. In the ebook I describe the study technique that I have developed as well as how to utilise the iPad for schoolwork. I have published the ebook on ZA Books for R50.

My goal is to reach as many students as possible and raise awareness about the benefits of using iPads in the educational environment. Would it be possible to arrange a meeting with you to discuss how I could go about this at your school?

Regards,
Tanya Meyer
www.tanyameyer.co.za

Tanya's book includes:
- a beginner's section that guides you into exactly how you get started with your iPad
- great tips on getting your iPad set up for school purposes
- a way to create summaries/study notes on your iPad
- an efficient, concise, productive and iPad-specific study method.

This is the kind of initiative that the Internet, tablets and apps make possible, and it does not have to be limited to tablets and apps! Anyone of any age can come up with an original book idea of their own.

IDEAS IN AN INSTANT

Today the average person has instant access to all the technology necessary to turn an idea into reality. Think about the #moonlightmass example that was conceived and launched over a cup of coffee. Nikki's ebook, *Parenting Matters*, was written over a weekend and uploaded a few days later. Hare-brained marketing ideas are dreamt up in an instant and executed within hours because email marketing campaigns are so simple to put together – if you have the basic technical know-how and an email list of followers. Here is a great example of an idea developed in an instant:

Lucrative Mobile Games Market Child's Play
Sunday, 30 March 2014
By Khanyi Ndabeni, *Business Day Live*

Staff at Cape Town-based company Thoopid, which developed the successful Snailboy game for cellphones, challenged developer RW Liebenberg to come up with a game concept – and an hour later he had Tap the Coin.

Players have to tap their cellphone screens to make a coin bounce. The aim is to keep the coin up for as long as possible, but each tap makes it move faster and higher – and you have to juggle more of them as you reach new levels. If the player does not tap in time, the coins fall off the screen.

"I wanted to create a game that is extremely simple to play and doesn't really need you to think much – something so simple that people can enjoy it while commuting or taking a break from a serious day's work. I think I have achieved that," said Mr Liebenberg.

The game is available for download to Apple and Android devices.

Last year, Thoopid released its debut game, Snailboy. After only a few months, it won the award for best cellphone game from the DevGAMM gaming conference in Kiev, Ukraine. Since then the game – in which a snail leaps and slides around a garden in search of his stolen shell collection – has been downloaded more than 100 000 times globally and is competing with the likes of the Angry Birds behemoth.

SOCIAL ACTIVISM

Thousands of local and global social-activism organisations use social media successfully in garnering support and in raising funds to fight for their causes in the courts and the media.

Social media gives people like us the opportunity to take on the role of 'armchair activist'. We are encouraged to sign petitions, spread the word to our friends in our networks, change our profile pictures to raise awareness and share videos and articles. In the digital age, making a difference is just a click away. However, recent research has shown that most click-throughs don't follow up with a donation. It can often just be an illusion of activism.

According to *The Guardian*, Avaaz is only five years old but has exploded to become the world's largest and most powerful online activist network. It was launched in 2007 with a simple democratic mission: organise citizens of all nations to close the gap between the world we have and the world most people everywhere want.

Avaaz empowers millions of people from all walks of life to take action on pressing global, regional and national issues, from corruption and poverty to conflict and climate change:

"Our model of Internet organising allows thousands of individual efforts, however small, to be rapidly combined into a powerful collective force.

"The Avaaz community campaigns in 15 languages, served by a core team on six continents, with thousands of volunteers. Action includes signing petitions, funding media campaigns and direct actions, emailing, calling and lobbying governments, and organising 'offline' protests and events. The intent is simple and stirring: 'to ensure that the views and values of the world's people inform the decisions that affect us all'."

VIRTUAL BUSINESSES

As our kids start their own businesses, they will increasingly be collaborating with people they have never met before in the real world. While there will be many dynamics around trust, this is the bigger picture and a new way of thinking.

Arthur's first company, Media Africa, was started on this basis in 1997 with three partners. He knew one partner personally but had only met the other online. If he was ahead of his time, then time had certainly caught up to the way he wanted to build a business: this company would never have been possible before the Internet.

Although personal relationships still provide the best basis for trust, this will, however, be a typical way to put a business together in the future. Geography is usually important and relevant when a business is initiated, but once the relationship between partners is established, being in the same physical space is no longer necessary.

So it is that most start-ups in Silicon Valley depend on their proximity to the venture capital giants of California for funding, but thereafter are able to build companies that have little dependence on a specific geographic location. At the same time, however, the continued gravitation to that area suggests that the funding dictates the location. For South African start-ups that depend on a wider range of funding, location will be far less of an issue – unless they choose to relocate to Silicon Valley to take advantage of that concentration of start-ups and funders.

PERSONAL BRANDING AND CREATING DIGITAL FOOTPRINTS

We live in the era of the Brand of You. Everyone today is a personal brand, whether they actively promote themselves or not. Everyone can become famous if they wish. When last did you Google yourself? Have you Googled your children? Whatever content you put online, from blogs to posts on social media to videos on YouTube or pictures on Facebook, everything is aggregated on the Internet to create your online profile. These tools are more powerful than the biggest ad agency could have imagined in the era of radio and TV. They give you the kind of audience reach that could only have been obtained in the past when dealing with big ad agencies, using radio and television – and at huge expense. Your digital reputation follows you wherever you go. Take time to look after it.

STAYING IN TOUCH

Online networks, both social and professional, will become increasingly important in the future. Social media allow for a continuation of connection, whether it be with someone with whom you went to school or someone you recently met at a conference. Your 'net worth' these days is very closely linked to the size and strength of the connections in your network. Knowing what they are doing, thinking and saying gives a sense of being in touch and keeping in the loop, which makes reconnecting virtually or offline in the future much easier because you have a 'sense' of each other.

In 2006, I attended my school's centenary celebrations in Bloemfontein, not having had contact with most of my friends from Brebner High School for many years. After the event, it looked like I would drift out of contact with many of those friends again. But then, in 2007, Facebook was made available in South Africa, and the picture changed almost overnight. Today I am in contact with almost all the people who were in my class at school, and with whom I was friendly at boarding school. Next time I see them, it won't again be a case of trying to figure out who they are!

Facebook and various apps have become wonderful tools for tracking down people who used to belong to a specific group, making school reunions and creating family trees so much easier.

SELF-EDUCATION

Few people today can say they have no opportunities to get an education or improve their professional development. Even if you can't afford to enrol in a physical academic institution, there is free courseware available online in almost any discipline imaginable (see Chapter 6). In addition, the web gives the ordinary person access to thought leaders and experts in their field from across the world. This is a 21st-century reality and an enormous advantage if you learn how to leverage it. There are so many ways to learn and be inspired.

TED is a non-profit organisation devoted to spreading ideas, usually in the form of short, powerful talks (18 minutes or less). TED began in 1984 as a conference where Technology, Entertainment and Design (hence TED) converged, and today covers almost all topics – from science to business to global issues – in more than 100 languages. Meanwhile, independently run TEDx events help people share ideas in communities around the world. TED is a global community, welcoming people from every discipline and culture who seek a deeper understanding of the world.

"We believe passionately in the power of ideas to change attitudes, lives and, ultimately, the world. On TED.com, we're building a clearinghouse of free knowledge from the world's most inspired thinkers – and a community of curious souls to engage with ideas and each other, both online and at TED and TEDx events around the world, all year long," states the TED website.

TED talks have occasionally been criticised for the easy wisdom they dispense, but even that is almost an art form. They represent not only powerful messages, but also powerful ways of distilling these messages for consumption by anyone.

In this context, here is a suggestion: both teachers and parents can show children a range of carefully selected TED talks about issues affecting children or society today, and then challenge them to come up with their own equivalents of TED talks. You would probably be surprised at some of the results.

Teddy talks? Not quite. But the world is certainly ready for a junior equivalent that showcases the bright minds among our youth.

We hope this chapter leaves you with more perspective, insight and appreciation for the connected world we find ourselves inhabiting with our children. For our children to take advantage of these opportunities effectively, they must have skills: high-tech to be able to plug in and play, and high-touch to be able to connect and relate.

So, before fast-tracking them into their increasingly digital future, let's make sure they first have solid foundations; that we understand their developmental and human needs, so that they will not just survive but thrive in the fast-moving world of what's to come.

- Technology has flattened the opportunity playing field for all.
- Anyone today can share their ideas with others, whether for profit or not, no matter their age, location, language or socio-economic status.
- Taking an idea to market can happen very quickly – overnight or even within a few minutes.
- Marketing tools with the potential to reach millions, quickly, are now available to everyone, without having to employ the services of advertising agencies, for example.
- The digital world is providing new ways to gain support for and funding of ideas outside of traditional formal channels. Today you can build a business or social enterprise, and launch or support a cause, all from the comfort of your own home.
- Education and professional development is available and accessible to everyone online and much of it is free.
- If you can plug in to the Internet, you can play the new game called 'Opportunities for All'.

CHAPTER 8

THEIR BASIC NEEDS

Before we let our imaginations run wild too far into the future, let's move back closer to home and make sure that we understand our children's basic needs so that we can marry them with the sometimes challenging decisions we will need to make around technology.

OUR PRESENCE

Children need parents. In an era of uncertainty and disruptive change, there has never been a generation of children that has needed its parents more. And yet many parents are hiding behind technology, using it as an excuse not to parent. In a time of maximum media, we are seeing more and more situations of minimal parenting. Parents are copping out and giving in to media on every side instead of claiming time for family life. If you don't create sacred family time, no one is going to give it to you. This is a personal choice. If you don't pitch up and create moments of togetherness, children will stop trusting you to be present.

One of the key desires of children is for a real and authentic relationship with us, their parents. This is what they long for most and it is what we find hardest to give in our warp-speed multi-tasking lives. The art of being present with our children when we are with them is a huge challenge to 21st-century parents. It's one thing to be with them physically, but another to be accessible emotionally at the same time.

Our heads are processing a million and one things at once, and we forget that the currency we trade with our children is time and attention. Today, when we are not present, the default setting for our children is to gravitate to a screen. They have discovered that the screen fills the emotional void – for a time, anyway. And our own default setting when we are busy is to send them off to watch TV or engage in some form of on-screen activity to keep them busy and quiet while we get on with our stuff. This has become a vicious cycle that can only be stopped and managed if we are more conscious of the choices we are making for ourselves and our children. Every choice we make has an impact on our children in some way, either positively or negatively.

Child and family psychiatrist Robert Shaw writes in his book, *The Epidemic* (HarperCollins, 2004): "Parents find themselves enslaved by a materialistic, over-achieving society that leads them to spend so many hours at work and so much money that they can't make the time to do the things necessary to bond with their children. They are worried that they might crush their children, stifle their self-esteem, or kill their creativity, to the extent that they lose all sense of proportion about the role of a young child in a family.

"They rarely put limits on their children or permit them to experience frustration, and they overlook their children's moral and spiritual development. As a result, essential values like empathy, effort, duty, and honour do not develop. And on top of that, they abandon their children to the influence of the media – children waste so much time on such mind-numbing electronic entertainment as television and video games that their literacy, social development, and creativity are all inhibited. These unbounded, untrained children agitate an ever-widening circle of behaviour until they finally bump up against real limits – which all too often have to be supplied by institutions such as schools or, eventually, the law."

We need to be present enough to see their need for strong, loving human connection, and to be able to fulfil it, while at the same time understanding that there is a place for their on-screen involvement and to take a balanced approach to finding our family's middle ground on the technology front. But first, we need to pay attention.

MULTI-TASKING LEADS TO PARENTAL INATTENTIVENESS

If we want our children to be media savvy – to manage the plethora of media in their lives responsibly – then we have to show them how, by managing our own arsenal of smartphones, organisers and electronic gadgets. We constantly allow these gadgets to interrupt the time we spend with our children; we find ourselves multi-tasking just to keep up. With the rapid pace of information assaulting our brains, is it any wonder that our ability to pay full attention to any one thing at a time is challenged?

This poses a problem to parents, quite simply because children require a whole lot of time, focus and attention – all in short supply in our multi-tasking lives. When our children pop into the study while we are answering emails, searching for the latest prices on a new car and downloading a podcast at the same time, do we stop what we are doing, make eye contact with our children and give them our undivided attention? Nine times out of 10 the answer will be no. This does nothing to build our relationship with our child.

It's interesting to note that, when we divide our attention and multi-task, we think we can get more done, but we are not necessarily being more efficient. Neuroscientists at the University of Michigan have found that switching back and forth between two tasks may decrease brain efficiency by as much as 50%, compared with separately completing one task before starting another one.[1]

There is mounting evidence that multi-tasking leads to stress and anxiety if not managed, and it also impairs our memory ability because it distracts us from paying full attention to what we need to learn and recall later. Interestingly, the coping strategies for managing your technological multi-tasking, reducing the stress caused by it, and improving your attention are fairly low-tech, including:

- Use a simple, low-tech, handwritten to-do list and prioritise what's on it.
- When your children are around, set time limits for tasks and don't get carried away. After X minutes, schedule to play a game with your child and show up. This is one way of demonstrating how you control your use of technology.
- Avoid task switching where possible and try and complete a task without distraction (adult ADHD is seriously on the increase). It's okay to tell your children that you don't want to be interrupted for the next half an hour if you are then going to be able to focus on them.
- Avoid interruptions when you are spending quality time with your children by putting your cellphone on silent for a period of time and switching off your email-alert function – or close the email app on your phone so that you are not watching for mails landing.
- Take power naps. They help us to refresh our multi-tasking neural pathways. They also help us to parent better, because we have more energy to pay attention, to listen and to make better choices – particularly in how we respond to our children.

According to Gary Small and Gigi Vorgan, authors of *iBrain* (HarperCollins, 2008), the key is to manage new technology and control the power it wields, rather than it controlling you: "All of us, Digital Natives [our children] and Digital Immigrants [ourselves], will master new technologies and take advantage of their efficiencies, but we also need to maintain our people skills and humanity."

Sage high-touch advice. After all, isn't that what parenting is really all about?

We know deep down that relationships and communication are key to a healthy family life. When it comes to our children, this means we should listen twice as much as we speak if we want to set a good example. But it's sometimes easier said than done, as I discovered when I made this New Year's resolution in January 2013. Some of these scenarios might sound familiar to you:

- *Due to my self-imposed personal deadlines around sorting and chucking and doing DIY around the house during the December/January holidays, I became a real nag. I threatened the children with all sorts of consequences, despite the fact that they had been amazingly supportive of, and involved in, the exercise. It was totally counter-productive. I stressed, my children got irritated with me and uncharacteristically tuned me out, turning to their smartphones instead. So much for fostering good communication, and proof that on-screen media provides an out for kids!*

- *My eldest son obtained his learner's licence, which meant I at last had the personal chauffeur I had been longing for! The problem was that I had taken to making calls on my cellphone while he was driving, even if we were in the middle of a conversation. In one such instance, I placed a call to my sister and she answered as my son was in mid-sentence, replying to a question I had asked him. I started chatting with her, cutting him off. When I had finished, I apologised to him and re-asked the question. He very firmly, and correctly, thanked me for interrupting him, and told me that the conversation was over. Mmmm, food for thought ... I would have been just as irritated if he had done the same thing to me without excusing himself from our conversation.*

The above scenarios made me take a hard look at myself as well as taking some remedial action! Here are three things I decided to do:

- *First, have more realistic expectations, slow down and keep things simple*

– my children don't operate at my pace just yet!
- *Second, my phone is being relegated to the cubbyhole of the car when my children are present. In fact, I am going to choose to turn it off in favour of conversation with the people who really matter in my life.*
- *Third, I will be an example of good manners where communication is concerned, excusing myself from a conversation if I need to take or make a call.*

To create listening children who respect others, and are fully present in their relationships, we need to lead by example. For those parents with children in the Foundation Phase, this means not taking your phone with you when you walk in to fetch your children from their classrooms or the playground. Be fully present, connect and savour the moment when you make contact with your child. Put your phone in the back seat.

EMOTIONAL CONNECTION

At the very core of being human is the need for emotional connection with others. We long for a sense of belonging and togetherness – to feel part of our tribe or community, whether that happens to be our family, our children and their peer group, special-interest groups or community or religious groups.

We need to believe that we are cared for and, on the whole, we also have a high need to care for others. Communication is the vehicle that helps us to express this need to care and be cared for. At the heart of this is a fundamental driver of human nature: the need to be noticed by others, to receive attention from them, giving us that sense of belonging and togetherness.

Everyone – adults and children – plays the attention game. It is the biggest game in town. If you can identify with this, then you will better understand your children, why they do what they do and why they are so attracted to social media and technology. So listen up.

Every human being is what I term an Automatic Attention-Seeking Device (AASD). Forget ADD or ADHD, we are all AASD: we are born this way and we don't change. Both adults and children – non-verbally and unconsciously – ask three questions of people they are close to every day:

- *Do you see me?*
- *Do you hear me?*
- *Am I important to you?*

When we get consistent 'yes' answers (which may also be non-verbal) to these questions, there is no need to resort to negative attention-seeking behaviour. But life is not perfect, and we all have strategies to attract attention should the need arise. Yes, even you! Think of what we do in the real world when our spouse or partner is preoccupied, or not paying attention to us. Strategies include:

- *ignoring each other*
- *picking a fight*
- *being funny*
- *crying*
- *getting ill*
- *dressing up or undressing*
- *feeding or starving each other.*

And so it goes on. Have you spotted yourself yet?

Children work exactly the same way. They, too, have strategies they employ when they are feeling lonely, left out or just plain invisible. Interestingly, they do not have to have this concept explained to them; they totally get it. I asked two children what they do when they are feeling invisible at home. The 13-year-old boy said he gets cheeky to attract attention, and the 10-year-old girl said she cries. You see, even negative attention is better than no attention at all when you are feeling short-changed. You just have to look at child abuse to understand how this plays out in extreme cases.

It is one thing for children to feel invisible from time to time, but it's an entirely different thing when they carry around within them an emotional void. For these children, who feel they are not getting their fair share of attention in the real world, the online world might become increasingly attractive. It's a place where they can find a tribe, and where they meet people who promise them the world, or at least a different kind of world to the one they want to escape from. They can try out different things to make them feel better, to fill the void, and they think they can do this with a fair amount of anonymity and secrecy.

We should remember that children have basic emotional needs that must be met in order to feel happy, safe and secure. Not only do we as parents need to support our children emotionally, but we are also responsible for ensuring that they develop into emotionally intelligent individuals, and this is something that most definitely cannot be done via a screen.

"If I know myself and I can manage myself, then I can know and manage you!"[2] This is a good summary of Emotional Quotient (EQ) and a very important aspect of both leadership and parenting. Do watch your emotional responses to your children and to life's challenges, as it will be a shaping force in the development of their EQ:

- Your children must see how you express yourself and keep your emotions under control, moderating your reactions to situations.
- When you talk about your feelings, label them.
- Become an attentive listener and your children will be far more likely to listen to what you have to say.
- Show your children how to reframe problems as opportunities.
- Co-parent consistently with your spouse, ex-spouse, step-parents and caregivers. This will result in respect instead of manipulation and power struggles.
- Say sorry to your children when you have made a mistake. This is a good example for them of you being self-aware.
- Allow children to experience the consequences of their actions. They may do things differently next time if they learn from their mistakes first-hand.
- Eat together and play together often, as these activities create opportunities for learning emotional intelligence.

The EQ journey starts face to face in discovering how others respond to the words we speak. A strong EQ will give your child a confident handle on life and will go a long way to creating optimism and happiness.

Arthur's daughter, Jayna, addressed this issue head-on when she was planning a small 16th birthday party. She tells the story in her own words:

"A couple of months ago my friends and I decided to take a break from constantly going to the movies as a form of socialising, as we realised that the group of us simultaneously staring at a screen wasn't very social. So instead we went out for supper, and to my immense disappointment, it still resulted in the group of us simultaneously staring at screens, albeit separate screens. The minute we had ordered our food, they had whipped out their phones to let their wider social circle know what they were eating, where they were eating and who they were eating with. This bugged me a lot, so when my birthday rolled round and I started sending out invites to a small get-together, I decided that I would not let the same thing happen on my special day. I wanted my birthday to be a day of proper, good old-fashioned, face-to-face interactions. So I thought for a bit and came up with a solution.

"People began arriving, and right at the entrance was a small box with a sign on it reading, 'Please put your phones in here so that we can be social for once!' A few people noticed it and laughed, as if the idea of giving up their phones was so shocking that I couldn't possibly have been for real. But they soon realised that I was very serious when I carried the box around and asked people to put their devices in it. I don't think that anyone quite understood how ironic it was that they were so unwilling to give up their machines that were intended to make social lives easier, in order to be social. But at last, the gathering was phone-free, and the result was incredible. For the first time in a couple of years, I fully enjoyed a social get-together in which I didn't constantly feel attached to something external, in which I wasn't getting FOMO of another party plastered all over Facebook. People who had never met before made real connections, laughter was heard everywhere, and we had a good solid game of Twister that didn't need to be posted on Instagram for us to enjoy it.

"Towards the end of the party, as people started leaving, they drifted towards the box and reattached themselves, but I didn't feel as if they were trying to evade the situation, they were merely phoning their parents to pick them up. I was quite proud of myself. When everyone had arrived, their phones were so much a part of them that I couldn't tell the difference between phone and hand. But when they left, I felt satisfied that I had made the right decision to confiscate them. Despite the fact that the box was empty, there wasn't a phone in sight."

FACE-TO-FACE TIME IS IMPORTANT

Face-to-face contact is diminishing daily as we:
- spend more time on our cellphones when we are with our children
- multi-task continuously, like working on our computers or sending and

receiving messages while trying to play with our children

- talk or shout through walls instead of walking into the room where our child is busy
- spend more time in our cars due to traffic congestion, so we are often side by side (rather than face to face) or our child is behind us in the back seat
- spend less time playing with our children
- allow our children to spend more time watching TV or doing some on-screen activity.

WHY IS MAKING EYE CONTACT IMPORTANT FOR YOUR CHILDREN?

- Eye contact means you take them seriously enough to make time to focus on them, which builds self-esteem.
- It conveys a non-verbal message of "I want to be with you right now", and "You are important to me".
- By watching your mouth movements, young children are better able to copy how you say and form words.
- By using both the visual and auditory senses, a child can tell if you really mean what you say. Is what you are saying congruent with the expression on your face?
- We role-model good listening by being good listeners ourselves. We do this by paying attention and not doing two things at once.
- When discipline issues arise, a child will take you much more seriously if you make eye contact while using a firm, low voice.
- It teaches respect with regard to relationships. It shows that we place value on them.

How good are you at family face-to-face time?

We are spending less face-to-face time with our children, even though we know how important it is for a healthy family life. Read through the following questions and see how you fare:

- How many times a week do you eat dinner together? ....
- How many times a week do you eat dinner together in front of TV? ....
- How many times a week do you eat together around a table? ....
- Is the TV on in the background when you are eating around the table? ....
- How many family hours per week do you spend watching TV together? ....
- How many family hours do you spend doing other on-screen activities together? ....
- How many hours a week do your children spend on a screen (including TV) without you? ....
- What do you do to connect with each other at home?
  ....
  ....
  ....
  ....

- How much time per day do you spend in the car with your children? ....
- What do you do to connect with each other in the car?
  ....
  ....
  ....
  ....

- What do you consider are the top three togetherness experiences/activities your family engages in on a regular basis?
  ....
  ....
  ....
  ....

- Do you think you have enough face-to-face time? ....

Now that you have had a glimpse of the status of face-to-face time in your family, consider your options. If you are happy, that's great. If not, then gather up your courage and make some changes to reclaim face-to-face time.

What three things do you need to change? You can use the above questions as a starting point.

(1) ....

(2) ....

(3) ....

PASSING ON VALUES TO YOUR CHILDREN

Says Robert Shaw in his book *The Epidemic* (HarperCollins, 2004), "The values you demonstrate in your day-to-day interactions will make all the difference in the outcome ... Everything we do teaches our kids something about the nature of life and how to be a human being. As parents, we should constantly ask ourselves, 'What does my action in this situation teach my children? What conclusions will they draw when we give in to their tantrums? ... What conclusion about life will they draw when their existence is all about entertainment or expensive gifts that substitute for loving attention?'"

As parents, we instil values in our children and a worldview. We do this by example. They see how we operate in the world and usually copy us. We also do this through conversation. Help your child experience your values by comparing things and discussing them: "Would we do that in our family? What do you think of how your friend responded? How do you think she or he should have responded? What do you think you would have done in that situation?"

How we spend our time and our money is an easy indicator for children to identify what it is that we value most, and they very often follow suit. Here are some easy examples:

- If we make time for dinner at the table we value conversation and hearing about everyone's day.
- If we regularly buy *Homeless Talk* or similar publications from a vendor at the traffic lights, we show we care for those less fortunate than ourselves, and likewise if we get involved in community projects.
- If we take care of our bodies, exercise and eat healthily, we show that we

value health and fitness and that we honour our bodies.

- If we make sure we are registered to vote and actually cast our vote, we show that we value democracy.
- If we walk out of a store and find that we have a product in the bottom of our trolley that we didn't pay for and return to the store to pay for it, we show that we value honesty and integrity.
- If we take time for prayer, contemplation, meditation and worship, we show that we value our spiritual development.
- If we take ourselves on courses and take time to work through our own personal issues, we show that we value personal development.
- If we are constantly reading, learning and updating ourselves professionally, we show that we value personal development and are committed to lifelong learning.
- If we go out of our way to help and comfort others in need – a sick family member or a friend in distress – we show that we have compassion and empathy for others, that we value helpfulness.
- If we don't text while we drive, we show that we value road safety over convenience.

We could continue, but you get the gist … Creating family values is not something that has to be done in a very formal way, like having a boardroom discussion. It can be done very simply by asking your children about how you as a family respond to various situations and what that reveals about what you value, and what is important to you. From this flows identifying desirable character traits in each other and principles to live by.

All this contributes to the EQ development of your child and is generated through repeated conversations among families throughout childhood, right into the late teens. It should become very obvious that values are created when we make choices about how to live our lives every day. And our ultimate goal is that our children should be able to make emotionally intelligent choices and take responsibility for them.

They need a value system: how we do things around here, what is okay and not okay, how we treat other people and ourselves, what we will or will not do. This will also help them to compare other value offerings that will increasingly come their way, both online and offline, as they move into the tween and teen years.

Bear in mind that children are continuously being bombarded by value-laden messages, from well-known commercial brands to celebrities, from school to friends, from TV shows to online games. The messages urge them to buy in to something, support a cause, follow a person or make a purchase. In the teenage years, hard choices may come up, such as whether to smoke something, take a drug, drink an unknown alcoholic mix, catch a lift with a stranger, meet an online friend in the real world, or have sex with someone.

What our children decide to do will be based on their values, their worldview and their relationship with their parents. Read more on how to prepare your children for these more complex choices in Chapter 11. Keep in the back of your mind the reality that teaching children how to make good choices in the early years is good grounding for enabling them to protect themselves by continuing to make good choices as they get older.

PARENTS, ARE YOU USING YOUR HIGH-TOUCH ADVANTAGE?

Families today compete with big commercial brands, whether they know it or not. We, like the big brands, are competing for our children's time and attention. But there's one big difference that gives you the upper hand in this equation. Because you live together under the same roof, you have the opportunity to engage, one human being to another. Do you know what a privilege this is and that global brands are green with envy at the advantage you have over them in engaging with your children? They would give their eye teeth and invest millions for the opportunity.

Our question is, are you using this advantage to deepen your relationship with your children, or does time and busyness get in the way? If you don't maximise your face-to-face potential with your child, someone else or a brand will, because every child is looking for connection and attention.

Online predators and big brands promise your children engagement, attention and inclusion in some way. Children with a void on the relationship or emotional front are the easy pickings here, while children who feel more emotionally secure stand a greater chance of not being sucked in, and of questioning things because they are not quite so emotionally desperate.

Lead and parent in a multisensory way and face to face; it's what most brands can't do and it's what will make your connection with your child unique and memorable. Be a human *being*, not a human *doing*, and you will be maximising your advantage in building a relationship with your child. Love, trust, respect and communication are basic protective factors for your children as they engage with the big wide world.

CHILDREN THRIVE ON ROUTINE AND BOUNDARIES

There is a time in the day for everything and children thrive when they have a routine and know what comes next. With the world going digital, there are now more things to fit into the daily routine and we have to decide how much of everything to allow in the day. If children are given carte blanche, the family routine that keeps everyone sane goes out the window and it isn't long before the children are calling the shots. If you give away control of the family routine, you will find it harder and harder to win back. Think of Arthur's example of setting the ground rules for TV-watching from the ground up (see page 31).

Children like the predictability of a routine and it helps them to acquire the skills of planning. A routine provides boundaries, a form of firm discipline rather than authoritarian discipline. Yes, children can go and watch television, play a computer game or spend time on social media, as long as everything else, such as homework, eating supper together, and tidying up, gets done too.

Implementing and maintaining a routine is about teaching them to have a balanced life, because technology can be all-consuming and addictive. Time just flies by unchecked when you are immersed in watching TV or playing Wii or PlayStation. We need to teach them, through our family routine and by monitoring their use of on-screen activities, how much is too much.

In other words, there is a strong link between routine and setting boundaries. Children really thrive on knowing how far they can go, how far they can push before someone pushes back, and shows them where the line is. In fact, they will often play up in their quest to find where the boundary is if no one is making it clear to them. Boundaries are about setting limits around issues such as:

- bathing before supper or bedtime
- eating dinner before having pudding
- what time they go to bed at night
- finishing homework before watching television
- how much television can be watched per day
- how long they can play computer games for each session
- how much airtime they get for their cellphones each week or month.

In 2013, at the Skylanders SWAP Force media launch in Nuremberg, I met Guha Bala, CEO of Vicarious Visions, the company that developed the ground-breaking Skylanders technology behind bringing toys to life on a screen. Multi-billionaire Guha, now in his thirties, started his company while still in high school, so he has been immersed in gaming culture for many years.

At the time of the interview, Guha had a daughter who was about to turn seven, as well as 10-month-old twins. I asked him how much time his older daughter spends doing on-screen activities each day. Guha said that he limits her to a maximum of one hour of on-screen time per day, which includes both gaming and television – she must choose. The rest of her afternoon is spent doing some form of physical activity, reading, writing and maths.

Considering Guha is one of the world's gaming gurus, it is telling that he has such balanced perspective and concern for his daughter's holistic development, agreeing that too much of anything is too much.

Children must learn to live within certain limits – for your own family sanity as well as for the good of their own development. Ultimately, this will lead to them becoming healthy and happy switchers from off-screen to on-screen activities, and vice versa. They can do this far easier if their developmental needs have been met in the early years. Even if your children are now in primary or high school, see Appendix 4 to remind yourself of the basics, as they are still important even in the latter years.

HOW MUCH SCREEN TIME IS TOO MUCH?

This is one of the most common questions asked by parents and it is not an easy one to answer because it depends on a number of variables including:

- the age of your child (the younger the child the less time they should be involved in on-screen activities from a developmental perspective)
- the type of on-screen activity (gaming, cellphones or TV, for example)
- whether it is term time or school holidays
- how much homework your child has
- how sedentary your child is, and whether he or she does a lot of physical activity or sport
- how technology affects your child's mood, behaviour and ability to concentrate (it can be different for every child)
- whether you use technology as part of a reward system for your child
- whether you use technology as a babysitter, and how often and for how long.

AVOID THE TRIPLE-S SYNDROME

Parents need to ensure that their children do not fall prey to Triple-S Syndrome: a Solitary, Sedentary, Screen-based existence. With our busy lifestyles, it is easy to fall into this trap:

Solitary

- **The danger:** On-screen activities perform the convenient role of both babysitter and entertainer, which is very useful for us but detrimental to our children on the whole. One of the key developmental areas in childhood is socialising, and this must be done through real, face-to-face play activities to have any effect.

The consequence: When you are too tired to play with your child or too busy to take your child to play dates or host other children in your home, the result is often a child who spends a lot of time alone, and in front of a screen for company. Even children who watch TV together don't necessarily interact and communicate with one another.

Sedentary

- **The danger:** When children are in front of a screen, they are leading an increasingly sedentary existence. The couch becomes their best friend or Siamese twin, if you will. Exchanging the couch for any movement-based activities becomes harder and harder the more time is spent in front of a screen.

The consequence: Movement helps to wire the brain for academic learning, which means a sedentary existence must be avoided at all costs or you will have even more demands on your time and wallet as you sign your child up for therapy to fill in the developmental gaps. Sedentary children also become more difficult to motivate and discipline, which will strain your relationship. Manage on-screen time for both your sakes.

Screen-based

- **The danger:** Children are increasingly viewing the world from a screen. Under the age of 12 a child has a developmental need to engage more with the real than the virtual world. Moderation and a good balance between on-screen and off-screen activities is important. When children spend a lot of time in front of a screen, on-screen activities can become addictive, because they stimulate the secretion of chemicals (dopamine) from the pleasure centre of the brain.

The consequence: One of the consequences is that children also experience a false sense of achievement without having done much. This becomes an expectation in other activities as they grow older, resulting in inability to complete demanding tasks.

It's a sad fact that many children now engage with on-screen activities rather than sharing a bedtime story, songs or conversations with their parents. The Triple-S Syndrome is eroding the very connections on which we build our families and our children's futures.

Prevention is better than cure. Vaccinate immediately with regular doses of screen-free time, characterised by the warm fuzzy features of play, movement, communication and connection, and don't forget the benefits of nature and spending time outdoors. The world is far bigger than the family media centre.

THE IMPORTANCE OF NATURE AND THE OUTDOORS

Screen-hungry children certainly do know how to tune nature out in their fascination with and addiction to gadgets and moving objects on a flat screen. There is a danger of this getting out of control, resulting in the concept of 'a world in one room', where children rarely go out, they move less, socialise face to face less frequently and don't fall in love with nature. Many babies, deprived of physical exposure to nature, such as crawling on all fours on the grass, cry when their sensitive feet first touch this green substance!

While "No child left behind" has been the mantra driving education reform in the USA for many years, there is a new twist that highlights children's increasing detachment from nature worldwide, and that is, "No child left inside!"

In Holly Korbey's article published on the Mind/Shift website in August 2013, she highlights the importance of getting kids excited about playing outdoors in the digital age: "In the opening pages of his moving book, *Last Child in the Woods* (Algonquin Books, 2005), journalist Richard Louv quotes a fourth-grader who told him, 'I like to play indoors better, 'cause that's where all the electrical outlets are.' Since the publication of his book in 2005, Louv has become famous for coining the term Nature-

Deficit Disorder – not as a medical diagnosis, but as shorthand for what's happening to kids who stay inside, away from nature, for most of their young lives. He uses compelling research to support his claims that rising rates of obesity, depression and anxiety, and ADHD symptoms, could well be linked to children's disconnection from trees, fields and streams."

I only have to take myself as an example to know that what Richard Louv says is true. One of the quickest ways for me to ground myself and feel happier after having spent hours working in front of my computer is to take my shoes off and walk barefoot on the lawn, looking at my garden, touching the bark of my big tree, listening to the buzz of the bees and the twitter of birds in the trees, and basking in the sunshine.

My office looks out over a lush garden with large trees and shrubs, teeming with bird life. Thanks to a bird-feeder close by, the beauty of nature is my constant companion. This is possible only because the office is part of my home. My research and consulting organisation, World Wide Worx, is run entirely virtually, across the Internet, with all my analysts working from their own personal environments too, and my writers also having their own home office set-ups.

Sometimes, when I have a meeting in my office, someone asks me when I am going to 'graduate' to a corporate office environment. I usually have to stifle my laughter, and try to be as polite as possible in explaining a simple truth: I spent decades investing in a career and creating a working style and organisation that would allow me the luxury of working from just this kind of environment.

Why would I abandon a spacious office overlooking a lush garden, visited by birds and small animals, for the cold, sterile walls of a corporate office park or cubicle environment? Yet this is the kind of thinking to which the modern office worker has been conditioned: the further you are from nature, the more business-like your business. Not everyone has the same choice of personal working environment, but everyone has the choice of developing a different perspective.

When visiting nature or game reserves, we feel a deep sense of peace that comes with openness, views and space. They feed our souls and strike an emotional chord within us. If children have no real point of reference, if they never interact with nature directly themselves and only see it in pictures, then what is the point of teaching them about saving the rainforests or the rhino, to which they will have no emotional connection whatsoever?

A further plea contained in Korbey's Mind/Shift article that is well worth heeding: "If we want children to flourish, to become truly empowered, then let us allow them to love the earth before we ask them to save it," says educator David Sobel, author of the book *Beyond Ecophobia* (Orion Society, 1995), which is about the fear of ecological deterioration. Korbey adds, "Backing this up, Richard Louv explains that Teddy Roosevelt and Davy Crockett became environmentalists not because they felt the world needed saving, but because of their joyful childhood experiences playing in nature. Most environmentalists fall in love with nature as children, and grow up wanting to take care of it."

"No child left inside" means making sure that our children get outdoors and have a hands-on experience with nature. This doesn't necessarily mean long-distance trips to game reserves either. What are you doing to connect your child with your closest nature reserve or botanical garden? Or even closer to home, do you watch for birds in your garden, putting out seeds or fruit to attract them? What about looking for earthworms when planting seedlings this spring? You don't have to look very far. Nature starts right on your doorstep.

A JOURNEY TO INDEPENDENCE

All of childhood is a journey to independence. Frustration and curiosity are what push children to learn more about their world and to derive meaning for themselves. One of our roles as parents is to balance their sense of satisfaction with their feelings of frustration; this is the learning process that leads to balanced growth.

Be interested in all their developmental transitions and celebrate them. There is something beautiful about each and every one. Get to know and understand your child's needs developmentally and emotionally. Be in touch as a human *being* not just a human *doing* who has to get through a very long list in a day. Don't just 'do' your kids because there is so much to be 'done'. Engage with them and connect. Slow down enough to experience the joy and keep sufficient perspective to help you make sound decisions out of love and understanding, not haste and fear.

- Children do need their parents.
- In an era of maximum media, children need maximum parenting.
- Children want a real and authentic relationship with their parents.
- They want more of our presence and happiness and less of our stress.
- Time and attention are what children need – these are the currencies we trade with them.
- Multi-tasking can lead to parental inattentiveness.
- We all need to manage the technology in our lives and keep people at the centre.
- Children need more laps and fewer apps.
- We need to role-model effective use of technology – our children are watching.
- When we are not paying attention, children use negative attention-seeking strategies.
- Face-to-face time with each other is important.
- Children need a value system against which to compare other value offerings.
- Children need to learn first-hand the consequences of their choices.
- Love, trust, respect and communication are protective factors that will help to keep your child safe.
- Switch off screens and *talk* your children clever.
- Unplug from technology from time to time in order to connect with each other.
- Children must not be reliant on a screen for soothing or falling asleep.
- Every child needs routine and boundaries.
- Play and movement are essentials for healthy development.
- Children thrive with time spent both indoors and outdoors and a balance between on-screen and off-screen activities.
- Facilitate your children's journey to independence by helping them make, and be responsible for, their own choices.

CHAPTER 9

Because most parents know little about the digital world and how both children and adults operate in it, we thought to give you a bit more insight to some basic principles before leaving you with some advice on how to keep your children safe and savvy. We'd like to imagine that if we were parents having a cup of coffee or tea together with you and chatting about our kids, these are some of the things – the 'Did you know?' – we might share with you.

THE INTERNET REMEMBERS EVERYTHING

In our regular digital safety presentations to learners in primary and high schools, one of the facts that shocks kids most is that the Internet remembers everything – even what they have deleted. It is a sobering realisation for many, to think before they post in future.

So how does the Internet remember? In just the same way as we do (or should do) regular backups of the content on our computers, search engines do exactly the same thing and they keep multiple versions over time. It's called a cache. The only way to have something permanently removed from a cache is through a legal process.

With regard to a social media platform such as Facebook, you may have removed something from your timeline but it can still come up in a search on Facebook because you don't know how many people might have it on their own timelines. In the same way, you can remove a tag on a picture someone else has posted of you but you cannot personally remove the picture. You would have to ask them to physically remove it – but it would still be saved in the Facebook cache.

There are also time-machine websites that have been tracking the development and history of the Internet since the 1970s and they cache, or backup, every version of every website ever created and published on the web.

The Internet remembers everything. We hope this is a good enough reason to have a conversation with your children about the importance of being a responsible user of social media and technology. Their digital reputation depends on it.

THEIR DIGITAL FOOTPRINT DETERMINES THEIR ONLINE REPUTATION

Whatever your child does or shares online, from the first time they open a profile on a social network to setting up a blog or website, creates a digital footprint. And, as mentioned, the Internet remembers everything, so they need to learn to be conscious and intentional about what they post online, which is easier said than done in the impulsive teenage years.

But, seriously, your digital footprint is much like a tattoo – it is very difficult to erase and will follow you around for the rest of your life. Employers and recruitment consultants actively check the Internet today to determine whether a person's online and offline reputations are congruent. The same goes for candidates who are applying for bursaries.

There is many a story of someone losing a job offer or, indeed, an existing job or position after an online search has turned up some unsavoury content. So it pays to look after your online reputation, a fact to which we can both attest as we often receive work opportunities via email from individuals at well-known organisations whom we have never met before in person, based on what they have discovered about us through a search on Google.

Reputation management just became part of your parenting portfolio! And your children will require regular reminders of its importance, as well as learning how to manage it for themselves by understanding that boundaries are healthy and will serve them well in the long run.

BECAUSE THEY CAN

Children are like a river – they will always take the path of least resistance. They are constantly on the lookout for loopholes, a way out, an easier option – they're human, after all. Whether eating sweets, watching television, playing computer games or surfing the net, they will do what we allow or enable them to do, for good or for bad, until we put up some resistance and give them some boundaries.

If you have no filters on the family computer and you don't activate parental controls on their phones, there are no boundaries and children will get up to things that they might not normally do, for the simple reason that they can – even nice kids whom you'd least suspect.

Wi-Fi at Wimpy, McDonald's and in other public spaces – kids will purposefully wait to do all their big downloads where they don't have to pay for the data. Clever! Or is it?

A common occurrence in many homes at the end of each month is that both kids and adults are becoming accustomed to pushing data downloads to the limit on the last day of the month when they can't get throttled, because throttling typically occurs on fixed-line networks each day when the cap is activated after midnight.

The problem with this is that children treat it as a right rather than a once-off occurrence, and it becomes an expectation. The complicity of adults in pushing access rights to the limit rubs off on other behaviour. It removes some of the barriers to self-regulation – the same barriers that would apply to, say, taking biscuits and sweets from the pantry.

In a similar way, they will try to hack into the school network and, once they have gained access, will push it to its limits too. This is bad manners, and they get their basic training for school network use at home. It is a sign of poor impulse control and is equivalent to running around shoplifting in the online space, and parents have condoned it, which, in turn, has conditioned kids.

If it's okay to do it at home then it's okay to do it at school or in other public spaces. Then peer-group learning kicks in – if they don't have it at home then they learn from their friends how to do it, much like kids share cheats for online games. And while you're at it, if you're visiting a friend's house and can gain access to their network via their Wi-Fi password, then you can steal from their data pantry too!

Parents need to give their children an understanding of netiquette – what is and is not acceptable behaviour when it comes to all things online. Sometimes kids push the limits in order to find out where the boundary actually is. We need to give them an answer. Families and schools need Acceptable-Use Policies for the Internet in just the same way as businesses do.

NICE KIDS CAN BE NAUGHTY ONLINE

Nice kids can be naughty online, and nice kids can even be nasty online. It is so much easier to be both naughty and nasty in the on-screen world than it is in the real world. Much of this is because there can be a reasonable amount of anonymity for the perpetrator of these acts. They can assume a digital persona that has its own name and wreak havoc in people's lives.

The screen creates a distance and potential anonymity between the perpetrator and the victim simply because it is a screen and therefore it's often seen as a game. In that context, succeeding at cyber-bullying is almost equivalent to winning at a computer game (see page 44 in Chapter 3 on gaming and the conditioning of soldiers for warfare). Because it's virtual, you don't see the face of your victim, you don't feel their pain and you don't realise you're hurting a real human being. But even when you do, the interface you are using, which is this impersonal screen, removes the human face and removes empathy for the victim.

The result is that even when you encounter the victim face to face you have already been desensitised to their feelings so it makes it even easier to continue the bullying in the physical world, and get off on witnessing the fear and confusion of the victim in the real world. This extends the power on the screen of scoring a hit and winning points into the physical environment.

It gives kids a real kick and an immense sense of power to be able to impose their will on others with anonymity, like a puppeteer pulling the strings of a puppet, and when they do, a surge of dopamine is released in the pleasure centre of the brain that creates a sense of euphoria. This is what fuels the vicious cycle of cyber-bullying. It is highly addictive, leading children to do it over and over again to get their regular fix. It can happen to the nicest of children in the same way as they can fall foul of drugs, alcohol or bad company in the real world.

They may also access inappropriate content such as porn, precisely because of the perceived sense of anonymity, enabling naughty or unsavoury behaviour. There have been cases of children getting hold of their parents' credit cards to enable them to pursue online activities that require payment. This can be as innocuous as an in-game purchase of virtual goods or as serious as paying for gambling.

STUPID THINGS PEOPLE DO ONLINE

Sometimes computers and digital media can make us adults feel stupid. But both adults and youngsters also do stupid things online that compromise their safety and security. We have highlighted some of the common ones below.

Parents:

- don't install filters on the family computer or activate the safe search filters on their search engine
- don't use parental controls that exist on their children's cellphones
- don't cap their children's cellphone accounts
- are often guilty of allowing their children to dictate their terms of usage of devices
- write down their user names and passwords on a piece of paper and stick it on their computer (especially dangerous if you work in an office or public environment)
- don't password-protect their list of passwords, which are saved in a document on their computer
- do online banking on public computers in Internet cafés or airport lounges
- engage in online gambling or porn
- give away too many contact and personal details on their social media profiles and in their posts
- do not activate their privacy settings on social media
- do not monitor their children's online activities.

Kids:

- don't have passwords, leaving their devices open to abuse by others
- use weak passwords that are easy to crack
- allow their friends to use their devices unsupervised or give friends their device or social media password
- leave their geo-location settings on, on their phones or social media platforms, allowing people to know where they are
- do not activate privacy settings on their social media accounts

- post inappropriate photographs of themselves engaging in compromising behaviour (even teenage girls posting innocent pictures of themselves in bikinis or in their nightwear is not a good idea if they are going public)
- download or watch porn online
- use free Wi-Fi in a restaurant or public space for downloading content (This is okay, but beware of pop-ups that simply say 'free Wi-Fi'. If you are in Wimpy, it should say 'Wimpy Wi-Fi', for example. 'Free Wi-Fi' could be someone sitting outside the restaurant masquerading as a hotspot. Logon through their link and they can see everything your child is typing, passwords and all.)

PERSONAL PRIVACY

Is personal privacy a thing of the past? Do our kids know what personal privacy actually is? Do they care? Should they care? Why?

There is a common perception that online privacy is prized by adults and ignored by children, but the real picture is a little more complex. Many adults are oblivious to online privacy issues while many children protect their privacy at all costs – from their parents. This is one of the most significant examples of the digital generation gap and the reason parents are often in the dark about their children's digital lives.

That said, children tend to completely disregard the rules of online privacy when dealing with anyone who is not their parent. From the seemingly innocuous, such as using their real names as user names in chat rooms and the like, to serious issues such as giving their address or phone number or school details to strangers.

One of the most potentially damaging things a child can do is something that seems completely unthreatening, namely giving their phone or computer password to a friend. These details can be shared as quickly as any photo over a social network. The consequences include causing trouble in your child's name (identity theft, cyber-bullying or embarrassing your child by offending their friends). It's also possible for fraud to be committed, such as making purchases in your child's name (worst-case scenario), and even something as seemingly innocent as messing around with the content of their phone can prove harmful.

These are obvious perils. Less obvious is the habit of not prizing privacy. The trends shaping the world of privacy are irrelevant here in terms of the argument that people don't regard privacy as important. Understanding privacy is essential to protecting reputation. Children need to understand that guarding their privacy online is part and parcel of guarding their reputation in the digital world.

The pursuit of maximum number of friends and followers in any social network is often a precursor to dropping one's guard to all forms of privacy. This form of oversharing can have devastating consequences in the real world. For example, it opens them up to stalkers and predators. A stalker is someone who establishes their identity and then follows them online with the intention of also tracking them offline and making physical contact. Stalkers want to be near or with the child as much as possible, and the very act of stalking is harmful. A predator is someone who wants to have physical contact with a child of a violent or sexual nature. And the Internet is a rich and fertile ground for paedophiles.

Cops Bust SA Porn Ring
Wednesday, 21 August 2013
By Lesego Ngobeni, *Eyewitness News*[1]

Police confirmed on Wednesday that they had cracked what was believed to be South Africa's biggest child pornography ring with links to various other countries. Six men were arrested in five provinces in connection with the case. Police confirmed that those arrested included a principal, who was also an award-winning author, two teachers, a lawyer, a dermatologist and a businessman. National police spokesperson Solomon Makgale said that five of the men had already appeared in court on various charges relating to the possession of child pornography. He said authorities also suspected that the men were importing pornography. "The initial charge was possession, but we suspect that they're involved in manufacturing, import and export as well as mass-distribution," Makgale told *AFP*. "The indications are there. They had cameras. They had these external hard drives," he added. "One of the people we arrested is involved in the export-import business." Electronic equipment, including 600 DVDs, memory sticks, laptops, tablets, and external hard drives, as well as 25 books believed to contain images of child pornography, had been confiscated. The images show children "suffering extreme forms of violence", *The Times* reported. Investigators said that the group had links with Canada, the United States, the United Kingdom, Western Europe and Australasia. Meanwhile, a prestigious private school based in Nelspruit immediately dismissed its principal. "The agreement follows his arrest for allegedly being in possession of child pornography," the school is quoted as saying in *The Times*.

DATA MINING – MARKETERS AND YOUR CHILD'S PRIVACY

A seemingly innocuous form of breach of privacy is also one that holds a more insidious threat. We are talking here about marketers who use data mining to find out more about your family's purchasing and other habits. This is often used to sell more products, sign you up to new services, get you to upgrade existing services, and upsell – essentially extracting more money from the same customers by getting them to commit to additional offerings.

That's all fine and well and there is nothing illegal about it, but it is fairly common for you to be targeted through your children. In the old days, it would have been a matter of phoning your home in the afternoon in the hope your child would answer, and then soft-talking them into giving away personal details ranging all the way from family behaviour through to holiday activities. Even back then it was unethical but not unusual.

The equivalent today is catching children online especially through social networks and in online games. This happens in the form of random adverts and offers but can also be more specifically targeted, based on details given in their profiles that they fill in for any site or service. This is a goldmine for the data miners, and ethics once again plays little role in this new privacy free for all. Parents and children should limit the information they provide online.

The first and most obvious rule is not to provide information in a public profile that would allow a marketer to trace you to a physical address or phone number.

Secondly, unless your business depends on it, your email address should not be publicly available. Times have changed. Making your details available online exposes you to far more unwanted contact than was the case in the past when your name, address and phone number appeared in the *White Pages*, a thick printed telephone directory that had a place in every home – and this is due to the skill of data miners who have access to ever more sophisticated technology and tools.

Thirdly, if your email address should be semi-private then your child's should be completely private.

And, considering the fact that an email address is so easily created or changed, how much more so their physical contact details? Your child needs to understand that when they are asked for these kinds of details when filling in an online questionnaire or competition entry form, contact details must be treated like a treasure. Children need to learn to be discerning or they will fall into potholes on the information superhighway such as spam.

CLICK-JACKING – PRESSING THE LIKE BUTTON COULD MEAN TROUBLE

There is a new category of spam on the Internet, and tweens and teens are highly susceptible to it. Hey, even we have been caught recently and maybe you were too! You get sent a video link from a friend you are connected to on social media. It has happened to both of us on Facebook. It says something like this:

- The worst traffic accident/aeroplane accident ever. To view this video click *Like* …
- This person was ordered to do … and what they did next will leave you speechless. To view the video click *Like* …
- To see what people are saying about a picture of you, click *Like* …

You click the *Like* button and there is no video – it never existed in the first place. These scams are being used to build up traffic via *Likes* to a particular product or service to which you are oblivious. The company behind this scam is trying to gather *Likes* for an online advert or page that is monetised. The more *Likes* they get, the more advertising they can generate from their clients and the more revenue they can earn off their site.

But that's not all, as they say in television infomercials … By pressing the *Like* button you give the spammer access to the password on your social media account. They can now access your Facebook page without your permission and send adverts for their or their client's product to your entire network. The next thing is you find yourself promoting weight-loss products and skin creams to your social network via posts that you never personally sent.

In other words, your account has been hacked! Reset your password immediately. Make sure you alert your children to this innocuous-looking form of scamming because they are suckers for catchy copywriting that is designed to grab their attention and pique their curiosity. Forewarned is forearmed. Protect your children and yourself from doing silly things online by sharing this insight with them and do change your social media passwords if you have been click-jacked.

SOFTWARE CAN'T PROTECT YOUR CHILD FROM STUPIDITY

You can't protect your child from bad choices but you can pre-empt them by teaching them how to make good choices. A bad choice online can be equivalent to the angst and challenges of reformatting a hard drive when a computer has crashed. Installing all the software and filters in the world without having conversations with children about digital safety and online netiquette is only half the battle won. Digital safety consists of a technical element as well as a human-behavioural element. The technical stuff is easy, and if it isn't then pay for a consultant to help you as you would in any other aspect of your life such as using an investment advisor for your financial affairs, a lawyer in legal matters and a psychologist if you should find yourself losing your mind.

The behaviour stuff – how you and your children actually use social media and technology – takes much more time and effort to crack. Many parents give up before they have even begun because the journey to being a responsible user of on-screen media takes many a conversation, and children who think they know it all may give you attitude. But having the conversations and using issues in the news as teachable moments are essential if you want to protect your children. Would you have let your toddler walk across a busy road unaided? We think not. Well, this is much the same. In this instance, the busy road just happens to be the Internet superhighway.

And you will have to have the same conversation from many different angles over and over again. Note that we use the word 'conversation', not lecture or speech. Children today do not respond well to the latter. They need more conversations that matter and fewer speeches that don't. At a talk Nikki gave to Grade 7–12s, a number of learners came to her afterwards and thanked her for not talking down at them, for meeting them at their level and for making it conversational rather than a lecture. She was blown away at their directness and ability to isolate what worked for them.

The Internet and social media give your children thousands and thousands of opportunities to practise making good choices. Watch what they are doing, applaud positive use of social media, and be there to guide and facilitate better decision-making should your child trip up or be on the receiving end of unsavoury online behaviour.

Digital safety and responsible online behaviour are not so much about high-tech but more about high-touch and the nature and quality of relationships and communication at home. It is you, not software, that will protect your child from their own stupidity online.

FROM THIS CHAPTER …

- The Internet remembers everything.
- Children will do whatever we allow them to do online.
- Children need boundaries – even if you trust them.
- Don't think it's beyond your child to be naughty or nasty online.
- Their grounding in acceptable behaviour online starts at home.
- Personal privacy is a choice.
- Software on its own can't protect your child from stupidity.
- Your relationship with your child, in addition to software, is their best form of protection online.
- They need to practise making good choices.

CHAPTER 10

DANGERS IN THE DIGITAL WORLD

Because we've lived most of our lives in the real world, we tend to have a handle on the dangers and instinctively and automatically raise our children with an awareness of them and with strategies of how to avoid them. We know this world.

The online world has, however, thrown us a curve ball because everything is new to us. We have not been faced with these dangers before and neither we, nor society as a whole, have much experience in dealing with them. We are writing the rule book as we go and we should not lose sight of the fact that we are as susceptible to on-screen threats and dangers as our children are.

We need to protect ourselves as well as our children. It really is a family matter. But take heart. Don't lose your common sense; it still applies in the digital world. And listen to your intuition; it can be a good guide when trying to get a sense of when things might be a bit 'off'.

Our aim with this chapter is not to scare you witless, but to enlighten you and put you in the picture. You need to know the dark side as well as the light side of this new-look world in order to help your children benefit from it, as well as to avoid the dangers. Here we relay a cautionary tale from our back yard, and one that underlines the importance of individuals and institutions working together to protect our children.

THE OUTING OF OUTOILET

It was the most abusive environment for children yet uncovered in South Africa, but its hosts were protected by distance, technology and anonymity. When authorities seemed powerless to act against Outoilet, individuals stepped in.

When Outoilet was first brought to the attention of Arthur's company, World Wide Worx, a few years ago, it was a mobile hub of bullying, abuse and humiliation for schoolchildren in the Western Cape. Confined largely to the Cape Flats, it was often described by teenagers as the 'best-kept sex secret' in the province.

It was hosted on computer servers in Russia, where little law and order applied to the online world. But the target was strictly South African. Chat rooms had been set up for dozens of schools in disadvantaged areas, and the chats fell into two categories: requests for information about members of the opposite sex, with a view to hooking up; and scandalous gossip or vicious accusations about fellow learners. The gossip became so virulent that it was blamed for destroying lives, literally and figuratively: some claimed that victims of this bullying had even committed suicide. Various case studies have emerged of children and adults reporting how the gossip had shattered their lives.

Then, during 2010, Outoilet took an even more sinister turn: adults began soliciting children for sex on the site. They also offered to share pornography with schoolchildren, and offered money and airtime for pictures of the children unclothed. In some cases, children offered their services to adults. And it wasn't long before the chat craze spread to schools across the country, invading Gauteng and KwaZulu-Natal in particular.

It was these developments that brought Outoilet back into the spotlight, and World Wide Worx found itself being called on to comment on the trend in numerous media, including *Eyewitness News*, *Rapport*, *The Citizen* and *Drum*. At the time, the consensus seemed to be that the only effective route that could be taken was via criminal proceedings: laying a charge with police, who would refer the matter to Interpol, which would refer the matter to the Russian authorities, who would be asked to investigate as well as close down the site. The Publications Control Board was also expected to initiate proceedings.

The breakthrough, for World Wide Worx, came with a suggestion by Kris Jarzebowski, CEO of recruitment portal CareerJunction, that the company use its influence to persuade Internet service providers to block the site. That was like a light bulb going on above someone's head: the vast majority of the activity on Outoilet was conducted via cellphones, and it would only take the major cellular network operators blocking the site to pull its abuse teeth.

The suggestion came at the same time as a discussion taking place internally on how World Wide Worx could support the Lead South Africa initiative, launched by Primedia Broadcasting to encourage "ordinary South Africans who continually seek to do the right thing for themselves, for their families and for their country". The Outoilet issue was a natural one to tackle in this context.

The World Wide Worx campaign was two-pronged: approach network operators and Internet service providers on one hand; and, on the other hand, advertisers on the portal.

One of the key issues at stake was the illegality of the site, and the abuse of children it promoted, rather than more general issues of pornography and sex chat among adults and children. Service providers do not see themselves as moral watchdogs or censors when the material in question is not illegal. It had to be shown that this was not a censorship issue, but rather a matter of protecting children from direct abuse.

This was not difficult.

According to the Constitution of the Republic of South Africa, learners have the right to a safe environment and the right to human dignity. The latter includes the right to be protected from bullying, sexual harassment, intimidation and victimisation. Any platform that encourages or allows behaviour that infringes rights to human dignity is therefore in violation of the South African Constitution, and can result in both criminal and civil action.

But there was also clear criminal activity on the site.

According to Childline, "taking pictures of persons under the age of 18 that are sexual and pornographic is illegal and … sending sexual pictures of someone of any age to a person under 18 years is also a criminal offence." Offers of such material to schoolchildren, including those in primary school, were common on Outoilet.

Following well-publicised allegations of a school-yard rape at Jules High School in Johannesburg, and the video recording of the incident on a cellphone, Outoilet took centre stage. Most of the postings in the Jules High chat room were offers or requests for the video, which the police had already declared to be child pornography. Money and airtime were offered by dozens of people for a copy of the video. Add to this the solicitation of children for sex and offers of remuneration for other favours, and the extent of illegal and abusive activity on Outoilet was clear.

The scale of participation varied from school to school. Some had up to a hundred postings a week, some only a few dozen messages a month. In many cases, especially those involving solicitation and offers of pornography or sex, cellphone numbers were provided.

There was no argument from either MTN or Vodacom. Both were fully supportive of the initiative, from the CEO down. And both networks officially blacklisted the site.

Equally important, though, was the immediate commitment by one of the biggest advertisers on the site, a mobile dating service aimed at over-18s. It turned out that the ads were placed via a global advertising network. The dating service immediately instructed the network to remove their ads from the site.

On 23 November 2010, *The Citizen* ran a front-page banner headline, "War on Outoilet", with the subhead, "Bid to block network over child pornography". Within two hours of the newspaper hitting the streets, the schools' chat rooms had been removed from Outoilet. It was clear that the combination of headline publicity and financial loss had done what police proceedings could not.

MTN issued a formal statement:

"Currently, MTN is using a service that prevents access on its network to websites that contain images of the sexual abuse of children. Launched in December 2008, the service supports the aims of the Mobile Alliance Against Child Sexual Abuse Content of which MTN is a member.

"The Internet Watch Foundation (IWF) provides MTN with a list that gets updated twice daily of websites identified as containing images of child sexual abuse. In addition to this service that helps protect MTN customers from inadvertent exposure to such content and minimise the perpetuation of the abuse of the child victims, MTN also has a Parental Control service. This enables MTN customers to choose and manage adult content and instant-messaging activities that can be received on the mobile phones of their children, employees, and themselves. This service can be accessed by dialling *101#.

"As a responsible corporate citizen, MTN has requested the IWF to block the Outoilet domains which have raised concerns in recent days. MTN can confirm that these domains have been blacklisted on its network."

One of the most significant consequences of the success of this campaign, aside from the blocking of the sites and the removal of some of their financial reward, was the extent to which it demonstrated that industry self-regulation can work.

Earlier calls by a government minister for a ban of all pornography online raised the spectre of official censorship of the Internet. This is typically the recourse taken by totalitarian states to control political expression, using 'morals' as their initial arguments.

World Wide Worx vigorously opposed the proposal. The role of the government, it argued, is not to act as a moral guardian over the activities of consenting adults. And no further regulation was needed to outlaw child pornography. Child pornography is illegal; soliciting children is illegal; exposing children to pornography is illegal. It merely requires the law to be enforced. And where the perpetrators hide behind anonymity of technology and the safety of foreign hosts, the industry showed that it could act a lot faster in this regard than government ever could.

Sadly, however, technology allows Outoilet and its lookalikes to keep resurfacing under different names, on different servers hosted in different countries, but we can all contribute to keeping it on the run, preventing it from reaching the same scale and impact it did when it was the scourge of our schools.

The Outoilet example highlights a host of different online dangers in a very practical way.

WHAT THE EXPERTS SAY

If you think your child is being cyber-bullied, before getting yourself in a state, here is some wise advice from www.connectsafely.org:[1]

• **Know that you're lucky if your child asks for help.** Most young people don't tell their parents about bullying – online or offline. So if your child's losing sleep, doesn't want to go to school or seems agitated when on his or her computer or phone, ask why as calmly and open-heartedly as possible. Feel free to ask if it has anything to do with mean behaviour or social issues. But even if it does, don't assume it's bullying. You won't know until you get the full story, starting with your child's perspective.

• **Work with your child.** There are two reasons why you'll want to keep your child involved. Bullying and cyber-bullying usually involve a loss of dignity or control over a social situation, and involving your child in finding solutions helps him or her regain that.

The second reason is about context. Because the bullying is almost always related to school life and our kids understand the situation and context better than parents ever can, their perspective is key to getting to the bottom of the situation and working out a solution. You may need to have private conversations with others, but let your child know if you do, and report back. This is about your child's life, so your child needs to be part of the solution.

• **Respond thoughtfully, not fast.** What parents don't always know is that they can make things worse for their kids if they act rashly. A lot of cyber-bullying involves somebody being marginalised (put down and excluded), which the bully thinks increases his or her power or status. If you respond publicly or if your child's peers find out about even a discreet meeting with school authorities, the marginalisation can get worse, which is why any response needs to be well thought out.

• **More than one perspective needed.** Your child's account of what happened is likely completely sincere, but remember that one person's truth isn't necessarily everybody's. You'll need to get other perspectives and be open-minded about what they are. Sometimes kids let themselves get pulled into chain reactions, and often what we see online is only one side of or part of the story.

• **What victims say helps most** is to be heard – really listened to – either by a friend or an adult who cares. That's why, if your kids come to you for help, it's so important to respond thoughtfully and involve them. Just by being heard respectfully, a child is often well on the way to healing.

• **The ultimate goal is restored self-respect** and greater resilience in your child. This, not getting someone punished, is the best focus for resolving the problem and helping your child heal. What your child needs most is to regain a sense of dignity. Sometimes that means standing up to the bully, sometimes not. Together, you and your child can figure out how to get there.

- **One positive outcome** we don't think (or hear in the news) enough about is resilience. We know the human race will never completely eradicate meanness or cruelty, and we also know that bullying is not, as heard in past generations, 'normal' or a rite of passage. We need to keep working to eradicate it. But when it does happen and we overcome it, our resilience grows. Resilience isn't something that can be 'downloaded' or taught. We grow it through exposure to challenges and figuring out how to deal with them. So sometimes it's important to give them space to do that and let them know we have their back.

Of course it goes without saying that in order to help your child, you need to consider the following:

- Know your child's passwords to be able to access their accounts in order to retrieve evidence – do not delete anything.
- Know and understand the school's social media policy.
- Once you have a clear picture of what has been happening, you will need to inform your child's school, especially if other children at the same school are involved.
- Contact your Internet service provider or cellular network to find out what support they can give you, especially if it concerns abusive websites that should be blocked or blacklisted.
- Contact the relevant social network via their reporting feature.
- Contact the police if physical threats are being made.

The Facebook Bullying-prevention Center (https://www.facebook.com/safety/bullying) includes not only insights and advice researched by Yale University, but also pointers to a wide range of additional resources.

The following are some useful websites that provide helpful content and/or details of protection software.

General

www.netnanny.com
www.mobiflock.com
www.virtuenet.co.za
www.theonlinemom.com
www.commonsensemedia.org
www.parentscorner.org.za
www.saferinternet.org
www.acopea.org
www.google.co.za/safetycenter/families/start/
www.google.co.za/safetycenter/tools/
www.microsoft.com/security/family-safety/default.aspx
www.doc.gov.za/child-online-protection-guideline/guidelines-for-parents.html
www.ikeepsafe.org/parents/
www.ikeepsafe.org/be-a-pro/beapro-research/
www.fpbprochild.org.za/internet-safety.aspx
www.vodacom.co.za/vodacom/services/convenience-and-security/account-services/vodacom-parental-control
https://www.mtn.co.za/everyday_services/useful_extras/Pages/parental-control.aspx
www.childlinesa.org.za
www.unicef.org/southafrica/resources_14002.html
www.unicef.org/southafrica/resources_10782.html
www.unicef-irc.org/publications/650
www.childnet.com/parents-and-carers
www.digizen.org
www.cyberbullying.us/resources/parents/
www.bullying.co.uk/cyberbullying/
www.parentsprotect.co.uk/internet_safety.htm
www.staysafeonline.org/stay-safe-online/for-parents/raising-digital-citizens
http://www.waspa.org.za

For schools

www.virtuenet.co.za

www.digizen.org/resources/school-staff.aspx

www.satnac.org.za/proceedings/2012/papers/3.Internet_Services_End_
   User_Applications/53.pdf

www.childnet.com/teachers-and-professionals

www.cyberbullying.us/resources/educators/

www.staysafeonline.org/teach-online-safety/

To block access to adult/selected content on your children's phones:[2]
- Vodacom: Dial *111*123# from the cellphone you want to block.
- MTN: Dial *101# from the cellphone you want to block. (MTN was planning on replacing this system, but it was still working at the time of going to print.)
- WASPA (Wireless Application Service Providers' Association).[3]

You can lodge a complaint directly with WASPA if you feel you or your child have been spammed, or wish to report misleading advertising for mobile services, or complain about billings related to premium-rate SMS services. You can check the WASPA Code of Conduct and the WASPA Advertising Rules to see which mobile industry regulations have been breached.

You can lay a complaint with WASPA online at http://www.waspa.org.za/code/complaint.shtml. Alternatively, you can contact WASPA via info@waspa.org.za call them on 011 476 7710 / 087 805 3328, or send a fax to 086 606 2016.

- Never disregard your own common sense or intuition when it comes to your children.
- Know the law and our children's rights:
  - Taking photographs that are pornographic or of a sexual nature of children under the age of 18 is illegal.
  - Distributing such material to children under the age of 18 is also illegal.
  - If you have children under 18 make sure that they know and understand the above and that if they are caught creating or distributing such material they will acquire a criminal record.
- Websites and domains known to be involved in criminal activity can be blocked or blacklisted by the IWF. For this to happen, you need to alert your service provider.

CHAPTER 11

HOW PARENTS CAN HELP KEEP THEIR KIDS SAFE & SAVVY

Owning a sophisticated piece of technology doesn't make a child a responsible user. As much as children are the chief technology officers in your home, they still need moral and practical guidance to ensure that they grow up into safe and savvy users of media. There is so much available to them and every day something new is launched onto the digital playground that grabs their attention. Just as families have unwritten ground rules about how to behave and how to treat others in the real world, so children need to acquire netiquette for the on-screen world. This doesn't mean you have to be a walking talking encyclopaedia about technology. What it means is that you need to care enough to ensure that your child has the skills to cross the information superhighway safely.

PERSPECTIVE = KNOWLEDGE + A HEALTHY DOSE OF COMMON SENSE

All this talk of technology can make parents panic and put them into a state of paralysis. So let's take a step back. This book is to help you to gain some perspective – to give you an understanding of how things have changed and what you need to do to stay connected while also passing on skills to your children to keep them safe in a digital world and in life in general.

So far, we have given you knowledge and insight into the new digital playground, important things you need to know and how your children operate both online and offline. Knowledge is an important element in understanding the changes going on in the world, to give your thinking and our arguments context. With such easy access to information today, ignorance is no longer an option, and neither can it be used as an excuse.

Unfortunately, when parents are paralysed by their fear of the unknown, or what they feel they have no control over, an element of tentativeness creeps in, undermining their intuition and often wiping out common sense. In a world of maximum media, parents need to strive to maintain some kind of balanced perspective to avoid either underreacting or overreacting to digital issues that have the power to help or hinder our children.

Strive always for perspective, hold on to your common sense, and you will find your middle ground in this brand-new world. In this chapter we will be sharing practical hints, tips and advice about what to do and what not to do to keep your kids safe and savvy, and to help you avoid a state of paralysis or panic.

BUILD ON YOUR GOOD FOUNDATIONS

In her regular presentations of 'The One Thing You Need to Remember', Nikki asks youngsters to tell her some of the lessons that their parents have taught them about how to live decently in the world and how to protect themselves. Children of all ages are always proud to put up their hands and share these things with her. These are the most common:

- Don't tear pages out of books.
- Don't write in library books.
- Wash your hands after using the toilet.
- Never catch a lift with a stranger.
- Don't talk to a stranger.
- Don't accept food, drink or sweets from a stranger.
- How to cross the road safely.

Interesting, isn't it? Now you need to build on those ingrained foundations you have already established. Add new information to pre-existing thoughts and patterns of behaviour. The anchor is already there, so why not use it?

As we explained in Chapter 4, children learn best when we give them concrete examples or experiences. 'Real' works because they can attach more meaning to it than they can to something abstract and removed from them. They need to be able to identify with what we are talking about if we are giving them advice or implementing boundaries, otherwise it will just go straight over their heads or be tuned out. Instead of just handing down a list of draconian rules with which they cannot identify, rather use real examples to give them context.

In my digital safety presentations for tweens and teens, after they have shared some of the lessons mentioned above that their parents have taught them to keep them safe, I then give them a few scenarios to which they can easily relate.

- **Scenario 1:**

"If your parents taught you not to tear pages out of library books, or cut out paragraphs or photographs from books to stick into your school projects, then please don't plagiarise from the Internet. It's too easy to just cut and paste someone else's writing from a website and drop it into your project, passing it off as your own. That's all very well and good until you get to matric when plagiarism monitors are in place. If you are caught, you will fail. Learn how to put things in your own words."

- **Scenario 2:**

"In the unlikely event that you went to the post office to post a real letter to a pen pal overseas, you would walk up to the counter, buy a stamp, lick and stick it onto the letter and then head off to post it in the big red post box. When you got there, and just before you drop your letter into the box, do you think it would enter your head to take off your clothes, take a picture of your private parts with a digital Polaroid camera and stick it onto the back of the letter before posting it?" At this suggestion there is always a gasp in my young audience who are incredulous that I could even suggest such a thing! I then go on to say, "Then don't photograph your naked body with your phone camera and send the pictures on to others via SMS, Snapchat, Instagram, WhatsApp, BBM or on Facebook. Even if someone promises they will never show anyone else, that's no guarantee, and social media platforms are a gazillion times more public than the back of a letter. Anything can go viral and be seen by thousands in seconds."

- **Scenario 3:**

Finally, I discuss stranger danger in the context of hitchhiking on a road. "Today, we navigate the information superhighway and catching lifts with strangers or picking up hitchhikers online is just as, or more dangerous an activity, than it is in the real world. There are only two types of people who hitchhike, in my opinion: those who are desperate and out of options and those who are ignorant and don't know any better. You need to make sure you are neither desperate nor ignorant."

During these scenarios, their heads are nodding, their eyes are wide and a flash of understanding moves across their faces. We have a connection and I can move on and discuss more sophisticated and complex issues because now they can relate and it makes sense to them.

Our job as the CEO of our family is to ensure that our children are neither desperate nor ignorant. Arthur uses two different analogies when talking to parents and learners to illustrate the fact that there are both good and bad to be had in the online world, in just the same way as both realities exist in the real world.

Social media can be like the shopping mall or the sea. Whatever dangers you would find in a local shopping mall are applicable in the online world too. There are fun and safe places to be in a mall, but there are also dark and dangerous places ...

Now think about the sea. It's a fun place to be – if you can swim and you adhere to the instructions of the life guards – but you can also drown.

We equip our children for offline realities and dangers. Today we must ensure they are also prepared for eventualities online.

Children learn through discovery and their curiosity about the world fuels that journey. But curiosity also killed the cat. Parents in the 21st century need to be aware of both the dangers and opportunities presented by the online world so that they can help their children not to allow their own curiosity to get them into trouble without dampening their desire to discover more about the world around them.

ACT MORE LIKE A CEO

So we've talked about how we as parents need to better manage the plethora of choices with which we are faced, and how we must teach our children the skills of making choices too. Now we need to look at parenting through the lens of a chief executive officer of a big business who needs to ensure that his or her company is prepared for the potential changes, dangers and opportunities that lie ahead, not fully knowing exactly what will happen or when.

If you were in this position, you would constantly be looking at the strengths, weaknesses, opportunities or threats that might be coming down the line, so that you could take advantage of the opportunities and minimise the threats. Right? Then why are we not doing this with our children and the changing landscape with which we are faced?

One of the very important management tools you need to use with your children is to do scenario planning with them. This needs to be done in a low-key way, around the dinner table at night or when riding in the car, for example. If you have children who are tweens and teens, think back to when your children were little and you discussed stranger danger with them when shopping in a big mall. You would tell them not to walk off with strangers, you would walk them through what to do if they got lost, who to approach, where to go and what to say. You gave them a game plan, a strategy of 'what to do if this happens to you', including screaming and shouting if need be. It was a 'what-if' scenario. We do this with our children for real-world situations, and we now need to do the same for them in the on-screen and online world of technology where many things can potentially happen to them.

My son Matthew, nine years old at the time, went to play at a new friend's house. When your kids are at this age you're no longer having tea parties with other parents to vet them before allowing your child to go and play. I had engaged with the mum a number of times on the side of the sports field and felt it would be fine for Matthew to go. On dropping him off, I made the following comment to him, "Matt, have a lovely time. I just want you to remember one thing. This boy has a 16-year-old brother. Now you have an older brother too and you know that he is allowed to watch TV programmes you don't watch and he plays computer games that are not age-appropriate for you because they're not good for you. I don't know what the rules are in this house but you know what's good for you." That was all I said and off he went. When I collected him a few hours later, he jumped in the car, looked at me with big eyes, and said, "How did you know?"

What transpired is that his friend had hauled out a computer game to play and Matt had noticed that it had a 16 age restriction for language and violence. He decided he didn't want to play but didn't want to lose face either, so he chose to use the art of distraction and said he didn't want to play inside and would rather kick a ball in the garden.

Now, apart from being blown away with Matthew's ability to make a choice to protect himself, I saw the power of presenting a 'what-if' scenario in action. Matthew was not taken by surprise. Somewhere in his mind he had been there before. He was empowered to make a choice even though I hadn't told him specifically what to do in that situation. Not only had I given him the scenario before his play date, but that was on top of many other conversations that happen spontaneously around the dinner table or while in the car.

Life provides parents with many teachable moments. We need to start using them for our own and our children's benefit. When you hear a story from someone about a child who has got into trouble in either the real or virtual world, do bring it up for discussion at home. Talk about what happened, and ask your children for their opinions and what they think they would have done in a similar situation. In their mind's eye they need to put themselves in situations and talk them through. It is great preparation for any eventuality, and while you can't guarantee the outcome, your children will have a blueprint somewhere in the recesses of their minds and will be more empowered to make the best choice they can when faced with a tough situation.

Scenario planning with children around real and virtual dangers takes place through casual, incidental conversations. We stress again that this is not a formal thing. It's much like young children who can't read; learning how to read words incidentally without being formally taught, almost as if they stumble upon some magic and then they understand for themselves.

Teachable moments are around every corner. Use them in your scenario-planning conversations. If you read about someone in a magazine or newspaper who loses a job or doesn't get the job they apply for because of something they posted on social media, this is a good topic to introduce at dinner. Or a story about a girl who gave out too much personal information and was the victim of a stalker, or the teenager who decided to meet their online friend in the real world and was abducted, without having a clue who they were really dealing with. What about the slut list that has been doing the rounds at school on WhatsApp or BBM? Is it okay to participate in this kind of activity and pass the list on to your contacts? What does that say about you as a person? Or the boy who lost his colours blazer for cyber-bullying a junior in the school? Questions to pose to the family include:
- What should one do in this situation?
- Where do you think they went wrong?
- What would you do, or how might you react?

Do remember that most parents have never been in this space before. This is brand-new territory. What we can say is that the more you chat, the more realistic you are, the more open your communication is likely to be. Position yourself as the parent and not a prosecutor in these discussions. You want a dynamic two-way conversation in which everyone feels free to participate and share their thoughts and ideas.

Do you see now why you need to get with the programme and become more tech savvy yourself in order to help and protect your child? You cannot do this from a point of zero knowledge or experience. A CEO isn't expert at every part of the business, he or she leans on others for that expertise, but has a good grasp of the whole picture. That must be our aim as parents, to get a handle on the changing world, what it means and how we need to respond.

But – and this is a very big but – having meaningful conversations with your children and doing scenario planning that will have any meaning for them, or impact on them, relies heavily on the fact that you have a relationship and that there is mutual respect between you.

RELATIONSHIP BUILDING IS KEY – KEEP IT REAL

We all have relationships with our children, but the depth, nature and quality of those relationships are largely determined by what we do or do not do in their early years. We are responsible for building the emotional bridge to our children and for building emotional collateral over the years. Daily we drop pennies of emotional collateral in an emotional piggy bank so that one day, in the more testing and turbulent teenage years, there is an emotional savings account to draw from. In other words, there is actually a relationship in existence.

With puberty starting earlier than ever – particularly for girls, with 40% starting between the age of nine and 10 years – we have a much smaller window in which to cement our relationships with our children before their peers rise in importance and start influencing them, which they can do with even greater impact in the digital world. Parents need to make hay while the sun shines, so to speak. Don't wait to connect with your child until you have the time, are less busy or less stressed. Connection is something that needs to take place on many levels between children and their parents every single day.

When children know they are important to you they feel secure and are much more open to listening to you and engaging face to face. This is part of positioning yourself as a brand of choice in their lives.

GET WITH THE PROGRAMME

To play and understand the digital game you need to be in the game yourself. You need to become used to and comfortable with some basic pieces of technology. To keep your children safe online you need to understand the technology, what it can do and how to use it. You don't have to be an expert, but you do need a basic understanding, or you will spend your life trying to read the label from inside the jar. By using these tools yourself, you will:

- understand their world
- understand technology and how it works
- be interested, not ignorant
- be able to access tools to monitor and protect your children
- be able to access tools and acquire skills to enable you to be part of the future that is rapidly unfolding
- gain knowledge and experience to grow your own confidence in the digital language.

Social media and technology are an extension of our children. This is their world and they need us to be a part of it and to understand the attraction. To not do so is to risk misunderstanding your children. We need to get with the programme and show our willingness to learn new things. Yes, this is difficult. We are the digital immigrants here and this is hard, especially as we, unlike our children, are not inclined to 'play' with technology.

One of the main reasons why our kids are so easy with technology is precisely because they play and experiment with it over and over until they have created a neurological pathway in their brain. We, on the other hand, learn how to do something on our computers, we do it a few times and don't do it again for weeks and then wonder why we cannot remember that darned shortcut! We never do it often enough to create that well-worn pathway in our brain, so we cannot retrieve that information and have to ask our children, the chief technology officers in our homes, how to do it all over again! Children learn through discovery. We should take a leaf out of their books.

As 21st-century parents we need to jump on the technology bandwagon, and fast. We need to get beyond being interested in our children's technological world – we need to become *part* of it. By all means, ask your children to teach you; they love that. But then you need to use what you have been taught or you will lose it. Children are quite proud of parents who are wired, because they feel their parents understand them better.

One of the comments Nikki received from an 18-year-old at a digital safety presentation she gave at a school said as much: "Nikki understands how important technology is to us; she understands our world, not like our parents who think we are just being rebels."

You need a smartphone. You need an email account. You need to be on social media if your children are going to be on social media. This is the only way you will have any appreciation of their online world. In addition, it is also a great way to keep tabs on what your kids are up to and who they are up to it with.

Essentially, you need to keep up so that you are not left behind in a fast-changing world. You need to keep up so that you can help your children to navigate the new world of work that is being reshaped as we speak by technology. We are literally growing up digital with our children. Let's take a peek into that future so that you understand the importance of getting with the programme now. So that you know why it is just as important for children to learn digital skills as it is to learn to read and write.

What you need to do:
- Get an Internet-linked computer.
- Open an email account.
- Open social media accounts.
- Activate your privacy settings on all media.
- Activate passwords.
- Install filters on your computer.
- Get a smartphone.
- Download instant-messaging programmes such as WhatsApp or BBM, for example.
- Get a PVR for your TV.
- Activate the parental controls on the PVR.

SELF-PROTECTION IS ESSENTIAL

It is a parent's natural instinct to protect his or her child. It is hard-wired into our very core. The reality, however, is that as our children get older they start spending more and more time away from us: at school, at extra-curricular activities, with friends, at sleepovers, at parties, at the movies, on school outings or camps. They are on a journey to independence – as they should be. In fact, one of our fundamental goals as parents is to let our children go. But to do so responsibly, we must prepare our children for that journey and that means letting go, little by little every day from the time they are born, and empowering them to make wise choices. Nikki found herself in an unexpected conversation with her children at the dinner table one evening when they were 11 and 15 respectively, that brought the topic of self-protection to the fore.

Matthew mentioned that one of his good friends had been boasting about having bought Grand Theft Auto, an inappropriate game for an 11-year-old, as it has an age restriction of 18. The game was purchased in the gaming section of a local toy store and, yes, nobody had questioned his age. The degree of violence in this particular game had recently put a client's 10-year-old stepson into psychotherapy after just two weeks of playing with it, so I was on red alert with this one. Our conversation moved from one thing to another, including the dangers of viewing inappropriate content, and I landed up summarising my children's responsibilities to themselves like this:

"You only really own three things in this life: you have one mind and you need to protect what it sees and hears; you have one body so look after it in the physical world and don't put yourself in risky situations (I alluded to drugs, smoking, alcohol, sex, hitchhiking, and meeting online strangers offline, for example); and you have one reputation consisting of both an offline and an online component. One mind, one body, one reputation – these are the three things you have to protect. Dad and I will give you the information and tools to do this but ultimately it is going to be up to you when we aren't there to protect you."

We cannot wrap our children in cotton wool; rather we must empower them by helping them to understand the pros and cons of many things, from social media to gaming, TV programmes and movies; teaching them the importance of personal privacy in an increasingly digital and connected world of decreasing privacy; teaching them that once they have seen inappropriate content they can never erase it from their minds; teaching them that they need to be savvy, rather than gullible – they must check out age limits on games and movies they are introduced to in other people's homes. We need to teach them that posting just one compromising photograph of themselves on the Internet could cost them their reputation and employment in the future, and that giving out personal information over the Internet and making friends with strangers could put them in physical danger.

Help them to develop a strategy for 'what-if' moments – when they would

*rather not play with a particular game or watch a certain movie, even if
everyone else is doing so. They have to know what is good for them and
that they will find themselves in situations where they must choose for their
own protection. If you prepare them without scaring them, by having regular
'in-the-moment' conversations around teachable moments, instead of giving
speeches or sermons after the fact, they will be able to take such situations in
their stride, always knowing that if they really need you, you are only a call
away and you will move heaven and earth to get to them.*

*Teachable moments are all around us, from stories in the newspaper,
movies, personal anecdotes and more. Your responsibility is to keep that
communication channel open so that they tell you what they are seeing,
hearing and noticing in their world. Understand the technology they are so
fond of and become part of their networks so that you know what is going on.
Commend any positive choices they make to protect themselves.*

If there is one thing we do understand about children, it is the fact that
this generation needs more conversations that matter and fewer speeches
that don't. If you lecture them they tune you out in an instant. You need to
have regular conversations over a wide variety of issues over time, to create
a context or backdrop to the family ground rules you want to develop
around the use of social media, technology (cellphones and online gaming,
for example), as well as how to behave in the offline world. You can't just
go in out of the blue, guns blazing, and lay down the law. That doesn't work
either.

In a sense, you have to till the fields of your children's hearts and minds
over time, and start sowing ideas and thoughts that will lead on to the
development of guidelines that will protect your children online as well as
help them to create a good digital reputation that will help them in their
lives and careers one day.

*The self-protection mantra, 'One Mind, One Body, One Reputation' was born
on a very ordinary day on my quest as a mother to help my own children to
protect themselves when I am not with them. It has subsequently become the
focal point of my parenting and learner talks on digital safety.[1]*

*'One Mind, One Body, One Reputation' is a short, sexy soundbite that
everyone can remember. It is only 27 characters and easily fits onto a
cellphone screen, or can even be used in a Tweet where you have only 140
characters available. It is the only thing that children need to remember from*

my presentation and I hope that it pops into a tween or teen's mind any time they have to make a decision about what to post online, as well as when they are making critical choices about what to do in the real world too. This mantra forms a simple and yet profound framework that parents and teachers can use when talking to children about making responsible choices in their lives. It opens the door to conversations that really matter.

It is also the safety mantra I use every time I say goodbye to my children if they are going off without me. In fact, I don't even say it to them anymore, I sign it. And it's just one finger to indicate the number one. The response of my boys is always the same, "Ja, Ma! One Mind, One Body, One Reputation!" No lecture on personal safety and good behaviour is required, and yet I feel secure in the knowledge that I have reminded them of what is truly important – the only three things that they are really responsible for in their lives – protecting their mind, protecting their body and protecting their reputation.

Says Susie Mesure in her article in *The Independent*,[2] "Catch them young and you'll be surprised what children will share with you: that's the straightforward advice of anyone working to help keep kids safe online. No, you'll never stop children typing 'sex' into Google pretty much as soon as they can spell it; nor will you prevent teenage girls from asking the Internet how they can be thinner, prettier, better liked. But you can get them to talk to you about it, which is often more than half the battle."

As parents we have many responsibilities to our children, but we also need to start passing personal responsibility and personal safety on to them, incrementally, so that one day we can let them go with confidence. Now it's time to lay down some tech-savvy family guidelines to help both you and your children to learn how to navigate the information superhighway safely and smartly.

- Owning a sophisticated piece of technology does not make your child a responsible user.
- Children need moral and practical guidance to help them to become safe and savvy users of technology.
- In a world of maximum media, children need maximum parenting – don't use technology as a parenting cop-out.
- Avoid overreacting or underreacting to technology – find your middle ground.
- Teachable moments involve real examples.
- Act like a CEO and do scenario planning with your kids for the digital world.
- Scenario planning provides children with mental blueprints or strategies for 'what-if' moments.
- Children need more conversations that matter and fewer speeches that don't.
- Connection is something that needs to take place on many levels between children and their parents every day.
- Position yourself as a brand of choice in their lives.
- Get with the digital programme to be in the game.
- Teach your children how to protect themselves so that you can let them go with confidence.
- Use the mantra: One Mind, One Body, One Reputation as a framework for conversations with your children.
- Till the fields of the hearts and minds over time, sowing ideas and values as you go.

CHAPTER 12

PRACTICAL PARENTING GUIDELINES

This chapter draws all our threads together into a practical guide to conscious parenting in a digital age. While we advocate maximum parenting in a world of maximum media, this does not mean hysterical helicopter parenting on the lookout for a threat around every corner, and neither does it mean laissez-faire parenting allowing children to do what they like. Rather, it really is about finding your middle ground to balanced and effective parenting that supports your child's development, grows and nurtures the relationship between you, and prepares them in the best possible way to learn how to make wise choices, protect themselves and thrive in a digital world.

We have divided this chapter into developmental stages, and each one will provide general developmental guidelines, advice on different media, issues to think about, regular questions we are asked, conversations to have and decisions to make.

0–2 YEARS

Physically, children in this age bracket are learning how to coordinate various parts of their bodies as well as how to defy gravity, which is a *big* thing. From birth to age two, the body takes the most phenomenal journey, from the warmth and comfort of the womb to opening up from the foetal position, activating and then shutting down various important reflexes that are part of human development, to learning how to roll over, kneel, crawl, sit, stand and walk. What drives most of this development is a curiosity to explore the world – to see what's behind the couch, to be able to reach what's on top of the coffee table and to chase a rolling ball.

Emotionally, babies and toddlers are bonding with their parents and caregivers, learning how to trust them. From 18 months of age they embark on the journey to independence by discovering that they are actually separate from their mothers. By the age of two they start to become more social and interact with other children. From birth, children need to hear their parents' voices and we need to talk them clever.

Things to think about
- How to encourage your children's curiosity in the world around them.
- Creating safe spaces in which they can move and explore their world.
- Their exposure to real, tactile and multisensory experiences.
- The fact that they are multisensory learners who need more than just a screen.
- Bonding with your child – they need your time, attention and physical presence.

Questions we are often asked
- Is it okay to give my baby or toddler my cellphone or tablet to play with?
- Will watching educational content on television or my tablet make my little one brighter?
- My child can't fall asleep without my smartphone or tablet in hand. Is that okay?
- The only way I can get my child to eat is in front of a screen of some sort. Is that okay?

Developmental and media guidelines
- Talk and sing to your child often. We must *talk* our children clever. The brain loves hearing the human voice, and babies and small children need to see your mouth move so that they can copy it when learning to vocalise and then to speak. The expressions on your face also give them the cues for their own emotional intelligence.
- Read to your baby often, from around six months of age or even earlier.
- Resist the temptation to put them to sleep by allowing them to watch a movie on your tablet or smartphone. It is easy to do but you are not helping them to develop the life skill of being able to put themselves to sleep. This is called self-regulation.
- Do not feed your child in front of a screen or you will need this as a continued crutch to get them to eat going forward.

- Create a regular routine for sleeping, playing and eating, for example. This is the beginning of discipline and will also keep you sane. Knowing what comes next keeps everyone calm.
- Keep TV watching to a minimum, if at all – it is not helpful for their brain and body development at this stage. It is only useful to you as it distracts your child for a while from needing you or quells their curiosity to explore their physical world, resulting in them sitting still.
- When choosing TV programmes, select ones with songs to learn, actions to copy and content that is calm and appropriate.
- Because your child sees you using a smartphone or tablet, they will want to play with 'your' toys. This is normal but do not give them unlimited access. Use them sparingly for really challenging moments, otherwise it will become a default setting for you both, replacing multisensory learning and quality connection time together.
- Babies need lots of human contact, including cuddling, rocking, touch, hearing your voice and smelling your scent. They cannot get this from a screen.
- Read to toddlers with them on your lap. This provides real, warm, fuzzy connection moments. Encourage reading and a love of books by providing them with a variety of board books, including touch-and-feel ones with different textures, sound buttons and clear pictures.
- They need more laps and fewer apps. This is a good mantra for this age and stage.
- Provide them with plenty of real toys and games that they can explore with all their senses. It is perfectly normal for them to put everything they play with in their mouth first, because this is how they map their world.
- Encourage movement as much as possible because the body is the architect of the brain, wiring it for all future academic and more complex learning later.
- Unplug from your own devices and your busyness regularly to focus on being present with your child. This is challenging but very necessary if your child is to feel important in your life. If they don't, you are in for a nightmare as they create negative attention-seeking strategies and learn how to manipulate you to get your attention.
- Bear in mind that all devices emit some form of radiation, posing a potential health risk from baby monitors and cordless house phones, to your cellphone, computer and tablet.

- Children at this age should be more off-screen than on-screen because the best way to learn about their world is through concrete, physical, multisensory interaction to help them to make sense of things for themselves.
- Frustration is an important part of learning and it is what galvanises a child to the next level of development. Parents often pass a device to a child who is showing signs of frustration, irritation or is upset. This results in taking away the desire to learn or the opportunity to learn how to resolve their feelings and self-soothe.
- Children at this stage are naturally very busy – and they should be. This is not a problem that needs diagnosis, remediation and medication. Your child is simply suffering from childhood! What they do need is lots of human attention, for both sensory input as well as their own sense of security. What they don't need is to be put in front of a screen to dull their curiosity and their need to move. They need engaging, multisensory life experiences with a parent, caregiver and toys. They also need lots of sleep to temper this.
- If your baby or toddler spends time with a caregiver or relative, make sure that the same media guidelines are used, especially if they are spending the majority of the day with that person. Consistency is very important from an early age when you are trying to establish healthy life skills and media habits.
- With regard to your own media usage, activate privacy settings on social media so that photographs you post of your precious child are only seen by people you choose to show them to and not to anyone who comes across your profile.

Conversations to have, decisions to make
- Who is going to be at home with your little one? Mum, Dad, a relative or a caregiver? At this stage of a child's life there is a strong need for lots of one-on-one attention. Whoever they spend the most time with is the person they bond with most strongly.
- How are you going to handle media in your home? This is as important as what you are going to feed your child and how much sleep they are going to get.
- How you will help your child to develop healthy media habits from a young age, such as not using on-screen media to get your child to eat and sleep. There is a time and place for a screen – be choosy how you use it.

3–5 YEARS

Physically, the pre-schooler is now trying to conquer their world, from jungle gyms, swings and slides to learning how to ride scooters and tricycles. Balls usually hold a lot of fascination and children start kicking and hitting very clumsily as they learn how to coordinate their body parts and make them work together. Good gross-motor coordination (movement of the head and large muscle groups of the body) is necessary for quality fine-motor control and eye-hand coordination.

Children need to move a lot and explore their world. At this stage they start to go to playgroup and eventually to pre-school. They acquire school-readiness skills with shape, colour and quantity, forming the basis for much learning. Sorting, matching, grouping and counting are learning experiences they should have with real toys and games. Puzzle building, playing with construction toys and fantasy play are essential for their development, as are creative activities such as playdough, painting, colouring and even playing in water and mud.

Emotionally, they are learning to separate from their parents when they go off to school, and they are becoming social beings who enjoy interacting with other children, learning to be comfortable with sharing and taking turns. Play dates start – initially with parents present unless a regular and consistent close friendship develops where there is a very comfortable element of trust. Through repetition of tasks they start mastering skills and this leads to the development of self-confidence. Your verbal and emotional input, as well as that of the teacher and other adults in a child's life, leads to the development of self-esteem. The less emotional stress and the more positive a child's environment, the easier it is for them to learn new things without emotion disrupting their brainwaves.

Things to think about
- Introducing children to movement activities, as well as a wide variety of multisensory learning experiences.
- Learning through repetition in a multitude of ways.
- Sending your child to playgroup or nursery school.
- Socialising your child at school and with play dates.
- How to help your child discover their world and maintain a sense of curiosity.

Questions we are often asked

- How much screen time is enough and how much is too much?
- Why does my child have a meltdown when I take away my smartphone or tablet?
- Why can't my child fall asleep on his or her own?
- Why does my child sit still in front of television?
- Why can my child do a puzzle on a screen but not in real life?
- My child would rather sit in front of a screen than run outside and play. Why is this?
- Why do children seem to concentrate better in front of a screen?

Developmental and media guidelines

- Limit on-screen activities and keep it real as much as possible. This means real games and toys and real friends.
- Encourage movement, fantasy play and exploration of their world, and allow them to get dirty and do messy play such as playdough and painting.
- Play dates are very important so that your child develops the social skills of sharing, taking turns, winning and losing. The closer they get to five years of age, the more time children will spend on setting down the rules of play when they are with their friends. This does not happen in front of a screen.
- Avoid too much sedentary on-screen activity. Children need to move in order to develop a strong body and visual system necessary for good muscle tone, enabling them to sit comfortably in chairs in a classroom setting for 20–30 minutes at a time. Movement develops a strong visual system, making reading easier.
- Be very selective about the content of TV programmes your child watches. This would be a good time to use the PVR so that your child watches what you want them to watch when you want them to watch. Pre-recording allows you to be selective, or use DVDs.
- From the age of four, children can play the 'Money or the Box' game (see page 181) to help them to make wise choices and to create a self-awareness of how much they are watching TV.
- Give your child limited use of your tablet or smartphone. Don't let it get in the way of your relationship, so be clear about when they are allowed to play on it and be consistent. If you give in at every turn at this stage, as with television viewing, you will find it harder and harder to regain control.

- Be prepared to play with your child – you are still the best toy in the box.
- Have a good selection of games and toys for your child. They need toys they can play with without you. These are toy-box toys they cannot break such as building blocks, animals, cars, dolls, shape sorters, action-reaction toys and more. Then you need special toys that are kept up in the cupboard that you take out when you are having quality playtime with your child.
- Construction toys enable a child to put together and take things apart. This is a vital skill that they need to learn in the real world. Being able to construct something or build a puzzle on a screen is no measure of whether your child will be able to complete such a task in the real world. Many teachers can attest to this. Your child needs to experience learning with their whole body at this stage and not just with their eyes and by tapping a screen.
- Whole-body, multisensory learning grows a wide variety of neurological pathways in a child's brain. The more neurological pathways wired in childhood the better. Those that aren't developed may never develop. Take a child who is not well socialised and kept at home in front of a screen. How do they develop the neurological pathway for empathy for others if they don't have a lot of human interaction? How do both left and right hemispheres of the brain integrate if a child spends more time sitting in front of a screen than crawling, walking, running, swimming and riding a bicycle?
- By all means use technology and child-appropriate programmes to reinforce what they are learning in the real world because repetition is vitally important in early childhood development to consolidate skills.
- This is the age of fantasy, which is necessary for the development of their imagination. If you constantly expose them to television, the fantasy of the mind will not be developed as they get used to prescribed images being provided for them and lose the power to imagine anything they have never seen. This is a travesty and also inhibits their ability when it comes to creative writing later on, and the possibility that they might ever come up with a ground-breaking original thought in the workplace that might have the potential to change the world.
- When you are looking for a pre-school, enquire about whether or not the school includes technology in the curriculum. It is unnecessary at this stage, and if they do, make sure it is for a very short period of time, such as 20 minutes.

- If your child is in aftercare, find out how much television he or she will get to watch, if at all. Once again, it is unnecessary.
- If you are using a babysitter or caregiver at home, make sure that they know what your family rules are around the use of media in your absence. How much and what your child can watch and engage with must be clear.
- The less variety your child has with on-screen media at home, the less pull the screen has for them and the more they will learn to entertain themselves with toys, games and books. Learning to be one's own source of happiness and knowing how to be your own boredom buster is a fabulous life skill to acquire that will stand your child in good stead, emotionally and developmentally, in the years to come.
- The radiation warning is important here as children start spending longer periods of time interacting with devices that emit radiation and could compromise their health if used without time limits.
- Do not use devices to pacify your child when they have a tantrum or they will never learn how to self-regulate or calm themselves down. They will always be reliant on a screen or device.
- Do not use screens as an antidote to boredom. Boredom and frustration are good. They encourage children to come up with creative solutions through play. This leads to a belief that success and happiness come from within.
- Encourage movement, not just because the body is the architect of the brain, but also for good health, to avoid obesity and diabetes.
- Children need to learn that there are moments for play and fun, and moments when they need to be quiet and still, such as when they are sitting at the dinner table or in a restaurant.
- If you are spending quality time together in a restaurant or public space, pay attention to your children instead of passing them a screen to interact with. However, if you need your child to keep themselves occupied in a challenging space, such as an aeroplane or when they have to accompany you to a meeting, these would be times to whip out that screen and let them play.
- Do not replace yourself or your relationships with a device. High-touch connection is still the best way to parent and build a relationship with your child that you can both trust. Bear in mind that their deepest need and desire is for belonging and togetherness – with you, their parent.
- As they move towards the age of five, you can empower them by giving

them more choice, but this still comes with limits and consequences. See instructions for the 'Money or the Box' game on page 181.

- Don't let your kids fall into the trap of only doing what they enjoy doing. They need to experience a wide variety of things in life, not all of which they will love. Some things just have to be done.
- Beware of what photos of your children you post on social media and who can see them. Activate your privacy settings and switch off the geo-location settings on your phone.

Conversations to have, decisions to make
- Are you going to install satellite TV and how big a bouquet are you going to get?
- What kind of programmes are you happy with your child watching?
- How many programmes a day will you allow your child to watch?
- When is it okay for them to play with your phone or tablet?
- Are you going to get a kiddie laptop for them?
- How do you protect your content on your devices?
- What kind of education do you want for your children?
- Are you going to eat dinner together around a table or in front of a screen?
- How many extramural activities will your child be doing?
- Who is going to look after them when you are not able to be there for them?
- Have you briefed your caregivers about your media policy?

6–9 YEARS
The move to primary school is a big thing. Learning is more formal and in a much bigger environment. Children have to establish themselves socially and physically, and they get to compete for the first time. All academic learning is now focused on literacy and numeracy skills to enable them to learn how to read, write and do maths. These important foundations will be established at school and you can reinforce them with everything from word games in the car to educational games at home or even computer games and apps.

Emotionally, children are now well on the road to independence and school has become 'their' place. Parents should no longer carry their children and their belongings to school but allow their children to do this themselves. While children love to spend time with you and your presence is still essential in their lives, they should also be encouraged to develop a circle of friends. Having friends and being part of various extramural groups are important for creating a sense of belonging that builds self-worth and self-esteem.

Things to think about

- How to create an independent, resourceful and resilient child.
- Fostering a love of learning.
- Reinforcing numeracy and literacy skills.
- Encouraging play dates and the development of friendships.
- Building your own social support structure that you can call on in times of crisis. These must be people who both you and your children can trust in your absence.

Questions we are often asked

- Is it okay for our children to be working with technology at school and then again at home?
- How much exposure to technology is too much and how much is enough?
- How do I identify over-exposure to technology?
- Should I give my child a cellphone?
- Why does my child want everything now? Why can't he wait?
- Why does my child always claim to be bored, except when in front of a screen?
- Why do children sit still and behave in front of television?
- Does my child still need to learn how to read and write?
- Can my child get into trouble on the Internet at such a young age?

Developmental and media guidelines

- Encourage your child to become a reader. Children need strong reading and comprehension skills in an era of so much information overload.
- Organise play dates. If you are a very busy working parent this may have to take place on a weekend. Please don't ignore this aspect of your child's life. Get to know other parents and children so that you know with whom your child is playing.
- Use teachable moments to illustrate your family values, such as giving old clothes to the needy, or returning an unpaid-for item to the supermarket to illustrate honesty, for example. Television advertisements and programmes can also provide points for discussion. Are they portraying

things that are aligned with your values or not?

- Acknowledge children for who they are and not just what they do. Being kind, persevering, trustworthy and reliable are just some of many character traits that are worth acknowledging and celebrating.
- Be alert about any environment in which your child is going to be, from school to a friend's house or even a shopping mall. Without being hysterical, you need to bring to their attention what they need to do and whom they should talk to if something goes wrong.
- Keep an established routine at home. Everyone will be more organised, sane and happy.
- Encourage involvement in the extracurricular programme at school to balance sedentary time spent in the classroom or in front of a screen.
- Watch what they are viewing on television. Use programme content as a teachable moment, such as characters being mean to each other. Help your children to be selective about what they watch. Decide together on a weekend what they will be allowed to watch the following week. Be clear about how many programmes and how many hours of TV they are allowed. Use the 'Money or the Box' game discussed on page 181.
- Monitor the impact of TV and gaming on their mood, behaviour, sleeping habits, language and choice of role models.
- What your child would never see in real life they shouldn't see on TV.
- They must ask permission to watch TV or play on-screen games. Do not give up control of the remote control.
- Switch off the TV when it is not actively being watched. This improves the word count between parent and child significantly.
- Be clear about when they can or cannot use your phone or tablet.
- Make sure you have activated parental controls on these devices.
- Activate or install filters on your home computer to protect them from inappropriate content.
- Teach them about not putting too much personal information on their profiles when playing Moshi Monsters, Club Penguin and other online games. These work similarly to social media platforms such as Facebook – they are just play-based.
- Make sure you implement limits to their ability to make in-app purchases on your phone.
- Know what games and apps they have downloaded onto your phone.
- Have clear time limits for gaming on the home computer, your phone or other gaming consoles in your home.

- Be selective about the on-screen games they play. Talk to other parents about what they do and do not allow their children to play.
- Eat meals together on a regular basis and, instead of watching TV, talk.
- Play games together. Play is the language of childhood and provides a wonderful bridge for connection while at the same time building great memories.
- Encourage children to help around the house by doing chores instead of doing them all yourself and banishing them to a screen to keep them out of your hair. If you don't, you risk never having helpers in the house and they will become couch potatoes you serve hand and foot. They actually want to help and do what they see you do. Often, we simply don't take the opportunity because it seems more expedient to do things ourselves – at our peril!
- Keep Internet-linked computers in a 'public' space where you can see what they are up to.
- Beware of what photos of your children you post on social media and who can see them. Activate your privacy settings and switch off the geo-location settings on your phone.

Conversations to have, decisions to make
- How many extramural activities are you going to allow your child to do?
- When are you scheduling play dates?
- What kind of technological risk management are you going to implement?
- When can they use your devices and what are they allowed to do on them?
- How much TV can they watch and when?
- What type of TV programmes and on-screen games will you allow them to engage with?
- Are you being a good role model when it comes to managing your own devices?
- Are you really emotionally and physically accessible to your children when you are with them?
- Who looks after them when you are not available, and do they understand your media policy?

Play the 'Money or the Box' game. Help your children manage their own TV viewing. We all get tired of nagging and reminding our children about the boundaries and rules concerning spending too much time in front of the box, but here is an idea that may go a long way to helping them to take personal responsibility for regulating their TV viewing.

If you want to limit your child's viewing to two programmes a day, for example, you would give them two tokens, such as poker chips, per day. For each programme they watch, they need to pay you a chip. Whatever chips they don't use up, they get to save, and then on the weekend they can exchange them for money. You pay them out R5 (or whatever amount you decide) per unused chip for the week. It works like a charm. You could, as children get older and programmes get longer, make it a chip for each half-hour of viewing. The point is that you need to establish exactly how much TV they are allowed to watch each day or week. This can also apply to the use of any other screen technology such as PlayStation, Wii or computer games.

10–13 YEARS

You now have tweens or pre-teens and they all want to be older than they are. Girls, in particular, are reaching puberty earlier – 40% by the age of 10. Although parents are still very important in their lives, the dynamic of the peer group is starting to kick in. They have a social life and should be very involved in extracurricular activities by now.

On the educational front, they are now reading to learn as opposed to learning to read and the world of information is suddenly their oyster as they start consolidating numeracy and literacy skills, adding more complex critical-thinking and problem-solving skills along the way. Innovation and creativity must also be fostered as essentials for the future world of work.

They are screen-hungry, and watching certain TV programmes and playing specific games are now conversation pieces in their social world, as are the latest devices. They may find themselves in or out of a social group on this basis. Children at this age are rapidly acquiring cellphones for their own safety and for their parents' convenience. These phones are increasingly smartphones to enable them to access apps such as WhatsApp, which facilitates low-cost communication and belonging to groups. This also means they can connect to apps, such as Instagram and Snapchat. A smartphone is a powerful device that can be used as a constructive tool or a weapon. These children are a big influence on the household spend – think devices, airtime and high-value purchases over which they have influence, such as the next cellphone, family holiday or new car.

Things to think about
- Implementing boundaries and limits when it comes to powerful devices they have access to.
- How devices can get your child included or excluded from various groups.
- What a device will enable your child to access, and who.
- How to ensure that devices don't detract from, but enhance, the work that needs to be done.
- Understand the addictive nature of an on-screen life.
- How to maintain close family bonds in a digital world.
- How to maintain a culture of play in the family.

Questions we are often asked
- What is the right age to give a child a cellphone?
- What sort of cellphone should we be giving our child?
- Do I need to purchase the latest device or gadget for my child every time a new one comes out?
- How do I protect my child from inappropriate content?
- How do I teach my child how to make wise choices?
- How do I keep up with technology?
- How do I make sure my child grows up healthy and happy in a digital world?
- How do I have conversations about digital safety with my child?
- At what age is it legal to be on Facebook?
- I don't understand their attraction to gaming. Why can't they stop playing when I tell them to?
- Why does television drain my child of energy?
- Can you come and speak to the school and tell *them* how they can keep *our* children safe online?

Developmental and media guidelines
- Movement and play are still essential. Children of this age, despite being tech-savvy, are still in the concrete learning phase and need real people and real games and toys. Some of their toys may now be tech-toys – say a remote control plane that uses a smartphone as the remote, or your

tablet incorporated in a board game.
- Play dates and socials are important. You need to have your finger on the pulse of things such as supervision, and what kids in other homes are allowed to watch or do that may be different to what happens in your home. You may not always be able to control this so ensure you have many a conversation with your child so that they know what to do to extricate themselves from an undesirable situation or how to contact you.
- Invest time in your relationships. These are the best defence in an unpredictable, risky and high-tech world.
- Your child should not yet be on social media. The legal Facebook minimum age is 13.
- Limits around gaming, TV watching and cellphone use are very necessary. Leaving limits unchecked, you could lose your child down the rabbit hole of technology.
- Familiarise yourself with age ratings on games, online TV, films and apps to check that your child is accessing only age-appropriate content.
- Teach them how to make good choices regarding their media usage. The more they practise making choices of their own the better they will get.
- Monitor the impact of TV and gaming on their mood, behaviour, sleeping habits, language and choice of role models.
- Install filters on your home computer to protect your child from undesirable content.
- You will probably give your child their first cellphone around this stage. Give them a contract to sign for phone usage (see Appendix 2 on page 214). Make sure it is password-protected and that you know the password.
- Provide boundaries around airtime on their phones and teach them how to look after their phone. See more on pages 214–216.
- Activate filters and parental controls on all devices, including cellphones.
- Be aware of what type of games they are buying and what apps they are downloading.
- Meet their friends in the real world.
- Be fun to be with, emotionally accessible and present – and, of course, you need to lead.
- Eat together around the dinner table – it is a great opportunity for conversation and teachable moments.
- Beware of what photos of your children you post on social media and who can see them. Activate your privacy settings and switch off the geo-location settings on your phone.

Conversations to have, decisions to make

- When will you give your child his or her first cellphone?
- What type of games will you allow them to play on-screen?
- How much time will you allocate to screen time?
- What filtering and parental controls should you install on your and your child's devices?
- How are you going to establish yourself as a hero in their life story long before their peers become a powerful influence?

We seem to need passwords for just about everything in life these days and it is a nightmare to remember them all. However, passwords are essential to keep our devices and content safe, much like locking our front door when we go out, or locking our car in a parking lot, to keep the contents safe.

Ensure that your children's cellphones, tablets and computers are password-protected. This will help avoid phone-jacking, which could result in:

- One child picks up another child's phone and sends a potentially embarrassing message, under your child's profile, to their entire BBM or WhatsApp list. While often done as a joke, it can also be done with the clear intention to harm.
- A phone that is not password-protected could be used by another child at a sleepover, at school or on a camp, to download inappropriate content such as porn. Your child will most probably be sleeping at the time and will be none the wiser, although it will appear on their browsing history and on your cellphone bill.

The most commonly used passwords are also the most commonly hacked ones such as: '1–2–3–4', 'password' and 'I love you'. Digital experts say it is best to avoid logical passwords, such as the name of someone close to you, a date of birth or favourite holiday destination. We put so much information about our lives on social media that those passwords would be relatively easy to crack if someone wanted to have a go. A good/strong password is made up of a mixture of letters or words, numbers and a capital letter. Some systems also call for the addition of a symbol into the mix.

Rather than creating too many passwords that will be hard to remember, have ones for different categories of information such as one for financial (banking and online shopping sites), another for all your social media sites, and another for general websites where you sign up for newsletters, for example.

And if you still battle to remember them all, and you keep a list of them on your computer somewhere, then make sure that that, too, is a password-protected document. As a parent, you need the passwords to all your children's devices. It is part of family digital safety and they should get used to it from the start. If they are not happy with you checking out their devices from time to time, then they are probably up to things they shouldn't be doing. There is a fine line between spying and concern, but it may be best to err on the side of caution.

What can parental controls help you to do?
• Track the location of your child or the cellphone.
• Filter content.
• Track the apps they launch or websites they visit.
• Content filtering: limiting the content they can access and websites they can visit.
• Limit in-app purchases paid for by airtime.

If need be, activate additional downloadable apps for protection, some of which are free.

14–18 YEARS

Teenagers are desperate for independence and have a biological need to socialise more. They are going through significant hormonal changes, which result in a roller-coaster of emotions. One day they can be up and the next they can be down. They are learning to be adults and that means they need to be allowed to practise being adults (under supervision, of course). Adolescence is not an illness to be cured but rather a stage they must go through and we must survive. To make matters more complicated, romance may be in the air.

They are tech-savvy but not yet responsible users of media. They are now well and truly navigating the information superhighway at a very risky time of their lives when they are trying on different personas and working out who they are and what they stand for, and testing your value system to see if it is a fit for them or not.

They need to be made very aware of how important their online reputation is because this will follow them forever. Everything they do offline and online has the potential to go viral.

They are also working towards completing their matric, which is an important gateway to what comes next. They live in a high-pressure environment, busy on all fronts and experiencing high expectations from every quarter.

Things to think about
- What were you like as a teenager?
- Does your child have a friendship group?
- The difference between spying and concern.
- Your child using devices as a weapon or a tool.
- What your child can do with the device they have.
- With whom your child can connect.
- Your child's digital reputation and how they can shape a healthy one.
- How to teach your child to be an upstander and not a bystander when it comes to cyber-bullying.

Questions we are often asked
- How do we protect our children online?
- Do our children want to be online more than they want to be with us?
- Are our children losing their literacy skills?
- Are our children losing their social/relationship skills?
- How do we help them understand how important it is to protect their digital reputation?
- How do we protect them when we aren't with them?
- Can they really multi-task and is it good for them?
- How is my child's value system being shaped by what they are exposed to by technology?

Developmental and media guidelines
- Help your child to find a good balance between home, school and technology. They *can* have it all, but not all at the same time.
- When studying, switch off all devices and alerts so that they can

concentrate without interruption. They won't like it, but it's essential when studying for tests and exams.

- Understand their need to connect to their peers and that they do it on-screen and mostly via text these days.
- Teach them to manage their voice and data usage by providing limits to contracts or airtime. They may need to pay in the difference.
- Teach them the importance of protecting themselves by learning how to make good choices about what they post online, from text to photos.
- Encourage them to be upstanders and not bystanders when it comes to cyber-bullying (see page 190).
- By having a healthy and high-touch, face-to-face relationship with your child, you can pass on the value of real offline relationships. This is how you teach EQ skills that you need to pass on to your child.
- Maintain your connection with your children by building a strong relationship with them, by understanding the role and attraction of technology in their lives, as well as their age and stage.
- Your children's best protection lies in the relationship you have with them and the values you have instilled in them. Keep going – this process takes time over many years and through hundreds of conversations.
- Be relevant. Keep up with technology and insist on being your child's 'friend' on social media, but just be in the background unless they engage with you.
- You need to be present both online and offline in your child's life.
- Understand the school's media policy and make sure your child complies.
- Teach your child netiquette. Online manners are important, such as your child not texting someone something they wouldn't say to that person face to face.
- Comprehension skills are not old-fashioned. In fact, in an era of information overload, they are essential. If your child has comprehension skills and can paraphrase or put things in their own words, they will be at less risk of plagiarising another's work by cutting and pasting information from a website into a project.
- Teach them good Internet-search skills. You have to ask the Internet very specific questions – teach your child how to phrase a question to get the information they are looking for. The rule is to approach the question from the specific to the general instead of the other way around.
- Always be available for a conversation with your teen. Don't just listen to the words, but also the spaces between the words – to what is not

being said or to what is being inferred. This is where you find clues to underlying issues they may not be discussing with you.

- Talk to them about how they might be exploring issues related to their health, wellbeing and body image online.
- Discuss how they behave towards others and what they post online, and don't shy away from tricky chats about porn, bullying, sexting and cyber addiction.
- Don't lecture and give sermons. Learn to master the soundbite.
- Do scenario planning with your teen about what could potentially happen in their world and possible ways to deal with it.
- Teach them not to delete text conversations because those are a body of evidence if something should go wrong in a cyber-bullying situation.
- Reputation, reputation, reputation. Google your children from time to time and see what comes up. Help them to create a positive reputation online. Their reputation will follow them and impact on them for the rest of their lives.
- Ensure they are using privacy settings on social networks and that they are being choosy about who they connect with online.
- Make sure they understand the consequences of abusing the technology they have at their disposal, such as making in-app purchases or downloading lots of data at someone else's house without permission.
- They still need to know what the limits are regarding gaming and watching television. Once again, it is about balance and the need to fit everything that needs to be done into a day. Social media and technology can provide a great diversion from the task at hand or what needs to be completed.
- Familiarise yourself with age ratings on games, online TV, films and apps to check that your child is accessing only age-appropriate content where possible.
- Don't let technology rob you of a family life. This also means, however, that you need to be fun and relevant, otherwise your children will not want to spend time with you.
- You provide the technology, so you set the boundaries and limits.
- There are times when you need to lead from the front and times when you need to lead from behind. Let your child go, little by little, giving more responsibility as it becomes appropriate. However, never fully trust a teenager, no matter how responsible they may seem, because they are at an age and stage that often results in risk-taking behaviour.

- Have a family charging station and don't let your child fall asleep with their cellphone close to their heads or under their pillows listening to music – as many of them do. This device emits radiation and can be a health hazard, apart from diminishing the quality of sleep they are getting due to interruptions caused by checking for messages and updates through the night, as some of them do.
- Take your family to places where there is no cellphone signal for the odd weekend to enable them to experience being totally offline in a world where they are always on and checking their devices. If they never get to feel the difference they will never know what it feels like – both liberating and odd at the same time.
- Help your child to get a dopamine rush in healthy ways that don't involve a screen. Part of the addiction to screens is that the content we can engage with stimulates the pleasure centre of the brain and we seek more of it the more immersed we become in on-screen culture, from gaming to online shopping to gambling or online porn or sex. Even downloading email is addictive, believe it or not!
- Make sure your child is not using technology to escape from everyday stress rather than facing the challenges of a face-to-face social life.
- Both you and your child need to be wary of the type of photos you post of them online and who can view them.

Conversations to have, decisions to make
- What risk-management arrangements will you make to protect your child online?
- How do you handle the fine line between spying and concern? In other words, will you check your child's cellphone or not, and will you tell them you are going to do it?
- How will you provide your child with sufficient access to technology so that they can participate academically and socially?
- What are the consequences of breaking an agreement with you regarding their use of technology? You need to be clear and have a contract with them so that they live by their choices.
- How will you help your child develop a healthy digital footprint?
- How do you intend preparing your child for their future technologically, as well as with the appropriate character traits and X-factors for success?

The key phrase is "Stop, block and tell".
When our children are in primary school they are taught about fire safety. The words, "Stop, drop and roll" are drilled into them because these actions could save their lives. In the world of cyber-bullying, the words "Stop, block and tell" are becoming an essential mantra to give our children for their own self-protection.

We need to do scenario planning with our children around the dining table. Discuss 'what-if' scenarios: "What if someone was sending you rude or nasty messages ... insulting you on social networking sites, blogs, and public websites ... posting embarrassing or revealing pictures of you ... forwarding your private emails to others ... spreading rumours and accusations about you ... impersonating you or starting an online fight with you? What would you do?"

Giving tweens and teens a plan of action is very empowering, and reinforcing it regularly is important. When they find themselves in trouble, an ingrained blueprint such as "Stop, block and tell" could help them to think clearly in a nasty situation. Here's the script:

Stop what you're doing and take a deep breath: do *not* answer or get into an argument online.

Block the person who's harassing you – for example, use the blocking feature on BBM or WhatsApp so that the bully can no longer connect with you.

Tell a parent or another adult you trust, otherwise no one can help you.

And if your children see others being cyber-bullied they need to know that they must stand up and do something about it instead of standing by. Experts say this is the single most powerful way to protect our children online because if they are not 'upstanders' then they become silent collaborators.

While technology has provided our children with powerful new ways of connecting and socialising, like all things it has a flipside and can be used to make others miserable. We need to teach our kids to be respectful and responsible in their online communication, the fundamental rule being to never say or do online what you would never do in real life. We need to encourage empathy for others and teach them to speak up and break the code of silence among kids about cyber-bullying. Even nice kids can be nasty online, albeit just by association. Get media savvy yourself and never forget the power of face-to-face communication with your children. Over and above self-protection mantras, online filters and privacy settings, their best protection lies in their relationship with you.

BEWARE OF THESE COMMON 21ST-CENTURY PARENTING TRAPS

In general, 21st-century parents are often:
- busy and starved for time
- suffering from information overload
- tired
- overwhelmed by responsibilities and choices
- stressed
- lacking perspective
- short of creative ideas
- disconnected from their intuition and common sense.

This can result in parents inadvertently falling into the following parenting traps that do nothing to help them protect and prepare their children for a fast-changing digital world. Subsequently, they may:
- overuse technology as a babysitter for their children
- use technology as a bodyguard, thinking their children are safe in front of a screen
- default to sending their children off to engage with a screen when they are tired or too busy
- use technology to substitute for time spent with their children
- use technology for peace and quiet in the home and to appease an upset child
- use technology to put children to sleep at night
- lack ground rules and boundaries when it comes to their children's use of technology
- not manage their own use of devices in front of their children
- give in to their children's nagging to use technology whenever they wish
- be overwhelmed by their own ignorance of the media landscape

- not be aware of the potential dangers and threats posed by technology
- use technology as a crutch and not a tool
- cop out of parenting and hide behind technology
- be hyper-vigilant to the point of being obsessive and denying access to technology by their children completely
- not care what their children are up to online or on-screen
- not share common ground rules around the use of technology with parents, partners, spouses or a caregiver such as a nanny, au pair or grandparents
- slip into unconscious parenting.

FROM THIS CHAPTER ...

- Plug into the age-appropriate section for your child.
- Understand their age and stage developmentally and emotionally.
- Understand the attraction of technology to their age and stage.
- Protect and build your relationship with your child.
- Teach them to protect themselves and make wise choices.
- Lead your child in their journey to being safe and savvy in a digital world.
- Make sure you are safe and savvy yourself.

CHAPTER 13

HOW CHILDREN CAN KEEP THEMSELVES SAFE & SAVVY

If your parents have given you this chapter of our book to read it is because they want you to be safe and savvy users of the information superhighway. They care about you and, likewise, you need to care about yourself in how you use all the screens in your life: your cellphone, tablet, the family computer, your gaming console and whatever other new devices have come on to the market in the few months since we finished this manuscript and it went to print.

Yes, you live in such an exciting world that is changing in some way almost every day. You were born into a digital world and are wired to use today's technology without having to read an instruction manual. You are the envy of every adult on the planet.

You are probably between the ages of 13 and 18 and you own sophisticated pieces of technology that you interact with every day, many times a day. Did you know that your smartphone has more computer processing power than NASA's *Apollo 11* when it made its trip to the moon? Now isn't that something?

You live in a plug-and-play world. If you can connect any of your devices to the Internet you can play, whether you are connecting to a friend on Facebook, playing Minecraft or The Sims, sharing information with members of your chat group on WhatsApp, sending information about a school project to someone via Dropbox or downloading information from your school server.

The world has changed considerably since your parents were children. The public library is now the Internet. The books in the library are all the websites (both good and bad ones), and the letters you write are in the form of emails, SMSs, social media posts and more. The post office consists of many different social networking sites such as Facebook and Instagram, for example, and pen pals have been replaced with 'friends' and 'contacts' online.

There are so many ways to engage with your world today and that's awesome, but owning a sophisticated piece of technology doesn't necessarily mean you are a responsible user of it. The world holds so many amazing opportunities for you to take advantage of, but there are also dangers that you need to be aware of so that you can try to avoid the potholes in the road, or getting yourself into trouble or a sticky situation.

You need to remember that you are a human being first, and a 'digital native' second. Celebrate all that there is to celebrate about being human and learn how to integrate the best of what technology has to offer. In the next few sections we are going to give you some guidelines on how to do this by sharing with you some things you need to know that may surprise you, some guidelines to help you navigate this new world wisely and some short soundbites to remember that will make all the difference to your future.

THINGS YOU NEED TO KNOW

We live in an increasingly high-tech era and are all linked to the digital skin of the world. All of this is new to us and hasn't been around for long enough for us to know everything about it so we are learning the rules of this new game together. One thing we are very sure of, however, is that the Internet remembers everything.

The Internet remembers

In our regular digital safety presentations to learners in schools, one of the facts that shocks kids most is that the Internet remembers everything – even what they have deleted.

In just the same way as we do regular backups of the content on our computers, search engines and social networking sites do exactly the same thing and they keep multiple versions over time. It's called a cache. The only way to have something permanently removed from a cache is through a legal process, which is costly and can take a long time.

Also, don't fall into the trap of thinking that if you delete a photograph from Facebook, for example, it is gone forever; it is only deleted off your timeline and remains on the timelines of all your friends who may have reposted what you posted. When you share something with a friend, know that they have the ability to share it with their friends too and this is how content goes viral. That's great when it is something you want the world to see, but if it is private you need to keep it so. It is your choice.

Anything posted in social media becomes permanently available, even if not on the site where it was first posted. Inexperienced users or those who are not very clued up on how social networks function will often create default settings that compound the problem. For example, they link Twitter and Facebook, so that anything posted on one automatically appears on the other (a big no-no, as material crafted for Facebook is usually too long for Twitter, and Twitter content like hashtags and user IDs make no sense on Facebook). The result is that when they've posted something inappropriate or embarrassing on one site, and quickly delete it when they realise their mistake, they often forget that it remains alive on the other site. If it's outrageously offensive, or sexual in nature, it will usually have been reposted or shared many times before the creator of the message realises what's happened. It is not a pretty sight!

The Internet is neutral – we are the problem

In 2014 the Internet turned 25 years old. It's been around for quite a while, for longer than members of the public have had access to it. It was originally developed for academics in universities to share documents with each other, but it is now used for so much more – both good and bad. But the point is that the Internet itself is not a place; it is just a communication channel – and a powerful one too.

The Internet is neither good nor bad; it is what you do with it that makes it either one or the other. Human beings have the choice as to what they share on the Internet – great ideas that might change the world, building web-based businesses, sharing friendly conversations or information about events and more, or it can be used for cyber-bullying, cybercrime, for sharing pornographic material, to stalk other people and other dangerous activities. All of this can be done on the same system. It is a matter of choice what you do and how much of it you do.

It might be helpful to think of the Internet as the sea. It can be a really fun place, especially if you know how to swim, but you can also drown.

Your online reputation will affect your future

Everything you do online contributes to your digital footprint, which shapes your digital reputation. And this follows you wherever you go. It's a bit like a tattoo: if you had a tattoo all over your face, it would be very hard and painful to get rid of. Your digital footprint is much the same. Whether you carve out a good or a bad one, you have it with you for life. This means you need to choose wisely.

The Internet is able to track all our online activities, remembering:
- what you say in your posts
- what photos you share
- what you buy
- what you recommend to others
- what you read
- what websites you visit
- the chat rooms you were part of
- and much more …

Employers and educational institutions are starting to do online background checks of potential employees or students. Examples abound where people are not getting jobs or are being fired for what they have said or posted online.

IMPORTANT QUESTIONS TO ASK YOURSELF
Before posting anything, quickly ask yourself these questions:
- What would my best friend's father/mother think if they saw this post? If you would be embarrassed or horrified, take this as a sign not to press the post button.
- What if this post landed up becoming the front-page story of the *Sunday Times*? Would you be proud of it? If the answer is no, then don't post it.
- Does this text or photograph portray me or my friends in a positive light, or is it embarrassing or degrading? If the answer is not positive, then don't post or send it.
- Would I say this to the person's face if he or she were here? If not, then don't post it.
- Am I being respectful?
- Is it good manners?

Rather be safe than sorry. We often post things when we are feeling emotionally charged. When you have just had a fight with your friend, a disagreement with your parents or have split up with a boy- or girlfriend, rather don't post anything rash because you may not be thinking straight.

It would be far better to go find a real shoulder to cry on or talk to. That's what human beings are there for, particularly your parents. Online pity parties can be a recipe for disaster so try to avoid them.

Fill in the blanks:
- If I want to be safe online ....
....
- If I want to be successful ....
....
- If I want to be connected ....
....
- If I want to be part of my family ....
....

THINK ABOUT HOW YOU WOULD ACT IN THE REAL WORLD AND BE CONSISTENT

- If you wouldn't say horrible things to people face to face, then don't do so online. It is cowardly and will most probably get you into trouble. It's not worth it for that brief instant of feeling vengeful.
- If you wouldn't stand up on stage in front of the whole school and strip naked, then don't post photos of your private parts online or share them via instant-messaging services, such as WhatsApp or Instagram. The online world is a far bigger stage and news travels faster than you can imagine. Even if someone dares you to send a naked selfie, you need to make a decision *now*, a pact with yourself, that you will *never* do this.
- If you would never cut out paragraphs from a magazine or book and stick them into a school project, then don't borrow content from websites and pass it off as your own. This is plagiarism and, in matric and when studying at tertiary education institutions, plagiarism software is used to detect what percentage of your assignment is copied content. You will fail if you do this. Don't be lazy. Learn to put things in your own words. Get into a good habit from a young age. It's a skill that will serve you well for the rest of your life.
- Always behave in a crowd as you would behave when you are alone. In other words, don't get so caught up in crowd behaviour that you forget who you are and how you live your life. Stand up for yourself and your

values. Ask yourself, "If I was alone, would I do this?" or "If I was feeling strong, would I do this?" The same goes for online behaviour: rather be a stand-out positive brand of one than follow a bunch of sheep into trouble.

UNDERSTAND THE ATTENTION GAME

People of all ages play the attention-seeking game – it is the most popular game in town. Understand this and you will understand what drives a lot of human behaviour, even yours.

Everyone wants to be noticed and everyone needs to belong to a group. One of the most upsetting things that can happen to anyone, but particularly to teenagers, is when they are shut out or left out of a group or ignored as if they don't exist. It can lead young people to do terrible things to themselves and others out of anger, spite, despair and loneliness.

When we feel these emotions we tend to resort to negative attention-seeking behaviour because we would rather get negative attention than nothing at all. This is what often happens in abusive situations. Being verbally or physically abused is a form of attention and if that is the only kind of attention the victim can attract they will accept it no matter how denigrating it can be.

Don't fall into this trap! If you are feeling empty, broken or lonely, find a real human being to talk to face to face rather than trying to fix yourself online by doing horrible things to other people to make yourself feel better, just as a weak bully would in the real world. When you are feeling down and looking for attention, you are at risk of visiting websites that encourage high-risk behaviour from violence to sex, drugs and more, and you could find yourself getting caught up in something that may be very hard to pull yourself out of.

DON'T HITCHHIKE ON THE INFORMATION SUPERHIGHWAY

Just think about some of the lessons your parents have taught you to keep you safe in the real world:
- Look left, right and left again when you cross the road.
- Don't talk to strangers.
- Don't catch lifts with strangers or hitchhike.
- Don't accept sweets from strangers.
- Don't swim anywhere if you are alone.

In just the same way, there are rules to help you to navigate the information superhighway safely. In the real world, there are two types of people who hitchhike: those who are desperate and out of options and those who are ignorant and don't know any better. When you make friends with strangers online, they might not be who they say they are. Photographs lie. Someone posing as a 16-year-old girl or boy may in fact be a 50-year-old adult. How are you to know unless you know them in the real world?

YOU NEED TO PROTECT YOURSELF

As you get older you will spend more and more time away from your parents: at school, on school camps or tours, at parties or sleepovers. When your parents are not around they cannot step in to protect you or help you to make a wise choice. This responsibility now falls on your shoulders and you need to make the best possible choice in whatever situation you find yourself.

When faced with a decision, bear in mind that there are three things you 'own' or are ultimately responsible for:

1. Your mind

You only have one mind, and your brain is like a sponge, absorbing your experiences – what you see/watch, what you hear, taste, smell or do. It all goes in and shapes who you are and what you become. Be selective about the computer games you play, the television programmes you watch, what you download and share.

Watching or playing excessively with violent or aggressive content on TV programmes or in computer games has been linked to aggressive tendencies.

Watching pornography online is highly addictive and can shape your attitude towards your own sexuality and how you think about others. Remember that porn is a fantasy – it is not what happens in real life.

When you are feeling down or upset, you become vulnerable to others who might promise you all sorts of things to get something out of you. "I'll never treat you like your mother, just send me a photo of yourself." You, therefore, need to protect your mind.

2. Your body

You only have one body and you need to protect it from physical harm or indecent exposure. Do not give out too many personal details about yourself on your profiles or online. The more you share the easier it is to track you down in the physical world. You do not have to fill in the name of your school or your home address. Making friends with strangers online can put you in physical danger. And don't ever arrange to meet an online friend without your parents knowing.

When people ask you to send them a picture of your private parts online, don't believe promises, such as that they will never show anyone else. Lies, lies, lies. Don't be fooled.

3. Your reputation
Your reputation will be determined by the choices you make both online and offline. You need to take responsibility for these choices because they will have an impact on your future.

So, to recap, you own three things – one mind, one body and one reputation – and *you* have to protect them. Your parents will give you the information and tools to do this, but ultimately it will be up to you when they aren't there to protect you. Use this easy-to-remember mantra to assess your thoughts, behaviour and actions online. It could save your life.

Be an 'upstander' not a bystander
If something were to go wrong with a friendship in real life or you had a problem at school, the likelihood is that you would tell your parents about it so that they could help you. If something horrible was happening to a friend, you might also share that with a parent or maybe a teacher who could help. Often such problems spill over into the online world and you may see a friend or someone you know getting dissed or cyber-bullied. Will you stand by and watch (be a bystander), or join in, or will you call for help (be an 'upstander')?

Choose to stand up and do something about it instead of standing by. It is one of the most powerful ways of protecting each other online. Have your friends' backs instead of becoming a silent collaborator in the crime.

Stop, block and tell
So, what if someone was sending you rude or nasty messages … insulting you on social networking sites, blogs, and public websites … posting embar-

rassing or revealing pictures of you ... forwarding your private emails to others ... spreading rumours and accusations about you ... impersonating you or starting an online fight with you? What would you do?

Do you remember how the words "Stop, drop and roll" were drilled into you in primary school so that in the event of a fire you could take positive action that could save your life? In the world of cyber-bullying, the words "Stop, block and tell" are becoming an essential safety mantra to help you to protect yourself. If you find yourself in any of the above situations, do the following:

- *Stop* what you're doing and take a deep breath: do *not* answer or get into an argument online.
- *Block* the person who is harassing you – for example, use the blocking feature on BBM or WhatsApp so that the bully can no longer connect with you.
- *Tell* a parent or another adult you trust, otherwise no one can help you.

Don't play tricks on people online
It might seem like a fun idea to play a practical joke on someone online, but these often backfire and you're the one who will get into trouble.

For example, phone-jacking is popular among younger teenage boys. While having friends over, a boy may leave his cellphone lying around. A couple of his friends get hold of it, and start sending obscene messages to the boy's social circle – boys and girls. One of the recipients is bound to show it to a parent, and the fallout can then be massive, ranging from social embarrassment – for the parents of the perpetrators as well as the children – to disciplinary action at school, to the extreme case of legal action.

RESPECT YOUR PARENTS
We know that sometimes you may think your parents are old-fashioned or too conservative, but one thing we know is that they love you and have your best interests at heart. Respect them – if only because they survived the world without Google! And they do know a thing or two about living successfully in the world.

- Teach them about technology and how to use it.
- Share your world with them. Keep them in the loop about where you are and what you are doing, even online, so that they can help you if need be. If you keep them guessing they'll probably think you are up to no good.
- Ask for help when you need it. Even if they don't know how to fix it, they

will find someone who can. If you can't approach your parents with a problem, find another adult you trust and confide in them.

DIGITAL SAFETY NO-NO'S

Your behaviour online and how you use technology are choices. You are responsible for each and every choice, each and every connection that you make. Here is a list of actions you should *avoid* in order to keep safe in the digital world:

- Don't create porn (videos or photographs). If you are under 18, it is illegal and you can get a criminal record.
- Don't send porn to anyone. If you are under 18, it is illegal and you can get a criminal record.
- Don't cut and paste directly from other people's work or websites without putting it into your own words – and even then you should acknowledge the source. Plagiarism is unethical and could cost you your matric or tertiary qualification.
- Don't open links in emails and posts from people you don't know. You could open yourself up to being hacked, blackmailed or scammed.
- Don't make friends with strangers.
- Don't give out too much personal information on your profiles.
- Don't diss other people. Words can harm so be careful what you say online.
- Don't overshare your thoughts and feelings online. If you are very upset or angry, rather stay offline and find a real shoulder to cry on.
- Don't post mean comments about others. Never text anything you wouldn't say to someone's face.
- Don't post embarrassing pictures of others. Only post things that put them in a good light.
- Don't spread rumours or lies about others.
- Don't play tricks on people online.
- Don't buy into peer pressure and following the crowd. Be your own person.
- Don't cop out and hide behind a screen – engage with real life.
- Don't text anything you wouldn't say to someone face to face.
- Don't fall asleep with your phone under your pillow while listening to music. Protect your brain from radiation and sleep with your phone far away from your head.

HOW TO STAY SAFE AND SAVVY

Actions you can take that will keep you safe and savvy in the digital world:

- For better sleep, switch your phone off completely so that you aren't disturbed by or tempted to check for messages or social media updates in the night.
- If you want to study better, switch your phone off completely.
- Keep your cellphone charged at all times. A dead phone cannot help you in an emergency.
- Make sure your phone – as well as any other device you may use – is password-protected, and don't share that password with anyone unless you want to be phone-jacked.
- Switch off the geo-location settings on your phone and don't use apps such as Foursquare. Geo-location tells people where you are, so that even predators will be able to find you.
- Make sure you implement privacy settings on your social media profiles to give you some control over who sees what.
- Make sure that what you post is a good representation of who you are as a person and what you and your family stand for. It is like an advertisement.
- Google yourself from time to time to see what comes up.
- Do learn how to block and 'unfriend' others.
- Do break the silence around cyber-bullying – be an 'upstander', not a bystander.
- Do let someone know if you get into trouble.
- Do be discerning about what is good and bad, what is okay and not okay for you. This might be different for someone else. Stand for something or you will fall for anything.
- Do think before you post.
- Do engage with social media as if the whole world is watching you.
- Do make wise choices by thinking through the consequences.
- Check yourself before you wreck yourself.

There are a number of ways in which you can break the law when you are online that could result in a criminal record. Paul Jacobson, director of Web•Tech•Law, lists 10 ways to get into trouble with the law online:

1 Share explicit photos and videos of yourself with others, especially adults

If you are under 18 and you share explicit photos and videos of yourself with others, you may be distributing what the law regards as pornography and both you and the person you are sending it to could be prosecuted under a number of anti-child pornography laws.

2 Share explicit photos and videos of other children with other people

The same child pornography issue applies here. In addition, you are also violating the other child's right to privacy and that can lead to your parents being sued (because they are responsible for you) or, if you are old enough, you being sued.

3 Share music, TV episodes and movies without permission

Most of the music, TV episodes and movies you enjoy are protected by copyright laws. It is illegal for you to make copies without permission and share them with other people. Unlike in the United States, where something called 'fair use' allows people to make copies for personal use, we don't have the same sorts of permissions in our laws. If you infringe copyright, you (or your parents) can be sued for losses and even prosecuted in a criminal court.

4 Take videos of kids fighting on the playground and posting them to YouTube

The law is getting pretty serious about tackling bullying in schools. If you take videos of kids fighting or bullying each other and post it for fun, you are probably violating their privacy and defaming them. If you see kids fighting and you want to capture the fight so you can report it to adults, take it to a responsible adult directly. Don't stop to share it on YouTube.

5 Make fun of other people, especially kids, on Twitter, Facebook or even in private chat groups

If you make fun of other people you are defaming them. This means you are harming their reputation – a reputation to which they have a right. What you are saying might be factually correct but that may not excuse you making harmful comments. Remember that whatever you say about someone online, even if it is in a private chat group on WhatsApp or Snapchat, can still be stored and turned over to law-enforcement authorities and used against you.

6 Impersonate your friends online and post embarrassing things on their behalf

Sometimes this is funny (if the prank is harmless), but when you impersonate your friends online you may be breaking the terms and conditions that govern use of the service, defaming them by publishing comments that appear to come from them and even infringing their privacy if you also go through their private communications and data.

7 Check in at schools and people's homes without their permission

Checking in at your current location is a great way to let your friends know where you are but not everyone likes that. If you check in at schools, you may be helping nasty people find new victims for their crimes and checking in at people's homes without their permission may violate their privacy.

8 Copy someone else's work and say it is yours

When you copy or use someone else's work and claim that it's yours, that is plagiarism and plagiarism is illegal. Always say where you got the material you are using and whether you have permission to use it.

9 Bully other kids online

Picking on other kids online and sharing embarrassing or offensive stuff about them is both harmful and illegal. Under recent laws, you could be prosecuted for harassment. It may seem like fun or you may think that your actions are justified, but think about the effect your actions have on others. There are many reports about kids who are bullied online and who hurt themselves or even take their own lives because of the bullying. It's not a game.

10 Share stupid stuff online

Posting photos of you and your friends doing foolish or even illegal things can really harm your future. What you post online is often permanent (even when you use services such as Snapchat) and can be found by future employers, police and other people who will use what you share to make decisions about you when you apply for a job or take part in certain activities. Photos or videos of you acting illegally can be used to hold you responsible for your actions by the police.

BE SAFE AND SAVVY ONLINE

There are so many amazing opportunities available to you that were never possible before simply because you were born in this era. We want you to be able to take advantage of new ways of connecting with people, innovative ways of building businesses and alternative ways of drumming up support for causes and funding for ideas. And you can: if you are smart and wise about the ways in which you put the digital world to work for you and not against you.

May you always remain curious about your world – that's the way you learn and get better at doing things – but never forget that curiosity also killed the cat, as the saying goes. Forewarned is forearmed and may you never forget the safety mantra:

One Mind, One Body and One Reputation.

We wish you good luck on your journey into cyberspace. Be successful and make yourself proud.

- One Mind, One Body, One Reputation.
- Be an upstander, not a bystander.
- People are more important than screens.
- Stop, block and tell.
- Think before you post.
- Check yourself before you wreck yourself.
- Tweet as if the whole world is watching you.
- Respect and manners, ladies and gentlemen.
- Social media is like a tattoo.
- Be your own hero.

CHAPTER 14

CONCLUSION

This book has focused on the choices you need to help your child make in order to be safe and savvy online. But the fact is that you also get to choose. More than that: you *have to* choose.

We decide what kind of childhood we want for our children – whether it will be driven by technology or by human relationships. How we incorporate technology into our children's lives flows from this decision. If you don't choose to focus on relationships, then technology will define your children's childhood. It will have an impact on their development and affect the relationships in your home and family. But if you remember nothing else, take this thought away: technology itself is neutral. What and how much we allow our children to do with technology is determined by us and the choices we do or don't make.

We need to acknowledge that all children are curious and look for excitement, attention and belonging, especially as they advance into the teenage years. Technology and the Internet have provided a new playground where all this can take place – even without you. All the while their parents are increasingly stressed and busy, and becoming less present and more inattentive to the children they are raising. Unless parents make a conscious choice to connect with their children, understand their age and stage and the realities of the new digital normal, disconnection may be the result. Ironically, in an age of increasing connection through devices, disconnection from your children is the worst route to raising tech-savvy children.

In a world of maximum media we need maximum parenting – without hysterical hovering.

When we talk about maximum parenting, what we really mean is that you need to learn how to dance the dance of digital connection with your child. This is a new layer that has been added to your relationship, and you need to get to grips with it. For a dance to be successful, both dancers need to learn their moves and positions – and find their rhythm. Throughout the dance, the space between the dancers gets wider and narrower; it has an ebb and a flow to it, but there is always a connection.

We hope that this book has caught your attention and has given you a practical understanding of the digital space and its applications, why your children find it so attractive, and what really makes your kids tick.

With a better perspective, you will be able to see the importance of combining knowledge with trusting your common sense. This combination will help you navigate this new-look world and help your kids thrive in it as responsible digital citizens with a high regard for personal and reputational safety.

We hope we have been able to give you practical handles and frameworks with which to help your children to connect with the world, protect themselves and celebrate their humanity.

We hope the book allows you to answer these tremendous challenges:

- Are you going to shield your child from the reality of a digital world, or are you going to teach them how to cross the information superhighway safely and intelligently?
- Will your children behave like hitchhikers who are desperate or ignorant, or are you going to help them to become tech safe and savvy so that they, in turn, can protect themselves in a digital world? In other words, will you help them become the hero in their own life story?

Our advice is to learn to understand the technology and the changing world, but don't get paralysed by it. Always, always keep the human in the middle. In a high-tech world, we need high-touch and conscious connection. Substitute yourself with devices when you are too busy to be with your children and you may well lose them down the technology rabbit hole.

Be teachable. Be curious. Be relevant. Be present.

The most practical step you can take has nothing to do with technology: ask your children what it is that you do that makes them feel loved. You will be amazed at the answers. Children are creatures of connection and what they want most is a real and authentic relationship with you, their parent.

The conversation that will flow from that simple question will at times be uncomfortable, and even painful, because you may be forced to acknowledge your own lack of effort or connection. But if you approach it in a spirit of rekindling or reinforcing relationships, it can be the beginning of real conversation.

It is *that* kind of conversation that will provide the foundation for raising tech-savvy children. To become a tech-savvy parent, don't start with the tech – start with parenting. And may the conversation with your precious and remarkable children be one that goes on and on.

Do you have a story to share about your journey to becoming a tech-savvy parent, or the challenges you've faced along the way? Please share it with Nikki and Arthur. You can email them on nikki@nikkibush.com and arthur@worldwideworx.com. Who knows? They may share them with other parents in a future book on the tech-savvy parenting conversation.

Nikki and Arthur are committed to supporting parents on their journey to becoming tech-savvy. Do collect your Reader Reward on the Resources page at www.nikkibush.com using the code TECHSAVVYBOOK.

APPENDIX I

COMMONLY USED TEXT ACRONYMS

8	– *ate*, or *oral sex*
1337 (or leet or L337)	– *elite*
143 (or ILU or 459)	– *I love you*
182	– *I hate you*
1174	– *nude club*
420	– *marijuana*
ADR	– *address*
AEAP	– *as early as possible*
ALAP	– *as late as possible*
ASL	– *age/sex/location*
CD9	– *Code 9 (parents are around)*
C-P	– *sleepy*
F2F	– *face to face (face time)*
FOMO	– *fear of missing out*
GNOC	– *get naked on camera*
GYPO	– *get your pants off*
HAK	– *hugs and kisses*
J/O	– *jerking off*
KFY (or K4Y)	– *kiss for you*
KOTL	– *kiss on the lips*
KPC	– *keeping parents clueless*
LMIRL	– *let's meet in real life*
MOOS	– *member(s) of the opposite sex*
MorF	– *male or female*
MOS	– *mom over shoulder*
MOSS	– *member(s) of the same sex*
MPFB	– *my personal fuck buddy*
NALOPKT	– *not a lot of people know that*
NIFOC	– *nude in front of the computer*
NMU	– *not much, you?*
P911	– *parent alert*
PAL	– *parents are listening*, or *peace and love*
PAW	– *parents are watching*
PIR	– *parent in room*
POS	– *parent over shoulder*, or *piece of shit*
pron	– *porn*

Q2C	– *quick to cum*
RU/18	– *are you over 18?*
RUH	– *are you horny?*
RUMORF	– *are you male or female?*
S2R	– *send to receive*
SorG	– *straight or gay?*
TDTM	– *talk dirty to me*
WSN	– *(I) want sex now*
WTF	– *what the fuck*
WUF	– *where you from?*
WYCM	– *will you call me?*
WYRN	– *what's your real name?*
zerg	– *to gang up on someone*

View more at www.netlingo.com

COMMONLY USED EMOTICONS

:) *or* :-)	smile
^-^	delighted or happy face
O:) *or* O:-)	smiling angel
:D *or* :-D	big, toothy smile
}:> *or* }:->	devilish grin
:X *or* :-X	lips are sealed
;) *or* ;-)	wink
:(*or* :-(	frown
:C *or* :-C	big frown, grumpy
:'(*or* :'-(	crying
:-/	sarcasm
:> *or* :->	big grin
:p *or* :-p	sticking out tongue
:* *or* :-*	kiss
:o *or* :-o	surprise, gasp, outcry
:O *or* :-O	scream
:V *or* :-V	talking, yakking
8) *or* 8-)	smiley (author wears glasses)
|:o	*Ooooohhh noooooo!*
O_O	shocked, surprised, bug eyes
O_o	confused
<_<	disappointed, ashamed, upset

APPENDIX 2

CELLPHONE CONTRACT FOR TWEENS AND TEENS

Dear ....

While you don't need a licence to operate a cellphone, you do need to take responsibility for using it wisely because this very powerful device can be used as a tool for good or a weapon for harming both yourself and others. You are about to set off on the information superhighway and, like on any road, certain rules apply. The contract below sets out both your responsibilities and ours, as your parents, to ensure that you keep yourself and others safe while upholding your reputation (and ours), which is important both now and for your future.

Our wishes for you
Our wish for you is that you ...
- enjoy all the functionality of your phone without compromising your own integrity
- maintain your high standard of manners and etiquette online as you do offline
- continue to value face-to-face communication more than on-screen communication – keep it real
- check yourself before you wreck yourself whenever you text or post anything – if you wouldn't want us to see it, then don't send it
- are an 'upstander' and not a bystander – help others in the online world as you would do in the real world, by letting an adult know that they are in trouble
- take responsibility for the choices and consequences that come with using a cellphone – everything boils down to what you choose to do
- know who you are and that your phone is not you – it is just a tool you use to connect with your world
- will always come to us first if you are in trouble or if you spot trouble – we would rather hear it from you than from someone else, and we can only help you if we know what's going on
- realise that we are on your team, no matter what, even if you mess up – mistakes are a chance to learn and then do it all over again, but differently
- remember that we love you and want the best for you, always.

Your responsibilities
- I will keep my phone charged at all times.
- I will not bring my cellphone to the family dinner table.
- I will stick to the airtime, voice and data limits that we have agreed on.
- I understand that I may be responsible for paying any additional charges and that I may lose my cellphone privileges if I go over the limits.
- I understand that I am responsible for knowing where my phone is at all times, and for keeping it in good condition, and that I will be liable for repair or replacement costs if I am irresponsible with it.
- I understand that my cellphone is a privilege and may be taken away if I talk back to my parents, or fail to do my chores, my homework or maintain my marks.
- I will respect others in public places such as restaurants, movie theatres or places of worship by making sure my phone is turned off or on silent.
- I will make eye contact with others, especially adults, when they are talking to me, instead of keeping my eyes glued to my cellphone.
- I will not text or make phone calls after 9pm at night.
- I will obey the school's cellphone policy.
- I will alert my parents when I receive suspicious or alarming phone calls or text messages from people I don't know.
- I will alert my parents if I am being harassed by someone via my cellphone.
- I will 'unfriend' or block anyone who harasses me rather than respond to them.
- I will not delete the conversations because they are a paper trail that may be needed to stop a bully or stalker, for example.
- I will not use my cellphone to bully another person by sending threatening or mean texts.
- I will not send embarrassing photos of my family or friends to others. In addition, I will not use my phone's camera to take embarrassing photos of others.
- I will not send naked pictures of myself to others regardless of the pressure my friends may put me under.
- If I hijack another person's phone and send mean or embarrassing messages or photographs on their behalf, I understand that I will have my phone taken away.
- I will not play tricks on people online.
- I will be an 'upstander' and not a bystander, and will alert an adult if I

know of someone who is being cyber-bullied.
- I will not send messages or photographs that I wouldn't be happy for you to see.
- I will keep you informed of password changes.
- I will try not to do anything on my phone that could harm my mind, my body or my reputation.
- I will not overdose on gaming on my phone and will respect the time limits we agree on, including in-app purchases – for which I need to ask specific permission.
- I understand that having a cellphone is a privilege, and that if I fail to adhere to this contract, this privilege may be revoked.

Our responsibilities
- I/we will make myself/ourselves available to answer any questions, or hear any suggestions you may have about owning a cellphone and using it responsibly.
- I/we will support you should you alert me/us about alarming messages or texts that you may have received.
- I/we will alert you should the details of your cellphone plan change in any way that impacts on the amount of airtime, voice or data allocation that you have.
- I/we will have a discussion before revoking any privileges relating to owning or using a cellphone should you disregard any of your responsibilities listed above.

Signed ....
(on behalf of the tween/teen)

Signed ....
(on behalf of the parents)

Date ....

Also downloadable at www.nikkibush.com

APPENDIX 3

SOCIAL MEDIA AND TECHNOLOGY POLICY

Every school, like every business, should have a social media policy, along with an acceptable-use policy for technology being utilised on the premises. The good news is that many schools around the world already have formal policies in place, and many of these are good sample policies or guidelines.

However, each policy takes into account the specific intentions, emphases or circumstances of the school or area it covers. This means that you cannot simply take a policy from Missouri and impose it on Mpumalanga. However, you can take the best out of a Missouri document and incorporate it into your own.

Here is a selection of guidelines and policies that you can use as a starting point.

TEACHERS' GUIDELINES
Best practices when using social media in education
from Model Social Media Policy for Missouri School Districts (USA)

- Be respectful: Realise that students might not be able to tell the difference between work and personal communications and adjust posts accordingly.
- Provide background/context: This can be done in the classroom or online, but make sure students know what you are posting about. Try to make posts connect with discussions and materials that have been shared in your classroom.
- Ask questions: Studies show that providing readers opportunities to interact with you (whether it be questions, links and photos, for example) is successful for actually getting them to interact with you.
- Sunshine is the best antidote for any problem – keep discussions in the public realm.
- Any information you would not be able to share is not allowable to share on a social network.
- Make it about education: Social media interaction with students should be treated the same as any other interaction with a student – focused on learning, transparent and meaningful.

- Make it part of your classroom culture: We're 14 years into the 21st century now. If you're not using the web, social media or texting, you're missing out on a truly powerful tool for learning. Teachers need to work to include new technologies into their rooms. Embrace the means of communication the lion's share of your students have and use technology to better prepare your students for when they leave your room.
- Be generous: One of the great things about social media is the ability to share with others, whether it be photography or links or anything else. Cultivate your network in the area you teach so you can use social media as a means for enhancing students' experience in your class.
- Be aware of hazardous material: There's lots of bad stuff out there and the line between what is appropriate or not is fuzzy and ever-changing.

Five dos and five don'ts of using social media with students
from Model Social Media Policy for Missouri School Districts (USA)

DO
- Do make use of social media as often as fits your lessons and curriculum.
- Do make social media a part of your classroom culture.
- Do encourage students to use technology (smartphone, laptop and iPad, for example) in your room, when appropriate.
- Do proofread and edit your posts. Verify sources. You want to look professional while online.
- Do consult with your superiors if you run into a potential problem, immediately, just as you would if you ran into a potential problem in the classroom.

DON'T
- Don't allow open access to social media. Students need to learn that there are appropriate times to use it. Set your privacy levels to the highest levels the medium allows.
- Don't post links to sites you haven't viewed yourself.
- Don't do anything risky, such as advocate politics, swear, or anything that can get you in trouble.
- Don't post things students may find offensive (politics and off-colour humour, for example).
- Don't post about anything you wouldn't share in the classroom.

Principles – be professional, responsible and respectful
from Seaford Head School, School Social Media Policy (UK)

- You must be conscious at all times of the need to keep your personal and professional lives separate. You should not put yourself in a position where there is a conflict between your work for the school and your personal interests.
- You must not engage in activities involving social media which might bring Seaford Head School into disrepute.
- You must not represent your personal views as those of Seaford Head School on any social medium.
- You must not discuss personal information about pupils, Seaford Head School staff and other professionals you interact with as part of your job on social media.
- You must not use social media and the Internet in any way to attack, insult, abuse or defame pupils, their family members, colleagues, other professionals, other organisations or Seaford Head School.
- You must be accurate, fair and transparent when creating or altering online sources of information on behalf of Seaford Head School.

Personal use of social media
from Seaford Head School, School Social Media Policy (UK)

- Staff members must not identify themselves as employees of Seaford Head School or service providers for the school in their personal web space. This is to prevent information on these sites from being linked with the school and to safeguard the privacy of staff members, particularly those involved in providing sensitive frontline services.
- Staff members must not have contact through any personal social medium with any pupil, whether from Seaford Head School or any other school, unless the pupils are family members.
- Seaford Head School does not expect staff members to discontinue contact with their family members via personal social media once the school starts providing services for them. However, any information staff members obtain in the course of their employment must not be used for personal gain nor be passed on to others who may use it in such a way.

- Staff members must not have any contact with pupils' family members through personal social media if that contact is likely to constitute a conflict of interest or call into question their objectivity.
- If staff members wish to communicate with pupils through social media sites or to enable pupils to keep in touch with one another, they can only do so with the approval of the school and through official school sites created according to ... requirements specified.
- Staff members must decline 'friend requests' from pupils they receive in their personal social media accounts. Instead, if they receive such requests from pupils who are not family members, they must discuss these in general terms in class and signpost pupils to become 'friends' of the official school site.
- On leaving Seaford Head School service, staff members must not contact Seaford Head School pupils by means of personal social media sites. Similarly, staff members must not contact pupils from their former schools by means of personal social media.
- Information staff members have access to as part of their employment, including personal information about pupils and their family members, colleagues and other parties and school corporate information must not be discussed on their personal web space.
- Photographs, videos or any other types of images of pupils and their families or images depicting staff members wearing school uniforms or clothing with school logos or images identifying sensitive school premises must not be published on personal web spaces.
- School email addresses and other official contact details must not be used for setting up personal social media accounts or to communicate through such media.
- Staff members must not edit open access online encyclopaedias such as Wikipedia in a personal capacity at work. This is because the source of the correction will be recorded as the employer's IP address and the intervention will, therefore, appear as if it comes from the employer itself.
- Seaford Head School corporate, service or team logos or brands must not be used or published on personal web spaces.

CHILDREN'S GUIDELINES
Guidance/protection for pupils on using social networking
from Giffards Primary School, Social Networking Policy (UK)

- No pupil under 13 should be accessing social networking sites. This is the guidance from both Facebook and MSN. There is a mechanism on Facebook where pupils can be reported via the Help screen; at the time of writing this policy the direct link for this is: www.facebook.com/help/contact/209046679279097.
- No pupil may access social networking sites during the school working day.
- All cellphones must be handed into the office at the beginning of the school day, and the Internet capability must be switched off. Failure to follow this guidance will result in a total ban for the student using a mobile phone.
- No pupil should attempt to join a staff member's areas on networking sites. If pupils attempt to do this, the member of staff is to inform the Head teacher. Parents will be informed if this happens.
- No school computers are to be used to access social networking sites at any time of day.

Cyber-bullying
from Giffards Primary School, Social Networking Policy (UK)

- By adopting the recommended no use of social networking sites on school premises, Giffards Primary School protects themselves from accusations of complicity in any cyber-bullying through the provision of access.
- Parents should be clearly aware of the school's policy of access to social and networking sites.
- Where a disclosure of bullying is made, schools now have the duty to investigate and protect, even where the bullying originates outside the school.

This can be a complex area, and these examples might help:
- A child is receiving taunts on Facebook and text from an ex-pupil who moved three months ago: This is not a school responsibility, though the school might contact the new school to broker a resolution.
- A child is receiving taunts from peers. It is all at weekends using MSN

and Facebook. The pupils are in the school: The school has a duty of care to investigate and work with the families, as they attend the school.

- A child is receiving taunts from peers. It is all at weekends using Facebook. The pupils are in Year 5: This is a tricky one. The school has a duty of care to investigate and work with the families, as they attend the school. However, they are also fully within their rights to warn all the parents (including the victim) that they are condoning the use of Facebook outside the terms and conditions of the site and that they are expected to ensure that use of the site stops. At any further referral to the school the school could legitimately say that the victims and perpetrators had failed to follow the school's recommendation. They could then deal with residual bullying in the school, but refuse to deal with the social networking issues.

- Once disclosure is made, investigation will have to involve the families. This should be dealt with under the school's adopted anti-bullying policy.

- If parents/carers refuse to engage and bullying continues, it can be referred to the police as harassment.

- This guidance can also apply to text and cellphone cyber-bullying.

Social media administrative regulation – students
from Pottsville Area School District, Social Media Policy (USA)

- Students are responsible for their own behaviour when communicating with social media and will be held accountable for the content of the communications that they state/post on social media locations. Use good judgement. Students are responsible for complying with the School District's conduct requirements. Students may not disrupt the learning atmosphere, educational programmes, school activities, and the rights of others.

- In addition, students may be required to comply with policies, administrative regulations, rules and procedures at the entity and/or programme in which they are assigned or in which they participate. If a student believes there is a conflict in the requirements (s)he is to comply with, (s)he must bring the matter to the attention of their teacher, who will in turn assist the student.

- This Administrative Regulation applies to all School District environments, whether the social media is used on School District property, or beyond School District property (including but not limited to, at a third party's contracted property).

- In addition to the regulations provided in the School District's Social Media Policy, some guidelines include but are not limited to the following. The School District reserves the right to determine if any guideline not appearing in the list below constitutes acceptable or unacceptable social media use:
  - Students must not promote illegal drugs, illegal activities, violence and drinking.
  - Students should state/post only what they want the world to see. Imagine your parents, the teachers, and the administrators visiting your social media. Essentially, once a student shares something it is likely available after (s)he removes it from the social media and could remain on the internet permanently.
  - Students should be cautious when they use exaggeration, colourful language, guesswork, derogatory remarks, humour, and characterisations. It is difficult for readers to determine the seriousness of the statements/posts.
  - Students should run updated malware protection to avoid spyware, adware, spiders, bots, crawlers and other infections that may be placed on their social media and computer to obtain personal information, breach security, and cause various technology problems.
  - Students should stay informed and cautious for new problems in the use of social media.
  - Students should comply with the rules that have been established for the School District's educational social media when they use it.

Acceptable-use and privacy regulations
from Pottsville Area School District, Social Media Policy (USA)

- It is the responsibility of all users to carefully consider their behaviour and what they place online when communicating with or 'friending' any individual. The Technology Director, or designee, is authorised to access users' postings on public locations and on School District servers, hard drives, systems, and networks under the direction of the Superintendent, and/or designee, law enforcement, a court order, a subpoena or other legal action or authority. Users may not coerce others into providing passwords, login, or other security access information to them so that they may access social media or locations that they have no authorisation to access. Users should note that information that they place in social media and designate as private can be accessed in litigation, can be distributed by their friends, and can be accessed in other various legal ways.

- The Superintendent, and/or designee, is hereby granted the authority to create additional administrative regulations, procedures, and rules to carry out the purpose of this Social Media Policy. The administrative regulations, procedures, and rules accompanying this Policy must include among other items guidance in implementing and using School District educational social media and commercial social media, and the responsibility of users for their own behaviour when communicating with social media.

- It is often necessary to access users' School District accounts in order to perform routine maintenance and for other legal reasons. System administrators have the right to access by interception, and to access the stored communication of user accounts for any reason in order to uphold this Policy, accompanying administrative regulations, the law, and to maintain the system.

- Users should have no expectation of privacy in anything they create, store, send, receive, or display on or over the School District's CIS systems, and the School District's authorised third-party systems, including their personal files or any of their use of these systems.

- The School District reserves the right to access, view, record, check, receive, monitor, track, log, store, and otherwise inspect and utilise any or all CIS systems, and authorised third-party systems, and to monitor and allocate fileserver space. Users of the School District's CIS systems, and third-party systems, who transmit or receive communications and information shall be deemed to have consented to having the content of any such communications accessed, viewed, recorded, checked, received, monitored, tracked, logged, stored, and otherwise inspected or utilised by the School District, and to monitor and allocate fileserver space. Password- and message-delete functions do not restrict the School District's ability or right to access such communications or information.

- Users are responsible for their own behaviour when communicating with social media. They will be held accountable for the content of the communications that they state/post on social media locations. Users are responsible for complying with the School District's employee, student, and guest conduct requirements. Users may not disrupt the learning atmosphere, educational programmes, school activities, and the rights of others.

- Inappropriate communications may not be included in users' social media, including but not limited to (i) confidential, personally identifiable, and sensitive School District information about students, employees, and guests; (ii) child pornography, sexual exploitation, bullying/cyber-bullying, inappropriate commercialisation of childhood experiences; (iii) defamatory or discriminatory statements and images; (iv) proprietary information of the School District and/or a School District's vendor; (v) infringed-upon intellectual property, such as copyright ownership, and circumvented technology protection measures; (vi) terroristic threats; and (vii) illegal items and activities.
- Users may not use their personal computers, devices, services, systems, and networks during the time they are required to be fulfilling their work, learning, school responsibilities, or volunteer requirements. The School District blocks all commercial social media sites on its computers, devices, servers, networks, and systems, therefore users may not use commercial social media during their work, school, and volunteer responsibilities unless approval has been granted by the Superintendent or an administrator, and the commercial social media has been opened for that/those person(s) and purposes only.
- Where users place their communication in 'privacy' marked social media, they cannot expect that their information will not be disclosed by a person within their 'private-marked group'. Such information may be disclosed by others within the 'private group', or the information may be discovered as part of the discovery process in litigation, or it may be disclosed by other means. The School District may be provided this information and be required to investigate it further. Information that the School District obtains may be disclosed without limitation for purposes of investigation, litigation, internal dispute resolution, and legitimate business purposes regardless of whether the particular user is involved.
- Information that a user deleted may be recovered indefinitely by the School District.

It is clear from the above that a school social media policy and acceptable-use policy for technology must cover not only use by children, but also by teachers and staff, and that parent behaviour must also be covered. Finally, any such policy adopted by the school must be accepted and signed, denoting acceptance, by students and teachers.

APPENDIX 4

DEVELOPMENT NEEDS IN THE FOUNDATION PHASE

This table covers some of the essential developmental needs of children and how the 21st century can interfere in that development. The table is part of Nikki's presentation called 'Connecting with Children through the Noise and Clutter', which deals with television usage, gaming, consumerism and changing childhood.[1]

A child's developmental needs	How the world is interfering
Children need freedom to explore, to find out how the world works, and to discover how they fit into the world.	Children live in a 'barbed-wire culture'[2] with limited access to the outdoors, playgrounds and nature. Technology is encouraging them to be sedentary screen slaves. Lack of parental presence or role-modelling is also affecting this need.
Children need plenty of physical movement in order to develop the neurological pathways that wire the brain for more sophisticated functions later. Physical exercise also develops resilience, perseverance and social skills.	The body is in fact the architect of the brain. Too much sedentary activity fails to stimulate the visual, vestibular and proprioceptive systems, which are the foundations for reading, writing and maths later in a child's life. Childhood obesity and diabetes are the most common problems, which relate to lack of exercise and physical movement in children as a result of an increase in on-screen activities.

A child's developmental needs	How the world is interfering
Children need to eat a healthy diet since their development and mental and physical performance are influenced by their intake of water and nutrients.	Much of our food today is depleted of nutrients for a variety of reasons – from overprocessing to sterile soil, among many others. The side effects of added growth hormones, for example, are also cause for concern. Most food advertisements on TV promote junk food rather than broccoli – the opposite to a healthy eating plan.[3] They encourage snacking on convenience foods, which are high in salt, sugar, trans-fatty acids, colourants and flavourants, while watching television.[4] Such foods, as well as fast foods, are also convenient for busy parents who are generally in a hurry. But all of them contribute to obesity, diabetes, food allergies and intolerances, as well as concentration and behavioural issues, and even disorders.[5]
Children need plenty of rest. Sleep is essential and important: • for physical growth and a strong immune system • to balance intense periods of physical activity, which should characterise a healthy childhood • to enable the body to balance sensory overload and prevent stimulation from overwhelming the child • to enable the child to process and consolidate what he or she has learned and experienced each day.	Children have so much packed into their day that it is often difficult for parents to keep a regular routine, including bedtime. Sometimes a child's routine is governed by a parent's diary, and parents today are very busy. Children can battle to fall asleep after spending time watching TV or playing on-screen games. The fast-moving light rays in these games affect the melatonin levels in the body, which are necessary for good sleep. Stress, anxiety and fear can also affect a child's sleeping patterns.

A child's developmental needs	How the world is interfering

Children need to develop their imagination and creativity in order to have original thoughts that will help them to solve the problems of the future that are not yet problems.
 	
   A strong imagination and creativity are highly useful in subjects such as English, Art, Maths and DT (Design and Technology).
	Excessive TV viewing and on-screen activities are limiting this development in an alarming way.[6] On-screen activities are replacing much of playtime, which is affecting social and emotional development, in addition to limiting creative and imaginative play.
	
	   The same can be said of children who are overscheduled from a very young age with extracurricular activities from lunchtime until dinner time, with little opportunity for rest, free play, alone time and reflection.
	
	   Even creative-art programmes are often so outcomes-based that there is little room for imagination, creativity and originality. In many instances, these programmes are being replaced by creative-craft programmes, which is far from ideal because of their prescriptive nature.

Children need to play. Play is the language of childhood. It's a child's work – it's how they learn about the world and find meaning.
 	
   Children also need play dates in home environments. Remember that they learn the most important things in the sandpit, or swinging from the jungle gym, and not in the classroom. And they learn them from you, their parents, and not from their teachers.
	Pre-schools today are falling into the trap of teaching via semi-concrete or abstract worksheets rather than providing a play-based curriculum through which children discover and learn for themselves through their own physical experience with their world.[7]
	
	   Some parents push their children into competitive sports and fast-tracked learning experiences at the expense of play.
	
	   Many children are enrolled in too many extramural activities from a young age, or spend their afternoons in aftercare, which means that play dates are impossible to arrange.

A child's developmental needs	How the world is interfering
	Qualitative research conducted among the upper-income groups in the primary school market in studies for K-TV (Project Rainbow and Project Punch, 2004) and for other youth brands reveals that children as young as seven engage in *four extramurals* on average *per week*, with some children participating in as many as *nine* over a seven-day period. This includes sports coaching and matches on a Saturday morning – the latter no longer being regarded as traditional leisure time for primary school children. As adults we question whether children as young as seven or eight still enjoy childhood pursuits and freedom in the traditional sense of the word. The majority of children report that friends do not visit or play at one another's houses during the week, and that socialising is limited to certain weekend timeslots in and among family activities and shopping.[8]
Children need real-life, real-time experiences, especially in the first seven years of life. It is only around the twelfth year that the brain is able to handle abstract learning with ease.[9]	On-screen activities are transporting children into a virtual world that is not real. This is fine in moderation and when balanced with plenty of concrete play experiences. On-screen activities should not be a young child's default setting.

A child's developmental needs	How the world is interfering
Children need to develop social and emotional skills in order to build solid relationships with their self and others. They learn this best by copying their parents and caregivers. They also need conversation, face-to-face contact and human touch. Emotional intelligence is a better indicator of how well a child will do in life than his or her IQ.	Children are being bombarded by thousands of messages from advertisers and marketers telling them that satisfaction is based on the consumption of 'things' rather than on relationships. On-screen activities are replacing conversation and affecting relationships, even among siblings.[10] Many families spend family time watching one screen or another instead of engaging in face-to-face conversation. As a result of more working parents and fewer parents at home with their children, there is less conversation taking place between the parent and child on a one-on-one basis as well as less spontaneous interaction. Much day-to-day living is scheduled to fit in with the demands of work.
Children have a driving need to feel that they belong. This is natural for all human beings. If children don't feel this sense of belonging within the family, they will look elsewhere.	This fundamental human need is being exploited by marketers and brands selling the latest in 'cool'. If you don't have it, you can't or won't belong! Owning or wearing the right 'things' now defines who you are and whether or not you fit in. Of course, what's considered cool changes daily, forcing children into a cycle of conspicuous consumption.[11] This also forces children into wanting to be 'the same' as everyone else instead of being unique individuals.[12] Our jam-packed schedules are threatening time spent together as a family and can impact on a child's sense of belonging.

A child's developmental needs	How the world is interfering
Children need to develop and own a healthy set of values. In a world of chaos and change, these will be their anchor and guide. Sound values help us to feel more secure in the world. They assist us when we have to make decisions or take action, even in the sandpit. Values are caught and not taught. They are demonstrated through our words and actions and it is essential that we be consistent in this regard.	Will children get their values from their parents or peers, as in the 'old days'? Or will the brash, noisy marketers, brands and media win their hearts and minds first? Some values being conveyed to our kids through various media include: • Adults suck, kids rule. • Don't worry about anyone else's feelings, just look after yourself. • Win at all costs. Yet children are also hearing the opposite – and sometimes from the same channels, such as: *Every day in every way, we are part of everyone.* They must find this rather confusing – and who should they believe?
Children need to feel safe and secure in order to access their learning potential. They need to be calm and have a steady heartbeat for optimum learning to take place. Children need information to be presented to them in many different ways to appeal to their different intelligences and learning styles in order to encourage and activate learning rather than inhibit or stifle it.	Constant exposure to inappropriate content via news programmes, reality TV and frenetic kids' programmes does not lead to feelings of safety and security.[13] When a child is stressed for any reason, his or her heartbeat goes up, which can affect the workings of the brain. Even fast music or computer game soundtracks that play above heart tempo (80 beats per minute) will affect a child's brain. At this point, the thinking brain shuts down and all input goes into the emotional brain (limbic system) where the child's values, culture and beliefs sit. The child is now totally open to suggestion without protection.

A child's developmental needs	How the world is interfering
Children need boundaries. Of course, this does not mean living in a straitjacket. But it does mean that establishing a regular routine (boundaries or rules by which we live) provides a certain amount of predictability, which can bring sanity into your household. Routine provides a feeling of safety and security for children, which is an optimum environment for learning. Routine does not mean inflexibility. Within routine there is plenty of flexibility and room for creativity.	With so much on offer today, parents need to be consistent in the boundaries that they set for their children. Where possible, choices for goods and services should be based on children's developmental needs and the family's values. Parents must learn to overcome pester power. Children thrive on routine from the earliest of days. This does not mean inflexibility. In fact it means quite the opposite. With parents being so busy and overscheduled themselves, routine is often overlooked or broken for convenience.
Children need parents and they need time. The importance of parental input cannot be over-emphasised. Children need as much time and attention as we can give them, and preferably in a way that they recognise as loving and supportive.	Due to economic factors and changing family structures, we are not giving children the time or attention that they need. Yet parents are the facilitators of their children's lives and play a pivotal role. As far as possible, therefore, they need to be present and accessible. Parents fill the leadership role. When they are absent, children will step into the gap and take control.

CHAPTER NOTES

Chapter 2

1. From James McNeil and Juliet Schor in *Facing the Screen Dilemma: Young children, technology and early education*, Campaign for a Commercial-Free Childhood, Alliance for Childhood and Teachers Resisting Unhealthy Children's Entertainment

Chapter 3

1. *Facing the Screen Dilemma: Young children, technology and early education*, Campaign for a Commercial-Free Childhood, Alliance for Childhood and Teachers Resisting Unhealthy Children's Entertainment
2. Cris Rowan, *ZoneIn*, http://www.zoneinworkshops.com/zonein-fact-sheet.html, retrieved 4 April 2014
3. Cris Rowan, *ZoneIn*, http://www.zoneinworkshops.com/zonein-fact-sheet.html, retrieved 4 April 2014
4. Adapted from an idea in Teresa Orange and Louise O'Flynn, *The Media Diet for Kids*, Hay House, 2005
5. http://www.vodafone.com/content/parents/get-involved/inappropriate_harmful_content.html, retrieved 2 April 2014
6. http://www.vodafone.com/content/parents/get-involved/excessive_use_of_technology.html#MainParSys_box, retrieved 2 April 2014
7. *Parents and Children's Media Usage*, Ofcom Report, 2013
8. http://www.vodafone.com/content/parents/get-involved/internet_mobile_security.html, retrieved 2 April 2014
9. https://www.netnanny.com/blog/which-websites-should-a-parent-block-based-on-a-childs-age/, retrieved 21 April 2014

Chapter 5

1. https://www.netnanny.com/blog/if-facebook-is-the-new-telephone-net-nanny-social-is-a-great-answering-machine/, retrieved 21 April 2014

Chapter 6

1. Don Tapscott, *Growing Up Digital*, McGraw-Hill, 1998
2. Mark Treadwell, "'Whatever': The conceptual age and the evolution of school (v2.0)", http://www.marktreadwell.com/Whatever_Notes, retrieved 19 June 2014

3. Carol Affleck, *The Rewired Generation: Stepping into the gap that is the digital divide*, www.youthfocus.co.za
4. Carol Affleck, *The Rewired Generation: Stepping into the gap that is the digital divide*, www.youthfocus.co.za
5. JG Isaksen, *Watching and Wondering*, Mayfield Publishers, 1986
6. Carol Affleck, *The Rewired Generation: Stepping into the gap that is the digital divide*, www.youthfocus.co.za
7. Don Tapscott, *Growing Up Digital*, McGraw-Hill, 1998

Chapter 7
1. http://www.destinyconnect.com/2014/01/23/share-a-coke-campaign-a-hit-in-sa/, retrieved 16 June 2014

Chapter 8
1. Gary Small and Gigi Vorgan, *iBrain: Surviving the technological alteration of the human mind*, HarperCollins, 2008
2. Pam Tudin, clinical psychologist and director of EQ in a Box

Chapter 9
1. http://news.iafrica.com/sa/876239.html, retrieved 25 April 2014

Chapter 10
1. http://www.connectsafely.org/tips-to-help-stop-cyberbullying/, retrieved 4 June 2014
2. http://www.parentscorner.org.za/industry-solutions/networks-protection-children, retrieved 4 June 2014
3. http://www.parentscorner.org.za/industry-solutions/lodging-complaint-waspa, retrieved 4 June 2014

Chapter 11
1. Nikki's parent talk is called 'Bridging the Digital Divide' and her learner talk is 'The One Thing You Need to Remember'
2. Susie Mesure, 'From Bullying to Pornography', *The Independent*, 27 March 2014, http://www.independent.co.uk/life-style/gadgets-and-tech/features/from-bullying-to-pornography-how-to-keep-your-children-safe-online-9129566.html, retrieved 9 April 2014

Appendix 4

1. Nikki Bush and Dr Graeme Codrington, *Future-proof Your Child,* Penguin, 2008
2. Youth Dynamix BratTrax, 2007/8
3. Juliet Schor, *Born to Buy: The commercialized child and the new consumer culture,* Scribner, 2004
4. *Born to Buy, ibid*; Campaign for a Commercial-Free Childhood, http://www.commercialfreechildhood.org/
5. Campaign for a Commercial-Free Childhood, http://www.commercialfreechildhood.org/
6. Martin Lindstrom and Patricia Seybold, *Brand Child: Remarkable insights into the minds of today's global kids and their relationships with brands,* Kogan Page Limited, 2004
7. Glynis Courtney, chairperson, Independent Schools Association of Southern Africa Pre-school Committee
8. Carol Affleck, "I Kid You Not", paper presented at Southern African Marketing Research Association Conference, 2005
9. Joseph Pearce, *Evolution's End*, HarperCollins, 1992
10. *Born to Buy, ibid*
11. *Born to Buy, ibid*
12. *Born to Buy, ibid*
13. Campaign for a Commercial-Free Childhood, http://www.commercialfreechildhood.org/

ACKNOWLEDGEMENTS

A book of this nature doesn't appear out of thin air. Being at the forefront of all things digital, Arthur is an early adopter of technology. I am somewhat slower, but getting there. On my journey I have been inspired by a number of visionaries and early adopters who have helped me to find my technology feet: Mike Stopforth, founder of Cerebra, took me under his wing nine years ago and set me up with my first website and encouraged me to blog; Dr Graeme Codrington, co-founder of TomorrowToday, an expert on the future world of work and co-author of my first book, Future-proof Your Child *(Penguin, 2008), continues to help me make sense of the disruptive changes technology is creating and how it is changing the world; the late Dave Klein, who was headmaster of HeronBridge College, was a pioneer in South Africa in introducing the digital school concept but, more than that, he understood the connection that children have with technology and the need to teach in a whole new way. Dave, thank you for sharing your vision – how I wish I could have shared this book with you.*

To Arthur: thanks for allowing yourself to be swept up in my wave of enthusiasm for helping parents to better understand the digital world. I so appreciate your insight, wealth of knowledge and the care you have taken not to inflame or incite unnecessary fear, but rather help to create understanding. Your calm and measured responses hide a mind that is working furiously but objectively in the background, connecting the dots and supplying answers that are accessible but not over-simplified. You have a profound way with words. It has been wonderful to work with someone who makes such use of the richness of the English language.

I'm deeply grateful for the role played by each of the unsung individuals who nudged me along the path into my digital adventure. I'd like to tell a little of that story, and give credit where credit is overdue.

Gus Silber awakened my interest in urban legends, which led to my foray into the life of an author. Anthony Gerada was the founder of Digitec Online, an electronic bulletin board that gave me my first experience of the Internet. William Ramwell came round to install the software that made it easier to explore what was then a very esoteric Internet.

Irwin Manoim, co-founder of the Weekly Mail (now Mail & Guardian), gave me a platform – called 'PC Review' – to begin writing about the Internet as it emerged in South Africa. Alison Lowry, first my editor and then publisher at Penguin, guided my urban legends books and allowed me to write Ink in the Porridge, about the 1994 South African elections. I relied on the fledgling Internet to research the book, and wrote about the experience in 'PC Review'.

Greg Gordon, then with the Sunday Times, interviewed me about "how the Internet wrote my book", which perked the interest of Nick Pryke, CEO of Struik. I was introduced to him by Karen Rostowsky on one of my visits to her pioneering computer store, Businessland, where she used to allow me to test and review software. Nick suggested I write "a book about the Internet" for the Struik imprint, Zebra Press. Marga Collings of Zebra shepherded The Hitchhiker's Guide to the Internet onto the shelves, and Jennifer Crwys-Williams presided over the book launch that helped launch me on the trajectory I still follow to this day.

Without each of these links in the chain, my digital life could well have been very different.

To Nikki: I have explored the impact of the digital world on schools, teachers and children for many years, and understood the crucial role of parenting in this arena, but listening to your experiences, deep insights and eye-opening perspective truly brought home to me the great need that exists among parents for the kind of guidance you have been providing. In the process, you guided me into my own deeper understanding of one of the most complex parenting issues of our times. Your determination, drive and efficiency in getting the book completed not only made it an easy collaboration, but it was also inspirational, and I thank you for drawing me into the project.

While the tight deadlines we imposed on ourselves due to the invitation to present a preview of this book at the 2014 Franschhoek Literary Festival nearly gave us both grey hairs, it was probably a blessing in disguise because we got the job done! Thank you to both our families for the support and the space they gave us to research and write Tech-Savvy Parenting.

Writing a book such as this demands intense focus and attention to detail, which meant writing late at night and on weekends (in between our normal workloads), Skyping and emailing on our respective holidays and business trips – thank goodness for digital communication!

To our publisher, Louise Grantham, at Bookstorm: your support for this project was instantaneous and absolute. You jumped in at the deep end and agreed to do the impossible. You turned a seven-month publishing process into a seven-week one, to ensure that we had a three-chapter teaser with a full-colour cover, to boot, ready for the Literary Festival.

Louise, thank you for being so flexible in your thinking and understanding the needs of speaker-authors such as ourselves. We needed a quick, nimble and fearless publishing team and Bookstorm has really come to the party in every way.

To your hard-working team who have been under the whip since the start: Russell Clarke, our editorial project manager, you have been our chief cheerleader, keeping us all on track and on time. Thanks for firmly steering the ship and dealing with our personal quirks. To Sean Fraser, our editor, thank you for turning the manuscript around so quickly and under great time pressure. To Wesley Thompson for his proofreading, and for taking the book through its final stages. To Nicola van Rooyen and the marketing team for their planning, publicity and promotion to get this book out there. Thank you to you all.

And finally, thank you to all our clients, particularly the parents, teachers, principals and business leaders who have asked the questions and shared their experiences. You gave us the reason to write this book. We hope we have given you the answers you were looking for.

To my precious sons, Ryan and Matthew: you really inspire me to do what I do and to understand this new-look world that will ultimately belong to you. Thank you for your patience once again as your mother put her head down and gathered her thoughts. You both know me so well and your support means the world to me. To my husband Simon, who quietly holds the space in the background so that I can express myself on the page, thank you for your endless love, the odd takeaway dinners and for accepting my very erratic hours that come with needing to work when the inspiration hits.

Finally, a big, wide and deep thank you to my family: to Sheryl, who put up with my working in the evening, on weekends, on holidays and in far-flung places, providing structure, support and love at a time when it was difficult to reciprocate; and to Jayna and Zianda, who were an endless source of insight, wisdom and experience in the digital world they have explored so responsibly with me. You are my most powerful inspiration.

INDEX

CPSIA information can be obtained at www.ICGtesting.com
Printed in the USA
LVOW07s0610040615

441152LV00003B/13/P